CW00419074

A Waste of Blood and Treasure

A Waste of Blood and Treasure

The 1799 Anglo-Russian Invasion of the Netherlands

Philip Ball

PEN & SWORD
HISTORY

First published in Great Britain in 2017 by
Pen & Sword HISTORY
an imprint of
Pen & Sword Books Ltd
47 Church Street
Barnsley
South Yorkshire
S70 2AS

Copyright © Philip Ball, 2017

ISBN 978 1 47388 518 9

The right of Philip Ball to be identified
as Author of this work has been asserted by him in
accordance with the Copyright, Designs and Patents Act 1988.

A CIP catalogue record for this book is available from the British Library.
All rights reserved. No part of this book may be reproduced or
transmitted in any form or by any means, electronic or
mechanical including photocopying, recording or
by any information storage and retrieval system, without
permission from the Publisher in writing.

Typeset in Ehrhardt by
Mac Style Ltd, Bridlington, East Yorkshire

Printed and bound in Malta
By Gutenberg Press Ltd.

Pen & Sword Books Ltd incorporates the Imprints of
Pen & Sword Archaeology, Atlas, Aviation, Battleground, Discovery,
Family History, History, Maritime, Military, Naval, Politics, Railways,
Select, Transport, True Crime, Fiction,
Frontline Books, Leo Cooper, Praetorian Press,
Seaforth Publishing, Wharncliffe and White Owl.

For a complete list of Pen & Sword titles please contact
PEN & SWORD BOOKS LIMITED
47 Church Street, Barnsley, South Yorkshire, S70 2AS, England
E-mail: enquiries@pen-and-sword.co.uk
Website: www.pen-and-sword.co.uk

Contents

Maps

Acknowledgements

I would like to take this opportunity to thank the numerous individuals who have given their time and lent their expertise to the production of this book. Firstly I must acknowledge the assistance of Doctor Jacqueline Reiter without whom this work would never have seen the light of day. I would also like to recognize the contribution of John Harcourt who worked so hard to translate my rough sketches into splendid maps and Romain Cames who translated Milyutin's history of the campaign from the original Russian. Finally I give thanks to my partner Tracy and my parents who helped to ensure the text was readable and all my friends and colleagues who have endured my obsession with this campaign over the last few years.

Introduction

The winter of 1795 had been especially harsh. The canals and ditches of Holland had frozen, compounding the misery of the Duke of York's broken army as they limped their way towards Bremen and their ships home. However, it was these same conditions that enabled the French Army under General Pichegru to surge across Holland. The natural defences of their country nullified by the winter ice meant the Dutch were unable to repel them. Resistance was quickly crushed and the Dutch ruler, the Prince of Orange, was forced to flee to Britain. The Netherlands became a satellite of the French Republic.

The Dutch had been a reluctant ally; British sources are replete with accounts of the unreliability of their troops and the hostility of their citizens but now they had become the Batavian Republic and an active foe. This was particularly galling to the British Government as not only had they entered the First Coalition, at least in part to protect the Dutch from French aggression, but the powerful Dutch fleet could now undermine the Royal Navy's hard-earned supremacy in the North Sea. Whilst this particular threat was diminished somewhat by Admiral Duncan's victory at Camperduin in 1797, the existence of the Batavian Republic remained a thorn in the side of the British administration, an affront to Britain's prestige and a reminder of their failure.

The United Provinces of the Netherlands was a peculiar political entity. Established by the Treaty of Utrecht in 1579, it was a loose federation of seven sovereign provinces, each of which sent representatives to the States-General who made the laws and ruled the country. Politics within this republic had been, from the start, defined by the struggle between the interests of the merchant classes, who through the wealth of the province of Holland (which accounted for sixty per cent of the Netherlands' total revenue) were able to occupy a position of dominance, and the supporters of the princes of Orange who sought to transform their hereditary role as figure head and military commander into something like the royal power enjoyed by the princes of neighbouring states.[1]

There had been a revolution in 1787 by middle class liberals (the 'Patriots') seeking to limit the power of the *Stadholder* and bring liberty to the people.[2] It had been crushed by the intervention of the Prussian Army under the Duke of Brunswick in extremely short order but the Patriots had merely gone to ground hoping for another opportunity to take power. The revolution in France had given many of them fresh hope and the forces that invaded the Netherlands in 1795 included a 'Batavian Legion' of troops raised and led by Patriots from exile in France.

There seems to be little indication that the ordinary Dutch were particularly thrilled about the institution of the Batavian Republic. Certainly they exhibited little enthusiasm for the allied cause in the war against France but to what extent this translated into wholesale republicanism is debatable. Support for the House of Orange had been traditionally strong amongst the poorer elements of Dutch society (the *grauw*) but this was at a low ebb by 1795, and certainly few seemed sorry to see the prince leave.[3] After four years, however, it had become clear that the Batavian Republic was little more than a puppet of France. The treaty that had created the Batavian Republic was particularly harsh on the Dutch, requiring an indemnity of 100 million florins plus the loan of a further 100 million at three per cent, the surrender of Maastricht, Flushing and much of the Scheldt as well as the imposition of a French garrison to defend their 'liberties'.[4] These measures were the cause of much resentment and Orangist agents found evidence of anti-French sentiment as they spied on their former state, but to what extent the people of the Netherlands were poised to rise in revolt to restore their prince remained to be seen. Certainly the Prince of Orange and his supporters believed that they would, and began to lobby the British Government for assistance.

The arguments put forward by the prince and his party were persuasive and backed by considerable intelligence so perhaps, when taken alongside the humiliation felt by Britain over the loss of their erstwhile ally, it is easy to see why these arguments found a sympathetic audience.

Britain was a maritime power and, apart from the Duke of York's ill-fated expedition to Flanders between 1793 and 1795, its efforts in the war up to this point had been restricted to snapping up isolated French colonies and launching limited coastal raids. As the MP and playwright Richard Sheridan put it, they had merely 'nibbled the rind of France'.[5] A party had emerged in the cabinet, which was intent on carrying the war onto the continent and its leader, William, Lord Grenville, was one of those listening closely to the Orangists' arguments. Grenville was foreign secretary and was close to Prime Minister William Pitt (in fact they were cousins) and he believed that liberating the Netherlands would not only restore Britain's tarnished prestige and strike a major blow against France but it would also open up the possibility for a wide range of other strategic options. Grenville felt that if the war was to be won there had to be an all out co-ordinated effort on the continent. He thought that action in the Netherlands would bring Prussia back into the war as Britain's ally, that a popular rising there would spark others and that these could be supported by the British Army operating on the continent, and finally that they would be able to act with the hitherto victorious Austro-Russian forces now sweeping through Italy towards Switzerland.

Grenville had already been looking for a chance for decisive action and seized this opportunity (as he saw it) with both hands. Easily persuaded of the feasibility of the Orangists' scheme, he sent out diplomats all over Europe (including his brother Thomas) to look for potential allies and began to draw up plans for an expedition. Eventually involving around 48,000 British and Russian troops, it was to be one of the largest operations undertaken by the British Government in the course of the French Revolutionary and Napoleonic Wars. Yet it was to end in abject failure. It finished the active service career of Prince Frederick, Duke of York, caused outrage both in parliament and the press and left the Netherlands under the yoke of the French Republic for another fourteen years.

Chapter 1

A New Coalition

The First Coalition of European powers had been formed in response to republican France's declaration of war and efforts to export its revolution. It had ended in failure with the Austrian capitulation at Campo Formio in 1797 but the war had continued. All attempts to negotiate peace with the ever-changing republican regime in France had failed so the British Government cast around for partners in a new coalition and began to ferment schemes to strike at their enemy in any way possible. Two opposing schools of thought emerged within the British Government; those championing a maritime strategy, aimed at sweeping up France's overseas territories and using Britain's formidable naval power to strangle France's trade, and those favouring a more direct, or continental, strategy which would seek European allies and aim to assist those allies by landing British troops on the continent to attack the French directly.

Even without the Austrian withdrawal from the war, 1797 had been a particularly dark year for Britain with the fleet paralysed by mutinies and a financial collapse looming. Though these immediate crises had been averted, the nation still found itself somewhat beleaguered at the start of 1798. There remained a constant fear of invasion; the French were known to have gathered a fleet of transports and the naval force at Brest continued to cause apprehension. The Irish had risen in revolt in May and the French had indeed landed in Ireland (at Killala) in August. A raid mounted to destroy the lock gates at Ostend had ended in failure and the French had launched an invasion of Egypt, capturing Malta on the way.[1] In India, the Sultan of Mysore Tippoo Sahib was confirmed to be plotting with the French. The Prussians had withdrawn from the war while Austria had suspended hostilities and was engaged in peace talks with France. The French had orchestrated a *coup d'état* and established another satellite state in Switzerland; the Helvetian Republic. However, all was not lost as despite an initially poor performance from the desperately undermanned British Army, the rebellion in Ireland was crushed and the French invasion defeated. Also, the increasing belligerence of the French Republic had begun to unsettle the as yet neutral Tsar of Russia.

Tsar Paul was extremely conservative and notoriously unstable. On his succession he had suspended all moves to assist the allies and stopped the expansion of Russia's army but he was deeply concerned by France's apparent disregard for the established order. He was angered by the establishment of republican satellite states on France's borders and the attempts to redraw the map of Europe following the treaty of Campo Formio, so he now looked to build a new coalition to restore the status quo. Recognizing the importance of Prussia and Austria to the future of any alliance, a delegation led by Prince Repnin was sent to Berlin in May 1798 to begin the four-power talks. All of the powers involved had reason to distrust one another but the rivalry between Austria and Prussia was seen as the major obstacle to establishing an accord. Lord Grenville particularly distrusted the Austrians because they had reneged on the terms of their previous treaty with Britain and the repayment of substantial subsidies remained outstanding. However, it soon became apparent that neither of the German powers were to be trusted as even before the negotiations began both Prussia and Austria were engaging in discussions with the French. In fact the French negotiator Abbé Sieyes was in Berlin whilst the negotiations were in progress.[2] The talks dragged on for weeks with no sign of consensus when something happened that would galvanize the opinion of the tsar and lead him to accelerate his march to war.

The tsar had seen the Order of St John, which ruled Malta, as a bulwark against liberalism and revolutionary excess, and was sufficiently appalled when the French seized the island in June 1798 to declare himself the knights' protector.[3] For Tsar Paul the attack on Malta was the final straw. He channelled his mounting frustration into action and contacted the British Government with an offer of alliance. He immediately sent 16,000 troops to Galicia to support the Austrians and promised a further 60,000 if hostilities against France were to resume. In return he asked for British subsidies to finance his war effort.[4]

The approach divided the British cabinet; Secretary of State for War and the Colonies Henry Dundas had lost all faith in allies but Foreign Secretary

Lord Grenville believed them to be essential to success. Secretary at War William Windham, already unhappy at the ministry's refusal to support the French Royalists, objected to the tsar's proposal as he believed that there could be no offensive alliance without the full co-operation of German powers. It must be an 'all or none coalition' he complained to his colleague George Canning; Britain should get agreement from Austria and Prussia or remain aloof from continental affairs. He believed that the country should 'remain as it is, upon a pure defensive, unless you can have a universal co-operation.'[5] However, despite Pitt's apparently poor grasp of military matters, Windham's objections were overruled and the government drew up a treaty and made plans to provide the Russians with a subsidy of £225,000 to be followed by a monthly subsidy of £75,000. These sums required extraordinary measures to cover them and other expenses caused by the war so on 29 November 1799 Pitt proposed the introduction of a new tax on income.[6] The British cabinet continued to harbour doubts that Austria could be induced to join the coalition and so came up with an objective that could be tackled by Britain and Russia alone. That objective was the liberation of the Netherlands.

Perhaps, initially, prompted by the entreaties of the former Dutch ruler, the Prince of Orange, exiled at Hampton Court, Grenville had settled upon Holland as the focus of Britain's next intervention in continental affairs. There was much sympathy for the Dutch in Britain. Both states were maritime powers with strong mercantile economies before the war. Britain and the United Provinces had been allies since the seventeenth century and the French seizure of the Netherlands, following the collapse of the First Coalition, was seen as a national humiliation in Britain. The dismantling of the French satellite regime, the Batavian Republic and the restoration of the House of Orange became major British war aims.[7]

The foreign secretary was further encouraged in his plan by a steady flow of intelligence from the Netherlands and the unrest there, which had led to a military coup. The coup had been led by General Daendels, whom the Directors had tried to have arrested for dissent, but had fled to France. Having confirmed French support, Daendels' return to Amsterdam in June 1798 was something of a triumphal procession accompanied by cheering crowds. Here, with the connivance of France's General Joubert, he placed himself at the head of a couple of grenadier companies and stormed the seat of government. The Jacobin Directors fled and more moderate representatives took their places.[8]

On the surface all looked quite promising and a draft treaty, containing a clause suggesting the liberation of the Netherlands as a possible secondary objective, was duly sent to St Petersburg via the British envoy Charles Whitworth.[9] However, by this time the Austrian ambassador had persuaded the capricious tsar that his nation was 'sincerely determined on war' and just needed to clear up the issue of the British loan before renewing the conflict. The Prussians too had made overtures; in an apparent reversal of policy, their minister Haugwitz had spoken to Russian Ambassador Panin 'about the possibility of a Prussian invasion of Holland and enquired what subsidies Prussia could expect from England'.[10] Believing, like Windham, that concerted action by all the major European powers stood the best chance of success, the tsar called the potential participants together in Berlin to discuss terms. The Prussians appeared to be the natural ally in a coalition against France, particularly one aimed at freeing Holland from French control: they were conservative; they were considered to be the pre-eminent military power of the age; the wife of the Prince of Orange was the King of Prussia's sister and they had intervened in Dutch affairs to put down a revolution in 1788. However, Prussia was not the power it had been under Frederick the Great. The new king (Frederick William III) was weak and his ministers vied with each other for control of policy, leaving the nation weak and divided.

The British nonetheless considered Prussian assistance to be pivotal in the success or failure of their Dutch venture. Lord Grenville sent his brother Thomas as 'envoy extraordinary' to Prussia to negotiate the formation of an offensive league between Great Britain and the leading monarchies of the continent 'to crush the subverting power of the revolution which had its seat at Paris and restore the system and landmarks its victories had swept away.'[11] Having already been forced to turn back once, when the frozen rigging of his first ship, the *Champion*, made it necessary to return to port, Grenville's second ship, the *Proserpine*, also met with disaster. Hitting a sand bank just off the German coast, she was struck by floating ice and sank. The passengers and crew had to abandon ship and make a harrowing six-mile journey across the ice, in freezing conditions, during which fourteen people died. However, Grenville eventually reached Berlin to carry out his mission.[12]

All of this political and diplomatic manoeuvring had been going on against a backdrop of deteriorating Austro-French relations. After Bonaparte's whirlwind campaign in Italy the Austrians had signed the treaty of Campo Formio in 1797, suspending hostilities and paving the way for peace negotiations to formalize the conditions of the armistice. These negotiations took place at Rastatt and were characterized throughout by double-dealing on both sides.[13] Even before negotiations had begun, the French were quietly continuing to acquire territory. Having consolidated their hold on Italy by establishing the Ligurian and the Cisalpine republics in Genoa and northern Italy respectively, they seized the Ionian Islands and then occupied the Papal States thus creating the Roman Republic. They then fermented a revolution in Switzerland and created the Helvetian Republic and occupied Piedmont having forced the king to abdicate.[14]

As well as approaching the tsar, the Austrians had made overtures to the British Government before the ink had dried on the treaty of Campo Formio. Austrian Chancellor Thugut believed that the resumption of hostilities was inevitable but had still hoped to gain something from the negotiations at Rastatt. He would probably have preferred the content of the talks to remain a secret but Prussian agents uncovered many details which scandalized Europe and ultimately made it hard for anyone to trust him.[15] Oblivious to, or perhaps unmoved by, the damage the conference was having on his nation's international reputation Thugut continued to negotiate with both sides whilst rebuilding Austria's army. Although the programme of reorganization made little headway, recruiting had gone on apace and an army of around 'two hundred and forty thousand men, supported by an immense artillery' stood ready to take the field by the start of 1799.[16] So although the Austrians were now distrusted by everyone, they would make a powerful ally and few were willing to make a move without their support. This distrust, engendered by what had been uncovered about Austria's negotiations, was deepened by their abandonment of Naples.

Seeking to rid his country of French dominance the King of Naples had joined the coalition. Encouraged by the presence of Admiral Horatio Nelson, fresh from his destruction of the French fleet at Aboukir Bay, the

Neapolitans jumped the gun and attacked the nearest French troops. Asked to assist, the Austrians sent only General Mack, an able administrator but a hitherto unsuccessful field commander, to lead the Neapolitan forces. The target of their offensive was Rome but Mack made no effort to exploit the dispersion of the French forces defending the Roman Republic and although the Neapolitans entered Rome on 29 November they divided their forces and were defeated in detail at various points around the city. In trying to retrieve the situation, the Neapolitans moved slowly and showed little fighting spirit; 'Mack despaired of success and instantly commenced his retreat towards the Neapolitan frontier … eighteen thousand veterans had driven before them forty thousand men, splendidly dressed and abundantly equipped, but utterly destitute of the discipline and courage requisite to obtain success in war.'[17] Mack, 'disgusted with the conduct of his soldiers' resigned and Naples fell to the French becoming yet another satellite state, the Parthenopean Republic, while the royal family fled to Sicily.[18]

The Austrians had stood by and watched while their supposed ally had been destroyed and their enemy became even stronger. Whilst they may have appeared a great potential asset to Grenville's coalition it seemed that their government's policy prevented them from realizing that potential. In fact Chancellor Thugut was infuriated by the whole affair and believed it to be a British plot to drag Austria into war. However, fortunately for Grenville's plans, events would conspire to push Austria off the fence and into direct conflict with France.

Whilst technically not at war, the French had never stopped their aggressive programme of expansion and annexation, and at the beginning of 1799 they crossed the Rhine to secure territories that they had been promised by the unratified treaty of Campo Formio and to threaten Austria itself. Though they had still not agreed to the terms of the coalition, particularly in regard to the repayment of the British loan, this proved too much of a provocation for Austria and they immediately moved to oppose this aggression. The war had begun.

The French opened hostilities by sending two armies across the Rhine on 1 March but their general, Jourdan, had been beaten by the Austrians under Archduke Charles in a series of battles between the Danube and Lake Constance, driven out of Swabia and forced back over the frontier. Jourdan's retreat had left the other French Army under Bernadotte dangerously exposed so they too returned to France. In Italy, the French Army under Moreau had suffered a serious defeat at Magnano at the hands of General Zach and, like their northern comrades, were on the retreat. Even this successful belligerence did not convince the British of Austria's honourable intentions and Grenville was to comment that:

> 'I have so total a want of confidence in everything Austrian that I look upon this only as a prelude to some patched up peace that will give to Austria a score of leagues more in Italy or in Germany, and may possibly (but not probably) restore the King of Naples; but will leave everything else exactly where the war found it.'[19]

The Russians however were sufficiently impressed to begin sending troops to assist Austria in Germany and Italy. On 15 April, Marshal Count Alexander Suvarov arrived in Italy and took immediate control of all allied forces. The effect was electrifying. Although the Austrians had been successful on their own in this theatre, Suvarov's army bought a new spirit of the offensive to their combined operations and a string of victories drove the French back more than 100 miles in ten days. The coalition forces entered Milan in triumph on 28 April and, working in concert with a popular catholic rising in Naples, were able to throw the French out of Italy entirely and by August were poised to cross the Alps into Switzerland. The still ambivalent Grenville was moved to exclaim: 'These Austrians are really going at a great rate in Italy, but as much as their armies delight me, so much am I disgusted with their cursed politics.'[20]

There was more to come. Diplomatic relations between France and Austria had collapsed; French Ambassador Bernadotte had provoked the patriotic citizens of Vienna and been forced to flee ahead of an angry mob, but the infamous negotiations at Rastatt had continued.[21] However with the increasingly hostile international situation, things soon turned nasty. French messengers were detained and their papers confiscated while in Rastatt itself, the French negotiators were given notice to leave within twenty-four hours and were packed and ready to go by eight o'clock on the evening of 28 April. They were held up at the gates of Rastatt for nearly an hour before being permitted to leave but only 500 paces down the road were stopped again by a group of Hussars of the Szeckler Regiment. Some later accounts suggested the cavalrymen may have been drunk but this is not mentioned in the account of an eyewitness who said they pulled three of the French delegates from their carriages one by one and massacred them with blows of the sabre. Though the survivors were escorted back to France, no explanation of this incident was ever given and it meant that diplomatic initiative was now clearly over.[22] Such an atrocity did little to raise Austria's standing in the eyes of their potential allies but it did mean that there was much less chance of them resuming their double game of secret negotiations with France. At least for the time being.

Meanwhile in Berlin the four power talks had made little headway. Not long after his arrival, Thomas Grenville had begun to send reports of the Prussian's disappointing recalcitrance, which became less surprising when it emerged that they were also in secret talks with the French. By April, Lord Grenville despaired of making any headway in Prussia and this made the liberation of the Netherlands impossible. He considered the plan dead in the water and even began to discuss sending Thomas to Vienna instead.[23] The Russians too were disappointed but as the war was now in full swing and Austro–French diplomatic relations seemingly irrevocably terminated, the tsar, impatient for action, gave up on Prussia and began to look for ways to strike at France without their assistance.

In addition to their military setbacks in Italy and Germany, the French were also facing serious opposition to their rule in several of the satellite republics and areas they were seeking to conquer. The decision to expand the system of universal conscription (the Jourdan Law) had led to widespread unrest which, coupled with the devastation wrought by French armies living off the land in territories through which they moved, developed into wholesale armed insurrection in several parts of Europe. The most serious of these were in Belgium, the Rhineland, and Italy as well as disaffected parts of France itself. Most of these risings were easily put down but they caused a great deal of disorder and showed that France, and its new satellites, were far from united in embracing the ideals of the republic. The success of the rising in Naples, which forced the French to abandon the south of Italy, had the side effect of adding weight to the suggestion that a popular rising in favour of the House of Orange would return the Netherlands to the allied cause with only minimal assistance from Britain.[24]

The idea that the Netherlands could be liberated so easily meant that the scheme might be initiated, at least, without Prussian intervention. Russian assistance in this area had already been mooted in Grenville's first draft proposal to the tsar and a landing in the Netherlands would enable him to strike at the French directly and act as a diversion from the main Russian effort in Italy and Switzerland. Whitworth was dispatched to lay the new proposal before Tsar Paul who, to his surprise (and discomfort) granted him a personal audience.

Intimidated by his personal meeting with the unstable tsar, Whitworth, through a misunderstanding, promised him the entire subsidy intended for Austria and Prussia and agreed to confirm his installation as Grand Master of the Knights of St John. This was not what Grenville had intended but the result was a treaty promising almost 18,000 men and the ships to carry them to Holland, which was specifically named in the treaty as the expedition's target.[25] The details of this agreement, thrashed out by Whitworth in circumstances that earned him the censure of the king and nearly cost him his career would be a bone of contention in the coming months but Grenville had his agreement and the Netherlands were to be liberated. The Orangist General Stamford and Captain Home Popham of the Royal Navy were sent to join Whitworth in St Petersburg to 'discuss the military objections which will, perhaps be put forwards by the Russian officers.'[26] It was not all that Grenville had hoped for but it was a start.

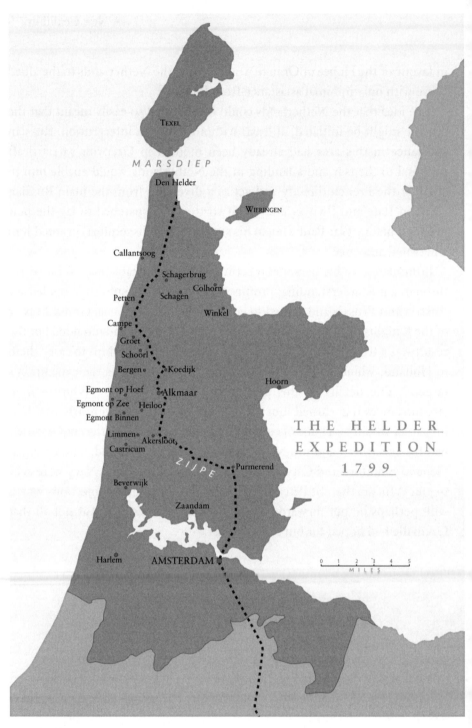

Map 1. The Helder. (*Produced by Pen & Sword for* The Late Lord: the Life of John Pitt – 2nd Earl of Chatham, *by J. Reiter*)

Chapter 2

The Secret Expedition

Although the war had now begun, the political wrangling continued. The liberation of the Netherlands was now a definite objective enshrined in treaty between Britain and Russia but how it was to be achieved had yet to be decided. An attack on the Netherlands made sound strategic sense; a large force would threaten to remove one of France's most important satellite states, forcing vital resources to be diverted from the main theatre of operations in northern Italy and Switzerland. It was felt that this diversion would greatly enhance the chances of Suvarov's army inflicting a decisive defeat on the French forces. Also, if the intelligence which was being laid before Lord Grenville and his cabinet colleagues was to be believed, this was going to be an easy victory for the Batavian Republic was on the verge of a counter-revolution.

As soon as the idea of liberating the Netherlands had been born, Grenville and the supporters of the House of Orange had tried to gather as much intelligence as they were able. Thomas Grenville wrote to his brother on 10 April that: 'The Prince of Orange has this moment left me, and has promised great activity amongst his friends for information from the Low Countries.'[1] As it was, the prominent Anglo-Dutch family the Bentincks had been gathering information on the government's behalf since the coup of 1798. Having received intelligence from the Netherlands for some months, Charles Bentinck stole across the border himself from Varel, in northern Germany, on 3 November 1798.

Bentinck was soon reporting that: 'In all the different places I have been at, I found the same disposition pervading all ranks of people with few exceptions.' Namely a yearning for the return of the old order. He also reported the weakness of the French garrison, which he estimated at less than 6,000 men and the loyalties of the Batavian Army:

'I have every reason to think that … the Batavian soldiers would not pay much attention to the orders of their commanders. General Daendels was, as I am told, consulted lately as to the expediency of sending a force to the frontiers of Brabant to watch the motions of the insurgents on that side. He said in answer that the government ought not to rely on the troops who would most likely join the insurgents.'[2]

On his return he continued to pass on optimistic reports from informants such as Jan Munniks and a Colonel Schutter. Schutter believed that many prominent members of the Batavian Government, and even General Daendels, could be persuaded to join the counter-revolution 'with very little trouble, some money and the hopes of pardon'. Munniks was so confident that he believed liberation could be achieved without Prussian intervention and that only a 'few English regiments' were required 'to establish and preserve internal tranquillity'.[3]

The Orangists were able to elicit the help of sympathizers who remained in the Netherlands. They channelled their information through the Dutch émigré Baron Fagel, who also employed spies and informants such as the exotic 'Alexandre'. The wisdom of relying on intelligence provided by those wanting Britain to mount an operation in their interests must be questioned and Grenville did employ professional agents (such as Monsieur de la Paule) to verify their optimistic reports as well as corresponding with well-placed nobles such as Baron Armfeldt and the Margrave of Hesse Homburg. Although these agents claimed to have canvassed the opinions of the *grands et petits*, they only seem to have reported what Grenville wanted to hear and a summation of opinion expressed in The Hague and other parts of Holland would prove of little military value to those planning the expedition.[4]

In addition to the apparent thirst of the Dutch people to throw off the yoke and restore their former rulers, Grenville had been persuaded that the Batavian Republic was almost undefended. Bentinck's claim the previous year that the French garrison was less than 6,000 men was backed up by Prussian reports claiming 'that there are not above 4,500 men in Holland, about the same number in Mayence'. However, the Orangist agent Fagel believed that even this figure was inflated.[5] There were also further reports of the unreliability of the Batavian troops with Fagel believing that 'the new levies which they are endeavouring to make there will join the Stadtholders's army whenever it shall appear.'[6] Grenville clearly took these reports at face value for he wrote to Dundas on 30 July that he considered the Batavian Army 'more with us than against us' and that they would be 'a source of more embarrassment than confidence to the leaders of the French party in that country'.[7] They were wrong on both counts.

Whilst there was no doubt considerable hostility towards the French, this did not necessarily equate to a desire to return to the rule of the notoriously conservative House of Orange and to risk everything by taking up arms against the regime. Even Fagel reported the 'reluctance and terror which he still finds to prevail so as to make every man, however anxious for a change, tremble at the idea of committing himself by any decided act.'[8] Not only were the Dutch unwilling to rebel on their own accord but other, less sanguine, agents reported deep divisions in Dutch society and that although they were united in their hatred of the greedy, arrogant French they did not all support a return of the House of Orange. So noticeable was the objection from some parties that the Prussian minister, Haugwitz, advised Grenville to avoid 'naming the Stadtholder in the first efforts to be made in that country'.[9] When taken in conjunction with Dutch suspicions of the motives of the British, who had been steadily acquiring Dutch overseas territories, it is perhaps unsurprising that the Dutch were lukewarm in their response to the expedition.

Any negative reports that did reach Grenville however were brushed aside and the planning of the operation began. The British military envoys in St Petersburg, General Stamford and Captain Popham, started to work with the Russians to decide how best to use the force at their disposal. Although they would not be on hand to advise the ministers directly, Stamford and Popham relayed their suggestions to London via Thomas Grenville.

Major General Stamford was descended from the English earls of Stamford and had served as an officer in the army of Frederick the Great before acting as a tutor in military subjects to the sons of the Prince of Orange. In 1794 he had been adjutant general of the Army of the United Provinces and had most recently been the Prince of Orange's emissary at the Berlin conference. He was therefore well placed to give the British Government advice on any plans for invading the Netherlands.[10] Captain Popham was a rising star in the Royal Navy and despite his involvement in the disastrous raid on Ostend in 1798 he retained the favour of his superiors and a reputation as an original thinker. It was his task to oversee the transportation of the Russian contingent. The two seem to have got on well though Stamford was to say of his colleague that 'I find myself wanting to take the bull by the flank, he by the horns.'[11]

Popham had not been in Russia long when he came up with the idea that the Russian troops should travel along the Eyder river rather than by open sea as spending less time at sea meant they would arrive 'fresh for service'. It was proposed that they would land at Delfzijl where Stamford believed they would 'be easily masters of the Schantz, Byrtang and Coverden, and thus have complete possession of the provinces of Groningen and Friesland, where they could long maintain themselves against any force.' Conversely, Popham reported that Stamford felt a landing in north Holland would be 'much more precarious in practice, and much more doubtful in success from the means of attack which the enemy might find in the ships of Amsterdam and the fleet of the Texel.' Finally it was noted that General Stamford considered 20,000 men 'amply sufficient for the whole object'.[12]

This all sounded very promising but Stamford made these recommendations in the belief that the Prussians would be participating in the operation. Although diplomacy with the Prussians had moved at a snail's pace, most in government believed that the Prussians would eventually come around and, as they saw it, see sense. On 20 June, Thomas Grenville wrote from Berlin that he believed the Prussians were merely dragging their heels over logistical matters and would 'soon quicken their march if they thought we were sailing to Holland as fast as I trust and hope we are.' On 22 July however, Haugwitz summoned Thomas Grenville and Russian Ambassador Panin to a meeting where, with apparent embarrassment, he informed them that the Prussian Government were no longer interested in joining the coalition as they had begun negotiations with France. Thomas was appalled, describing the event as 'a picture of shame and disgrace' and said he would 'rather have died on a dunghill than have undergone the humiliating scene which Haugwitz had yesterday to pass through in his evening conference.' All hopes of Prussian assistance were at an end or, as Thomas Grenville put it 'vanished into idle air'. There would be no Prussian troops, no passage down the Eyder and no landing at Delfzijl as all would contravene Prussia's neutrality. The sole responsibility for planning now passed to London.[13]

The non-participation of Prussia was a bitter blow as all plans had depended upon it and all had believed that it would eventually come about. However, so convinced was Grenville by the optimistic tone of the majority of the intelligence he had been receiving, he believed the main aims of the expedition to Holland could be achieved without Prussian participation. The expedition was to go ahead. Measures to gather the required resources now stepped up a gear.

As part of their treaty obligations the Russians had agreed to devote 20,000 men to the task of liberating Holland and Britain had agreed to supply 13,000. But there was a problem. By 1799, Britain had only around 16,000 infantry at home available for service overseas and the number of those volunteering for service had slowed to a trickle.[14] Since the outbreak of the French Revolution in 1789 the British Army had been 'scattered over the habitable world by half regiments, in different garrisons, or frittered away in detachments in Ireland.'[15] Fevers in the West Indies had further reduced numbers and those raised for the Duke of York's Flanders campaign in 1793 were of very poor quality, with one staff officer describing them as 'worse than any I ever saw.'[16] Even this inadequate force had been decimated by the campaign so a new army would have to be raised. Fortunately for Pitt and his colleagues there was a source of readily available manpower: the militia. They would just have to change the law.

The militia was a large force raised by ballot in times of war specifically for the defence of the nation. It was the closest that Britain had to a conscript force but its soldiers were prohibited from serving abroad by law. The terms of their employment had been changed before to allow militia units to serve in Ireland during the rebellion the previous year and so, although Britain was still under threat of invasion, Pitt and Dundas felt that these conditions could be changed again to provide them with the force they needed to liberate the Netherlands. In order to tap this rich source of healthy, partially trained, soldiery they proposed reducing the establishment of the militia and offering substantial inducements to the now redundant militiamen to enlist in regiments of the line. Though previous attempts to introduce such a measure had failed, the Militia Reduction Act was passed by parliament on 12 July 1799. It proved very successful and 24,977 men were transferred to the regular army by the middle of August.[17] Yet this was a drop in the ocean compared with the manpower that the French Republic could call upon. Since the introduction of mass conscription through the *Levée en Masse* (1793) and the Jourdan Law (1798), the French had been able to add hundreds of thousands of men to their armies each year.

There was also an issue of quality. Whilst the militiamen were relatively fit and healthy and could perform the drills necessary to form up on the battlefield and fire their weapons, they were not fully trained soldiers.[18] The British Army's official historian Sir John Fortescue would later write: 'The Ministers, after all the bitter experience of the past six years, had not yet learned the difference between an army and an assembly of men in red coats.'[19] The men were not given time to train, recognize their officers or even, in some cases, adopt the uniforms of their new regiments.[20] Nor was sufficient provision made for their supply and transport and many sailed without even greatcoats. The government were not entirely unaware of their inadequacies. Windham wrote that they were 'in a state which no officer would describe as fit for service'[21] and even the eternally optimistic Grenville called the use of the militia battalions 'unpromising and difficult'. There was a sense in some quarters that the whole thing was being rushed. Windham, still hoping to support the French Royalists, believed that 'this expedition to Holland will destroy in the bud … an army that, with a little delay, would have exceeded anything that we have seen since the first years of the war.' Yet, for all the misgivings about the force, it was the only one available if Britain were to fulfil its obligations and achieve its aim of liberating the Netherlands.

By 19 July, Grenville was able to report jubilantly to his brother that 'militia enlisting goes well, and will I trust give us from 15,000 to 20,000 men.'[22] Whilst the army was slowly starting to build at their camp on Barham Downs there remained the issue of how to transport them to their objective. Even by using revenue cutters from the North Sea and reusing the ships bringing troops from Ireland, the Board of Transport was only able to provide enough ships to transport 10,000 men.[23] This problem was exacerbated by Popham's report that the craft intended to transport the troops from Russia were unsuitable for the open seas. This meant that British ships would have to be diverted from landing their own troops, complicating matters considerably and possibly making the whole operation impossible. Fortunately Popham was able to secure the tsar's approval to provide ships to be converted to transports on the British model. He reported: 'I have not left one idle man in Cronstadt.'[24] The immediate problem with the Russians had been solved but the shortage of transports meant that the British contingent would still have to be moved in successive waves, which would have an impact on the planning of the expedition.

On 10 July, Dundas wrote to the king announcing that the ministry had appointed a commander for the expedition, Sir Ralph Abercromby, though he felt it to be politically expedient that the king's son, the Duke of York, would take over once the second wave arrived. Dundas wrote that it would be unjust 'if the deliverance of Holland and perhaps of the Netherlands, should be accomplished without the personal participation of the Duke of York.'[25] Although Abercromby would only command the initial contingent, the responsibility for planning the military side of the operation rested solely with him and he was soon to make his presence felt around the planning table.

Abercromby made his position clear from the start:

'The object of the present armament is the conquest of that part of Holland to the northward of the Waal. The advanced season of the year demands the greatest promptitude and vigour in the execution of it. No operation which does not immediately tend to the accomplishment of this object ought to be undertaken.'[26]

Stamford's plan to land in the province of Delfzijl had been made impossible by the defection of Prussia but now it was suggested that the force could menace large parts of the Netherlands by capturing a series of islands and coastal areas. Walcheren, Goree and Ameland were suggested as well as a possible landing in Groningen to take that province and perhaps attack Friesland, Overyseel and Coevorden. Abercromby rejected them all. He could see no purpose in seizing small islands, particularly Walcheren, which he described as 'extremely unhealthy' and he believed too little 'remains of the season to land in Groeningen'. His meetings with the navy and what local experts he could find did nothing to dissuade him from this view. His contention was that Holland must be attacked in force along the Meuse river, possibly capturing the island of Voorn where they could 'act on the Waal and the Rhine' and be safe from any French attempt to dislodge them. He also urged the mobilization of several regiments of cavalry to 'add to the uncertainty and increase the alarm.'[27] This plan was rejected after a meeting on 2 August with men who knew the area (Captain Flynn and Colonel Sontag) who felt it would be impossible to get the fleet and the transports close to the coast or to supply the troops once they were landed.[28]

Grenville believed that because of the transport problem, the first contingent should strike a blow independently at a small target such as Walcheren island.[29] Abercromby, already engaged ordering ammunition and artillery from the Board of Ordnance as well as moving his troops towards their ships at Southampton, added detail to his objections:

'The Island of Walcheren is of small extent and is flat; at this season of the year every movement, every object may be seen from every steeple. The enemy therefore cannot be easily distracted or deceived. The disembarkation very probably must be effected by force, a strong co-operation on the part of the navy will be necessary.'

He went on to add that flat-bottomed barges and gunboats would be required in some quantity, which in practical terms ruled out Walcheren as an objective though it continued to be mentioned in government dispatches right up until the actual landing.[30]

Meanwhile things were moving on apace in the rest of Europe with fresh French forces bearing down on Suvarov in northern Italy and Grenville chafing at the bit, feeling that time was slipping away from him. Further reports from his brother Thomas led him to believe that the Netherlands were by now a powder keg that could ignite at any moment. He complained about what he perceived as obstructiveness on Abercromby's part, accusing him of being possessed by the spirit of the famously cautious Duke of Brunswick. When the general suggested that it might be prudent to wait for the Russians, who were not scheduled to sail until 22 July at the earliest, he exploded: 'Were all the Generals on earth unanimous in that opinion, I am sure nothing they could say would weigh a feather in my mind.'[31] His impatience to get the expedition underway was clouding his judgement. He had known all along that the force was possibly inadequate and the task difficult but he feared that, at this rate, the campaign would not commence before September when deteriorating weather conditions would inevitably hamper operations. He could not understand why the military men would not just take what they had and attack a smaller target, such as Walcheren.[32]

Grenville's fury and Pitt's impatience to get the expedition underway prevailed. On 2 August, Pitt smugly reported that 'all military objections have been overruled … and that we shall now hear of no more difficulties.' Ready or not, the best and most prepared of the army's battalions began to embark upon the available transports. Even as they boarded, Grenville was beside himself with worry that the operation might have to be cancelled following the dire news that a French fleet of 40 ships of the line had left Cadiz on 20 July for an unknown destination. Yet to his relief there was no further delay.[33] The fleet finally left harbour on 10 August and it was perhaps a measure of the haste in which the expedition had been dispatched that even at the point of sailing it had no fixed destination. Dundas sent Abercromby an urgent dispatch outlining the possible objectives for the expedition:

'In the first place I must state to you that the advices lately received from the continent render it a matter of the most urgent necessity that the expedition should, without a moments [*sic*] further delay, proceed to the coast of Holland, and as there appears very little doubt of your being able to take possession of the island of Goree, you are in any case to consider it as the first objective to be attacked.'

He added that 'should the attempt appear altogether impracticable, or so dangerous as to induce you to forgo the prospect of the superior advantage to be derived from it, the next in point of immediate importance is to attempt to get possession of the Helder and the Texel Island.' Finally, he left the whole thing up to Abercromby and Admiral Duncan and said: 'I think it right to add that I do not wish to exclude the exercise of your own discretion, in concert with the Admiral, either in respect to modifying each or either of these plans, or in adopting any other.'[34]

Even while the fleet was at sea the execution of the campaign continued to be a matter of great discussion. Abercromby was troubled by the task before him and Adjutant General Alexander Hope, who believed that their force was inadequate, wrote to him with a list of suggestions. These were largely aimed at disrupting Dutch trade, so that the expedition may gain credit and prove to be a 'public utility' without putting it at risk of destruction, which, he wrote, had been causing the general some apprehension.[35]

It was perhaps as well that the actual destination was unknown for despite the fact all parties involved knew it was necessary to keep the expedition a secret, it had proved impossible to do so. French agents had been reporting to Paris about the marshalling of Orangist sympathizers in June and even if their spies had not been keeping them up to date, full details of the 'secret' expedition were regularly reported in the British press.[36] *The London Chronicle* had reported the review of the troops on Barham Downs by King George III and the Prince of Orange and on 5 August it wrote that: 'part of the troops had begun to embark on board transports at Dover: Admiral Mitchell, who is to have command of the foreign expedition, arrived in town yesterday from the Downs.' On 10 August it was reported that 'The Earl of Chatham in the course of next week, sets off for the encampment at Barham Downs, to accompany His Royal Highness the Duke of York; his lordship is to have a command in the secret expedition.' Two days later, if anyone was still in any doubt, the paper gave a full organizational breakdown of the invading army and revealed the object of the expedition as 'to re-establish the government of the *Stadtholder*, which the great body of the Dutch anxiously desire.' Not only did it report on what it actually called a 'secret expedition' but it also said that the French knew all about it. It added that on 2 August, the French Directory decreed General Guillaume Marie Anne Brune to command the Batavian Army because 'the British government in several ports of the channel are preparing a secret expedition.'[37] Richard Sheridan, the playwright and radical MP, was later to mock the secrecy of the expedition in parliament saying: 'Never was such an undertaking conducted in such ostentatious mystery – never did the object of a secret expedition obtain so much universal notoriety.'[38]

Therefore, although the exact landing point remained undecided, the French knew roughly where the expedition was headed and frenzied preparations to meet it were made throughout the republic's dominions. The expedition, based on the flimsiest of unverified intelligence and comprised of raw, barely-trained troops with insufficient supplies or transport, sailed to an unspecified part of Holland to act in concert with an untried ally to ferment a revolt – which it could not say for certain would occur – against an enemy that was now fully apprised of their approach. Military considerations had been outweighed by the political and the consequences were perhaps inevitable.

Chapter 3

Red Coats and Gherkins – the Anglo-Russian Army in 1799

The force which set sail for the Helder in August 1799 was essentially a new army, composed largely of men transferred from the militia only weeks before. It was very much untried and whilst contemporary accounts praise their performance and talk at length of their potential, that praise was qualified and the troops' best years lay ahead of them. Their commanders, however, were (with a couple of exceptions) experienced soldiers with many years campaigning behind them.

The commander of the first wave of the expedition was Sir Ralph Abercromby. Born in 1734, he had been in the army since 1756 with his first commission in the Third Regiment of 3rd Guards (3rd/Guards) taking him to Germany during the Seven Years' War, where he served as a staff officer. Having risen to the rank of colonel, he retired on half pay in 1783 when his regiment was disbanded.[1] Rejoining the army at the outbreak of war he was appointed the Duke of York's second in command during the 1794 Flanders campaign, where he masterminded the harrowing winter retreat through Holland following the recall of his chief and 'his coolness, intrepidity, and indomitable resolution were of the most essential service'. In 1796 he commanded the expedition to the West Indies, which resulted in the capture of St Lucia, St Vincent, Demerara and Berbice. The following year he took Trinidad and made an unsuccessful attempt to capture Puerto Rico but returned home, protesting ill health, just in time to take command in Ireland, which was teetering on the brink of revolt. Here, in spite of numerous political difficulties he laboured to bring discipline to an army he famously described as 'formidable to everyone but the enemy'.[2] Following a political row over the role of the army in the province, he resigned before the outbreak of the rebellion itself. It was acts such as this that gave Abercromby a reputation as undiplomatic and led the Duke of York's biographer, Alfred Burne, to call him 'the give up general'.[3] Whilst he was, by 1799, quite advanced in years and certainly cautious this was by no means a fair assessment. Abercromby's performance as a military commander was solid and largely successful, prompting Pitt to describe him as 'standing higher than any other officer in general opinion'.[4] In planning the Helder expedition Abercromby had shown a high level of strategic acumen and displayed great knowledge of the needs of such a task. The objections he presented to the ministers were entirely sensible and even Grenville admitted that 'It is very right for a military commander about to undertake an important expedition to make his demands upon government as on the most unfavourable calculation that can by any possibility be made of the resistance he is to meet with.' Throughout the expedition, Abercromby acted with great professionalism and guided the troops under his command with determination in spite of their inadequacies and the many difficulties they were to face. His character was summed up by one who knew him well: Henry Bunbury, aide to the Duke of York, described him as 'An honest, fearless, straightforward man; and withal sagacious and well-skilled in his business as a soldier … respected and beloved by all who served under his command.'[5]

The man appointed to overall command of the expedition was His Royal Highness Prince Frederick Augustus, the Duke of York, second son of King George III. He had received military training at a young age in Prussia and had commanded the army during the campaign in Flanders in 1793–5. Despite misgivings about his abilities, it was felt that York was the only general who, as a prince of the blood, would be acceptable to the Russians as commander.[6] The historian Simon Schama claimed that the Batavians greeted York's appointment 'as the one ray of hope in an otherwise murky outlook' and many have been critical of York's abilities as a general.[7] Bunbury, for example, wrote that 'he was not qualified to be even the ostensible head of a great army on arduous service' and this view was echoed by numerous others.[8] Perhaps as a measure of their lack of confidence in his leadership, Pitt and Dundas appointed a council of war to be consulted in any decision, although it wasn't widely used.

Perhaps York's most important failing as a commander was the handling of his Russian allies. Despite his biographer Burne's attempts to portray him as an eighteenth century Eisenhower, his personal conflict with the Russian commanders (especially Essen) ensured that they co-operated grudgingly at best and greatly diminished the expedition's chances of success.[9] Although he may have been aware of the need 'to ensure harmonious dealings and smooth co-operation between the three nationalities in his army' and publicly wrote in diplomatic terms of his allies, his personal interactions with them were actually divisive. Bunbury, who served on his staff, reported that after Bergen the duke lost faith in his allies and was openly rude about them. The result was that by the end of the campaign 'the Russians were angry, sullen and scarcely to be counted as allies.'[10] Whilst the Russians had not proved to be all that was hoped for, York's poor handling made them less than useless and reflected badly on his qualities as a coalition commander.

By the professional standards that had become increasingly common by the end of the Napoleonic period, the Duke of York was (even by his own admission) perhaps not amongst the best generals of his day.[11] He was ponderous in his manoeuvres and lacking in initiative and flexibility but he was really just a product of the eighteenth century school of warfare in which he had been trained. Whilst it could be (and has been) argued that Wellington or Napoleon would have been more successful, it cannot be said that his leadership cost the campaign. Even the acid-tongued Sheridan didn't go that far.[12]

Abercromby confessed to being pleasantly surprised by the performance of Sir James Pulteney, the man appointed his second in command in the first wave. 'Sir J Pulteney really surprised me,' he said. 'He shewed ardour and intelligence and did himself honour. I have reason to be satisfied with all the general officers although they did not all shew the same intelligence.'[13] Bunbury, meanwhile, described Pulteney as 'a very odd man' but added that he was experienced and knowledgeable, 'good tempered, cool, unpretending, utterly indifferent to danger or to hardships'. According to Bunbury, the only things that prevented him from becoming a commander of the first order were his 'awkward manners' and his lack of confidence in his own opinions.[14]

Sir David Dundas replaced Pulteney as second in command with the arrival of the Duke of York (though the wound Pulteney received at Callantsoog did not keep him from his duties for long). Dundas was the author of the controversial regulations which had been brought in only a few years before and introduced a uniform system of drill to the British Army. As you would expect, Dundas was an expert in moving troops on the battlefield and Bunbury described him as 'a brave, careful and well skilled officer'.[15]

Apart from Colonel MacDonald, commander of the reserve, who divided opinion (Abercromby called him 'a brave and skilful officer' whilst Moore clearly believed him too reckless) the subordinate commanders of the British contingent performed with adequate professionalism and attracted little comment.[16] They included Sir John Moore, later a hero of the Peninsular War, who was highly praised for his conduct in this campaign in the course of which he was wounded three times. Lord Chatham, the brother of Prime Minister William Pitt was lambasted by later historians but performed creditably and was praised for the expert handling of his brigade at Egmond. He was also wounded and was probably not even present when his brigade got lost in the dunes at Castricum. The role of General George Don is more complex. In addition to commanding a brigade in Pulteney's division, Don had a diplomatic role. Using contacts that he had established before the expedition sailed, he tried to make contact with the Batavian Directory to negotiate their surrender. It was a mission that was to land him in the dungeon of the French fortress at Brest. There were numerous casualties amongst the brigade and battalion commanders throughout the campaign but control seems to have been maintained and there were few lapses at this level.

As for the troops themselves, much has been written about their discipline and performance in this campaign, most probably because of the controversial (or at least unusual) origin of the majority and because they went on to become what many historians believe to be one of the finest armies ever to have been deployed by Great Britain.

Regiments of the British Army at this time were divided into battalions of roughly 1,000 men and this campaign was one of the few occasions in history when several battalions of the same regiment served together and at almost full strength. Each battalion was split into eight 'centre' companies and two elite 'flank' companies; one of light infantry for skirmishing and outpost duties and one of grenadiers whose job it was to lead attacks on the enemy. It was common practice in this period to combine flank companies to create elite battalions and for the Helder expedition, two battalions were created from the grenadiers and light companies of the militia regiments deemed unready for service. Although commanded by experienced officers, they proved something of a mixed blessing during the campaign.[17]

At Callantsoog, Abercromby extolled the virtues of his force: 'I could not yesterday sufficiently admire the spirit of the British soldier. Without any sort of discipline, they did in their own way as much as could have been expected from veteran troops.'[18] However, the units of the first wave were the cream of the army, largely composed of the more experienced troops and little diluted by militia recruits. Much has been made of the potential of the militiamen and how well they performed considering that they had spent very little time with their new units and in many cases didn't even know their officers. Those in the army's lower echelons reported a more patchy performance than that seen by their commanders, particularly in terms of their discipline.

Private William Surtees was shocked by what he saw as indiscipline in men of the 35th Regiment of Foot (35th foot):

'This regiment, after coming ashore, was drawn up close to us; they had not long landed before the men began with their knives to cut off each other's hair, which was then worn in the shape of a club; this was done without any orders from their officers, and appeared to me, such a breach of discipline, as I could not have anticipated … had stricter discipline been enforced from the outset, I feel assured the army in general would have benefited by it.'[19]

Surtees also recounted how a rumour spread that the Duke of York had said they could discard their packs to ease their advance and he believed it and promptly did so, to his later regret.[20]

Abercromby wrote to Dundas to say the discipline of the troops was good: 'The troops continue healthy and behave extremely well; no instance of outrage or even of plundering has occurred.'[21] Adjutant General Hope however, reported of at least one instance of theft by a soldier of the 17th Regiment of Foot (17th foot) from a Helder butcher who was unable to identify the culprit.[22] An anonymous officer, who served as a lieutenant with the Grenadier Battalion, also recounted a tale of rounding up stragglers who were looting a village on the outskirts of the sandhills: they had drunk milk left out for pigs, overturned beehives, ripped up mattresses and ransacked the post office in search of plunder and even divided up the internal works of a clock.[23]

Ill-discipline was not confined to the private soldiers, for the lieutenant had an anecdote about a junior officer who had joined his regiment from the militia and been captured by the French apparently hiding in a barn while his regiment went into action.[24] Hope's daily reports also contained details of officers falling out amongst themselves, behaving dishonourably and being absent from their regiments during the campaign.[25]

The performance of the British battalions was also variable. On many occasions throughout the campaign, the British infantrymen demonstrated the fighting prowess that had made them famous in previous conflicts. In others they pursued the enemy heedlessly, losing their formations and exposing themselves to counterattack. On some occasions their inexperience enabled the enemy to get the better of them and they fled in disorder from the field of battle. The slowness of Abercromby's flank march at the Battle of Bergen has been attributed to the poor discipline of the militiamen but there were very few in his force and it was the veterans of the 23rd Regiment of Foot (23rd foot), who broke and fled following the confusion at the gates of Hoorn. All in all, it is fair to say that the army Britain sent to the Helder were not equal to the difficult task to which they were assigned but they did demonstrate their potential. Abercromby's conclusion is probably the most apt: 'The troops behaved as well as I could wish. ... The militia men are, I think, a superior race of men, and a great acquisition to the army at this time.'[26]

Whatever the shortcomings and inadequacies of the British contingent no one would blame them for the failure of the campaign. Sadly the same cannot be said about their allies, as many British accounts laid failure squarely at the feet of the Russians. By the end of the campaign, public opinion had turned against them to such a degree that one witness who saw them on the Isle of Wight after their evacuation exclaimed: 'I do not wonder at their having been beaten. ... They are really not human, and their filth is shocking to the greatest degree. ... The convicts in the galleys in France or in the hulks in England come nearest to them in general resemblance and dress.'[27]

Things had begun well, with the Duke of York reporting that he had inspected the Russian contingent and that:

> 'I have the great pleasure in assuring you that, from their appearance in every respect, the most happy consequences may be expected from their co-operation with His Majesty's arms in this country: Lieutenant-General D'Hermann seems to enter most heartily into our views, and I form very sanguine hopes of receiving assistance from his zeal and experience.'[28]

Even at this stage many British commentators wrote of the strange and even 'repulsive' appearance of the Russian troops but it was the way in which their army was disciplined that provoked the most comment.[29] Abercromby felt 'The Russians, entre nous, seem to be a strange kind of people. There may be bravery but there is no discipline. The general may cane an officer, but he does not prevent plunder and robbery.'[30] The robbery was a particular problem for an army operating in what was supposed to be friendly territory. Whilst the British Army had their own looters, which were largely kept under control and punished if caught, the Russian Army considered plunder part of war and the Cossacks in particular considered it a way of life. This problem was exacerbated by the fact that the Russian troops were hungry as they had been unable to stomach the rations the British provided, resorting to spreading axle grease on their bread and drinking the oil out of street lamps in Yarmouth after the campaign.[31] Nonetheless, many in the British contingent saw that the behaviour of the Russians would dampen any enthusiasm the Dutch population might have for the counter-revolutionary cause. One-legged engineer, Major John Finlay, wrote to his wife that: 'Their unextinguishable love of plunder will, I foresee, create us many enemies.' The anonymous lieutenant added: 'the wholesale plunder practised by our allies was small inducement to Mynheer [a Dutchman] to stir himself in our favour.'[32]

The Russian's bad behaviour was not confined to robbing the locals. Although they were harshly disciplined in camp and gave all the appearance of 'absolute subordination', the Russian officers could exercise little control over their soldiers in battle.[33] At Bergen they had advanced impetuously, apparently giving no heed to their flanks and fi ring at any target that presented itself. In the subsequent battle at Egmond, attempts to keep them under control meant that they advanced slowly and with apparent timidity.[34] The Dutch officer C.R.T. Krayenhoff, writing in 1832, believed initially that British accounts were biased against the Russians but after questioning eyewitnesses agreed that the behaviour of the Russians, on this occasion at least, was 'eccentric, weak and wavering'.[35] By Castricum they were back to their old ways, attacking recklessly and provoking the French counterattack. From the British perspective they were unreliable and entirely unpredictable allies, a great disappointment for Pitt and Grenville who were hoping for a repeat of Suvarov's waltz through northern Italy.

Although the tsar's soldiers lacked discipline they did fi ght bravely throughout, only generally giving way after suffering massive losses (some self inflicted) and being outmanoeuvred by the nimble French. Although some blame for their mishandling must fall on the Duke of York, it is with the Russian's own generals that the fault must lie. The anonymous lieutenant believed that the Russians were capable of great 'passive courage' but lacked confidence; 'as regards all the morale of an army, they were utterly destitute' and this must be attributed to leadership.[36] In the Italian theatre, the Russians performed apparent miracles under Suvarov and the Duke of York believed that Herman, the senior Russian general in the Helder, was attempting to emulate him.[37]

Major General Ivan Herman Von Ferzen was a Russian officer of Saxon descent. He had served in the Russian Army since 1769 and had fought the Turks in the wars of 1769–1774 and 1787–1791, where he had served with great distinction, repulsing the Turkish invasion of the Kuban Valley. He had also participated in the 1794 partition of Poland, where he served as a corps commander. When he arrived in Holland in 1799 he was an experienced leader of men.[38] According to the treaty, the Russians retained 'direct command' of their own troops, which were to be kept together as much as possible, and 'no important operation was to be undertaken without a Council of War in the presence of the Russian commander.'[39] York reported that Herman was in complete agreement with his plan for Bergen and in fact insisted on detaching some of his troops.[40] Though many believed the general was an amiable and co-operative ally, some took his sanguine attitude as mere bluster. Lieutenant General Moore had little time for him:

> 'The Russian General Herman, who at first commanded them, despised all assistance, held everybody cheap, and certainly had too much boast and pretension for a man of sense. His action fell short of his talk as much as it generally does with men of that description. He displayed nothing but personal courage, and was at last taken prisoner, as some suspect purposely to cover his misconduct.'[41]

Although he may have suffered from inflated belief in his own abilities, as well as those of his troops, Herman was a joy to work with compared to his successor, Ivan Nikolayevich Essen. Essen was also an experienced officer, having served against the Swedes in 1788–1790 and in several battles during the Polish Partition 1792–1794. Promoted to major general in 1797, the Helder campaign was his first experience commanding a large formation.[42] Essen was to prove particularly unpopular with his allies, even refusing to land his division because he 'did not see on the shore any preparation to receive the emperor's troops with honour, and that he could not be so regardless of the dignity of his sovereign as to disembark in such an unceremonious manner.'[43] It was not a good start. On Essen's promotion to command of the Russian contingent, Bunbury was moved to write: 'D'Hermann, who remained a prisoner in the hands of the French, was probably a bad general but he was a brave, zealous and straightforward fellow. His successor in command of the Russians, General Essen, without possessing more military abilities, was false, intriguing and ill-disposed towards the British.'[44] The most damning description came from the Russian Ambassador Vorontsov, who considered Essen to be 'the most stupid and malignant of men', adding that he had 'made the greatest efforts to persuade his whole corps that the British were seeking only to cause the Russians to perish' and that he personally had found their correspondence to be entirely disagreeable.[45] On taking command he admonished his troops and imposed stricter discipline, insisting that his troops maintain their formations. As a result they moved at a much slower pace prompting Moore to write: 'The present Commander of the Russians seems as cautious as the other was imprudent. Whether he is too much so for the bold undertakings our situation requires will be seen hereafter.'[46]

The clash of personalities was not helped by the Russian perception that the British considered them expendable, having abandoned them to be slaughtered at Bergen, provided them with inedible rations and not honoured their treaty promises, particularly in regards to the allocation of horses.[47] As we shall see it was not to be a harmonious relationship and the conflict between the allies was to impede operations throughout the expedition.

Chapter 4

The Enemy – the Franco-Batavian Forces

Whatever the inadequacies of the invasion force, the army tasked with thwarting it were believed to be worse. Grenville's intelligence reports had convinced him that there were only between 6,000 and 10,000 French troops in the entire Netherlands and that the forces of the Batavian Republic were said to be weak and disenchanted, more likely to join the invaders than fire on the Orange flag. Early reports had indicated that the commander of the Batavian Army would be open to negotiation and could possibly be bribed into defecting or at least adopting a neutral stance. However, by the time the expedition sailed, this opinion had changed and he was considered 'a most determined and active enemy'.[1]

Lieutenant General Herman Willem Daendels was that commander. He was born in Hattem in 1762 and had studied law before joining the Patriot Revolution in 1785. He quickly rose to prominence in the Patriot ranks, leading the defence of his birthplace and the capital before their capture by the Prussians, after which he fled to France under sentence of death and continued to work against the Orangist regime. In 1794 he joined Pichegru's invasion of the Netherlands at the head of the Batavian Legion and helped to bring about the transformation of his homeland into a satellite of the French Republic, where he remained a prominent political and military figure. He was popular with the people but more importantly with the common soldiers of the army, which enabled him to play a leading role in two coups in the Batavian Republic to bring about a more liberal form of government. Although the state of his personal finances may have led some to believe he was open to bribes, Daendels remained a liberal and a staunch republican and although his defence of the Helder has been criticized in some quarters he actively opposed the invasion throughout the campaign.[2]

Daendels enjoyed a good relationship with his colleague, Lieutenant General Jean-Baptiste Dumonceau. Daendels had seniority but the two men had been comrades in arms since the invasion of the Netherlands. Dumonceau was Belgian and slightly older than Daendels; he too was a failed revolutionary having experienced his first action in the Brabant Revolution in 1789. He retained a healthy disdain for politicians when he transferred to the service of the Batavian Republic and wrote to Daendels in 1798 describing the government as anarchists in the pay of the English. Dumonceau was a career soldier and had served in the Brabant Chasseurs, fighting in numerous major battles including Neerwinden and Tourcoing. Perhaps because he wasn't Dutch, he didn't feature too strongly in the politics of the Batavian Republic but Dumonceau was an active and conscientious officer. One of Grenville's intelligence reports spoke of him as talented, adding that 'he has an authority, a simplicity which inspires the love and confidence of the soldiers. He is a zealous republican by conviction and is loyal to the party he has embraced. He is not jealous of Daendels and even has attachment and devotion for him.'[3] He gave Daendels little cause to complain of his conduct during the invasion, marching his troops hard to oppose the landing and suffering a wound at Bergen that put him out of action for much of the campaign.[4]

The brigade commanders of the Batavian Army were not especially noteworthy, many being descended from foreign mercenary officers who had served the old United Provinces since the seventeenth century. They seemed to have been unfortunate rather than incompetent, though their reluctance to obey Brune's orders regarding the reduction of their regimental baggage hampered their ability to deploy with the same alacrity as their French allies. Amongst the most noteworthy Dutch officers in the army were Chief Engineer Colonel Krayenhoff (who wrote an insightful history of the campaign) and the outstanding Colonel Crass, commander of the advanced guard who was in the thick of it whenever the Batavian forces were engaged.

At the time of the landing, the Batavian Army were around 20,000-men strong (organized on French lines in 'halve-brigades' of around 1,500 men) with something in the region of 13,000 available to defend the beaches. The Batavian Government had been frantically raising troops since they got wind of the possible invasion and had voted to conscript 20,000 extra soldiers and to create a National Guard of 32,000 to support them.[5] The existing army was based on that which had previously served the Prince of

Orange but was reorganized into French-style demi brigades (DB), called halve brigades (HB) in Dutch. The conscription introduced on Brune's insistence was not popular, with many of the potential soldiers hiding in the forests to avoid joining up, and the quality of the existing troops was rather lacking. About sixty per cent of these were foreign (mostly German) mercenaries or ex-prisoners of war and they were little trusted by their allies or their own government.[6] During the campaign the performance of these troops was extremely varied; they fought well under certain circumstances and earned the praise of their British opponents whereas at other times they disintegrated, fleeing in panic at the mere rumour of the enemy.[7] This particular trait earned the contempt of French General Brune who had been appointed to command all forces in the Batavian Republic, even though such behaviour had been common in the forces of revolutionary France only a few years earlier.[8]

For Lord Grenville it was the loyalty of the Batavian troops that held the most interest. Orangist agents had informed him that the soldiers would not fire on the Orange flag but although there was an almost hysterical fear of treachery in the Batavian camp, the soldiers did fight. There were a number of deserters; Abercromby reported fifteen by 4 September, all Germans, and within a week he'd received around 300 more. 'The Dutch took every opportunity to desert,' he said. Some of those captured during the campaign were also prepared to put on an Orange cockade and join the Hereditary Prince of Orange's makeshift battalion on the island of Texel. This formation was bolstered by volunteers from the naval mutineers and reached around 2,500 men by the end of the campaign. Despite the Grenville brothers' great faith in the utility of such units, they were considered a nuisance by the expedition's commanders who had to feed and arm them. They were put on Texel Island to keep them out of the way as their motivation for turning their coats provoked some suspicion and their reliability in action was doubtful.[9]

Although the Batavians fought better than anyone had expected in the defence of their republic, the driving force behind the thwarting of the expedition was undoubtedly the French contingent under General Brune. Later to become one of Napoleon's 'less-distinguished marshals', Brune was born in 1763 and had enjoyed a meteoric rise through the ranks of the republican army, thanks in part to his friendship with the leading revolutionary Georges Danton. Joining the army as a volunteer in 1791 on a wave of patriotic fervour, Brune was general within two years and served under Bonaparte in the Army of Italy, where he gained a reputation for leading from the front. He had played a part in the transformation of the Swiss Confederation into a French satellite commanding the Army of Switzerland against the defending forces. His actions in this theatre were notorious for his political meddling and use of extortion to line his own pockets. After a brief stint as commander of the Army of Italy, where he continued in much the same vein, Brune was appointed to command the French Army in the Batavian Republic.[10]

The arrival of such a notorious, revolutionary firebrand alarmed the conservative Dutch and at first there was little co-operation. Orangist intelligence described him as a money-grabbing looter who would make every effort to sustain the revolution as he profited so much from it.[11] With increasing fears of invasion and the intervention of Fouché, the French ambassador at The Hague, his demands for extra troops and stockpiles of military supplies were eventually heeded. Having been given command of both the French and the Batavian forces, Brune conducted a spirited defence with limited resources and was hailed as the 'saviour of the Batavian Republic'.[12]

Brune remained controversial even after his appointment. Following the Battle of Bergen he 'sent squads of his prisoners through the town as if they had been so many wild beasts just captured' but such displays may have helped dissuade Dutch waverers from putting on the Orange cockade.[13] The Duke of York's biographer, Burne, called his actions at Castricum impulsive but his defences were well constructed, his troops well placed and his reaction was aggressive and decisive, catching the Russians overextended (again) and routing them.[14] That he led, in person, the counterattack on the allied right is again the cause of criticism from Burne but this can be contrasted with the behaviour of the Duke of York who was dining at Alkmaar at the time.[15]

Brune was an inspiring commander, well liked by his troops for his bravery and liberal treatment of them. He exhibited a fearsome temper and a hearty distrust of the Dutch but he clearly understood his troops and their needs and his outbursts were either in private or positively channelled. A certain amount of invective and deflection of blame are perhaps to be expected from a general schooled in the revolutionary way of war.[16]

Brune's subordinates were a mixed bunch, most of whom were to find fame in the later Napoleonic Wars. Chief of Staff Charles Dumoulin was described by one intelligence report as a 'Jacobin without talent or spirit' but he went on to play a prominent role in Napoleon's Brumaire coup and served as a brigade commander at Austerlitz.[17] Another report described Brune's second in command Reubell as 'an imbecile, incapable, and despised by the soldiers'. It is perhaps understandable therefore that he played little part in the campaign. The commander of the artillery was General Jean de Seroux du Fay, a nobleman who had served with the Royal Army in the Seven Years War and had come to embrace the revolution only to save his head and his family, having served eighteen months in a republican prison.

One of the most prominent Napoleonic generals to see action on the Helder was Dominique Vandamme. Born in 1771, he had served as a private soldier in the Royal Army and at the outbreak of the revolution had formed a company of volunteers, which he led through the 1792 campaign. Like most of his colleagues in this campaign, Vandamme had risen rapidly through the ranks and was a general de brigade by the end of the year. By the time he reached Holland in 1799 he was an experienced commander having served with the Armies of du Nord, the Sambre et Meuse, and the Haute Rhine, where he distinguished himself during the passage of that river under General Moreau. He had fought against the Duke of York and the allied army at Tourcoing in 1794 and would be one of Brune's greatest assets in the campaign that was to follow, in which he commanded a division.[18]

The other prominent general de division to serve under Brune was Louis-Jean-Baptiste Gouvion. Born in 1752 to a military family, Gouvion joined the Royal Army as a lieutenant in the artillery in 1768 and rose slowly but surely through the ranks, reaching that of lieutenant colonel by the outbreak of war. As an experienced, professional officer he found promotion accelerated in the course of the war and having served with the armies of Italy, du Nord and the Sambre et Meuse he had risen to the rank of general de division by 1799. In Holland he was also to prove a great asset to his commander.

The brigade and battalion commanders were also to prove competent and brave, often inspiring their conscript soldiers by fearless personal example and suffering serious wounds or paying with their lives as a result. General de Brigade David died at Krabbendam, shot through the neck at the head of his troops. Chef de Brigade Mercier died at Egmond, shot through both thighs under similar circumstances and Adjutant General Maison was seriously wounded whilst carrying out his duties. The need to lead by example in the republican forces caused a high level of officer casualties, but it must be noted that both the British and Russian armies suffered similar levels. In order to lead on an eighteenth-century battlefield, officers simply had to put themselves in the same mortal danger as their men. The French troops themselves were variable in quality. The impression given by most British sources is that that these were dashing, experienced troops whose light infantry tactics enabled them to run rings around the brave but inexperienced British and their allies.[19] However, in reality the French Army in Holland were comprised of some of the worst units in the French Army. An anonymous British officer wrote:

'The year 1799 had been the most disastrous to the French armies since the revolution … when the alarm took place in Holland, they were obliged to send off whatever they could get together, and that portion of their force opposed to us was certainly inferior to the general run of their armies.'[20]

One of the few credible intelligence reports received by Grenville prior to the expedition sailing gave French numbers as around 20,000 but added that there were very few old soldiers, the rest being conscripts amongst whom were a 'prodigious number of sick'.[21] Certainly their commander privately expressed a lack of faith in their fighting spirit: 'We cannot win with discouraged soldiers who do not want to fight.'[22] Some of the reinforcements rushed to Brune were veteran troops but many of those sent to Holland had been raised recently, specifically for the campaign, such as 90 Demi Brigade (raised in Lille after the landing) and, as such, behaved as erratically in action as the militia battalions on the British side.

One area in which the French infantry excelled was that of light infantry tactics, although (despite Private Surtees' claims to the contrary) there is little evidence that French soldiers received specialist light infantry training or practised marksmanship.[23] However, following the outbreak of the war the French had found that their troops were naturally predisposed to skirmish. Whilst eighteenth-century tactics required rigid discipline and hours on the drill square, taking cover in folds of ground and behind trees and walls to take pot shots at the enemy required little preparation, and in fact came easily to the majority of conscripts. When accompanied with the mass charge, often in huge columns, it went some way to compensate for the inadequacies of the republic's mass conscript armies in other areas.[24]

A great deal was to be seen of these tactics throughout the war and the Helder campaign was no exception. Describing the French attack at Krabbendam, Moore said: 'A number of the enemy's Yagers and light troops, taking advantage of such cover as presented itself, commenced a fire. Some artillery also began to play upon us, and under the cover of their fire a large column attempted, with shouts and drums and bugles to charge us.'[25] Again at Egmond it was noted that: 'The French troops were more experienced, and quicker amongst the hummocks and waves of this great sand sea; nor did the British know anything about light infantry tactics.'[26] However, it should be noted that none of the French attacks were successful and another British witness to the campaign reported that:

'[T]hey were not much better than ourselves in terms of discipline, being from the last levy of the conscription and not half drilled. We could see, during the day, the Officers plying the men with canteens of gin, and three parts of their wounded, and the prisoners we took, were drunk.'[27]

Although the level of intoxication was quite common in French armies of the time and was also reported in Egypt a couple of years later, it may have been an indication of low morale amongst the recent conscripts.[28] Following Bergen, Brune expressed concern for his men as 'the fatigue of the men, and I know not what dispositions which I had not before seen in the minds of soldiers, told me if the enemy … attacked us next day, weariness might occasion a real reverse.'[29] Though the soldiers may have been new recruits, this was nothing unusual in the French Army, which had been absorbing vast quantities of conscripts annually since the war commenced (the 327,000 in 1798 was in fact the lowest number since 1793). The tactical doctrine and regimental structures into which they were inducted were designed to cope with them and to make allowances for their shortcomings.[30]

One of the most serious problems facing the Anglo-Russian army in the course of the campaign was that of supply, particularly feeding the troops. However, this issue was not confined to the allies. The French Army were famous for their ability to live off the land but this had made them few friends in the countries they passed through and had contributed to the discontent, which had led to anti-French risings in many parts of Europe. This issue was particularly pertinent in the Netherlands where there was a danger of counter-revolution and the depredations of the invading army had such propaganda value. Therefore Brune had set up a series of magazines and organized chains of provisions with local victuallers, although when they were forced to retreat from Bergen those supply lines were disrupted leaving the French conscripts to starve and lowering their morale further.

So the invasion of the Netherlands was to be prevented not by the highly-motivated armies of the revolution, which had swept all before them in earlier campaigns, but with conscripted dregs gathered in haste and led not by the *crème* of the republic's generals but by experienced and active commanders who were used to making the most of what they were given. Similarly, the Batavian forces, though riven with internal conflicts and fears of treachery, did not desert to the enemy but in fact gave a good account of themselves on most occasions.

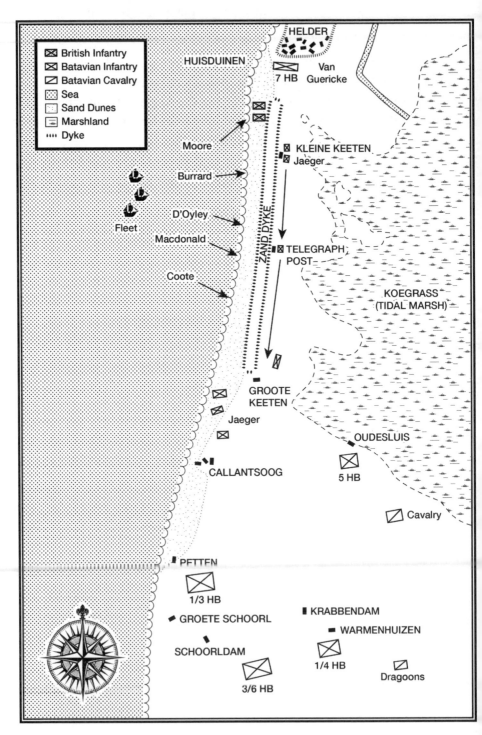

Map 2. The landing at Callantsoog. (*Produced by John Harcourt*)

Chapter 5

Callantsoog – the Landing

As General Abercromby prepared to sail on 10 August, Dundas sent him his final orders.[1] These in effect gave Abercromby *carte blanche* to land wherever he saw fit and in consultation with Naval Commander Admiral Duncan he decided that, of the options available to him, the west coast of the Helder region was the most practicable.[2] This area is a narrow peninsular above Amsterdam, with a west (North Sea) coast that has long sandy beaches, suitable for landing troops. On the north-eastern side below the Island of Texel, where the North Sea meets the Zuider Zee, is the small town of Helder, which had a safe harbour protected by strong batteries pointing to the sea. The beaches themselves were overlooked by a series of steep sand dunes, from fifty to 300 foot high, which ran parallel to the sea for the length of the coast and in some areas formed an almost impenetrable maze. In the particular spot where the troops landed, the dunes were bounded on the east side by a feature called the Zand-dike. This was an old dyke against which sand had piled up over the years in a distinct ridge; indeed Daendels believed this feature to be the basis of the sandhills themselves. Beyond this dyke was a further area of sand described as 'a great, dry beach', which proved to be difficult ground for cavalry and artillery.[3] This terrain was to present numerous difficulties for both sides and have a significant impact on the course of the campaign.

Unfortunately, bad weather, which was to plague the expedition throughout, prevented the army from landing. High winds and tumultuous seas with huge waves crashing against the shore meant that the fleet – 'fifteen ships of the line, forty-five frigates and brigs and one hundred and thirty transport vessels' – had to ride at anchor off the coast of Holland for several days.[4] The fleet was so close it was reported that the flags used to signal between the ships could be clearly read from the shore.[5] Any chance of surprise which may have remained following the appalling lack of security surrounding the expedition's preparation was now completely lost. Batavian Commander Daendels could lay his plans with some confidence as to where the assault would take place. According to his report, he ordered Major General Van Guericke to place his 7 Halve Brigade (7th HB) on the right, near Huisduinen and 'to dispose the remainder of the troops in such a manner that they might line as close as possible the great dry beach, which lies between the Helder and the Zype, and that they might have it in their power to march suddenly upon the points of the coast which was [sic] threatened.' The left was covered by 'the 5th demi-brigades by the Zan, upon the two Keetens, and the whole brigade of Major Zuylen Van Nywelt, by Callants-Oog.' Daendels concluded: 'Thus the troops were placed so as to have it in their power to arrive speedily on the coast in two great debouches.'[6]

On the morning of 27 August the weather improved sufficiently to allow the landing to begin. A signal was fired from Admiral Mitchell's ship, the *Isis*, and a host of small ships set out towards the shore covered by an enormous naval bombardment. Francis Maule, an officer in the Queen's Regiment (Queen's) was present and later recalled: 'A cannonade, tremendous and well supported, incessantly commenced from all the line of battle ships, frigates and gun boats, and bomb vessels. One hundred pieces of cannon without cessation opened over the line of boats, and hurled defiance upon the hostile shore.'[7]

The seas were still rough, however, and many soldiers and sailors were drowned as the ships' boats ferried the assault force ashore. A party of the 92nd Regiment of Foot (92nd foot) – also known as the Gordon Highlanders – led by Sergeant Evan Cameron, was lost when their boat stuck on a sand bank and they tried to wade ashore.[8] Even allowing for the conditions, the lack of experience in mounting this kind of operation became quickly apparent. The landing had been given detailed consideration; Edward Walsh, who landed with the 29th Regiment of Foot (29th foot) said it was intended that all the launches 'should rendezvous under the stern of such frigates as lay nearest the landing place' and they were then to land in order of the planned deployment at a signal from the admiral's ship.[9] The plan of operations, however, 'was not precisely executed, for the first boats that received the men from the transports, having been taken into tow by wherries and schooners pushed on directly to the beach, under a press of sail, without attending the general rendezvous.' As a result, the landing was shambolic in the extreme, with units attempting to form up under the harassing fire of the Dutch *jaegers* (light infantry) operating in the tall sand dunes overlooking the beach. The units were mixed up and the assault force had to be formed from a variety of regiments 'chiefly of the third brigade' and the reserve.[10]

The only thing that prevented complete disaster at this stage was Daendels' fear of the potent supporting fire that the fleet could bring to bear against his troops if they attempted to attack the British on the beach. Some commentators have criticized Daendels' lack of enterprise and claimed that the dunes would have covered his movements until the last moment.[11] Moore believed, for example, that 'the ground was such as to render the fire from the shipping of no avail. Had we been opposed we must have been beaten with little resistance; but the enemy had made no disposition to oppose the immediate landing. Some picquets to my front retired as I advanced.'[12] There are however, extensive gaps in the dunes, which Daendels felt would have exposed his men whilst forming up, and any units coming down on to the beach would surely have suffered heavily. Other witnesses believed that the fire of fleet, although it did little damage to the enemy, protected the invaders whilst they were at their most vulnerable.[13]

As it was, covered by the fire of the fleet, the British invaders reached the beaches virtually unscathed. However, they soon came under fire from the light infantry of the 1st and 2nd Batavian *jaegers*, which Daendels had posted in the dunes to cover his centre. The ad hoc units on the beach took cover and returned fire at their near invisible assailants whilst the Grenadier Company of the Queen's (supported by those of 29th foot) were sent up the dunes to flush them out.[14] Their commander, Lord Dalhousie, realizing that they were opposed by a considerable force, sent his Light Company to support the outnumbered grenadiers and a series of confused skirmishes broke out with the British being slowly reinforced by fresh troops landing from the fleet.[15] The numbers began to tell and the British charged up the dunes against the *jaegers* who were now being outflanked by Dalhousie's companies and too dispersed to resist a concerted attack. They broke and despite the efforts of their officers, fell back towards Groote Keeten fighting 'every inch of the way'.[16] Their commander, Lieutenant Colonel Lucq, had made a valorous attempt to stop the retreat; trying to encourage his men to remain he 'exposed himself with a boldness which cost him his life' and in their haste to escape the *jaegers* they abandoned his corpse on the dunes.[17]

Daendels' plan was to refuse (hold back) his centre to draw the invaders deeper into the dunes, away from the covering fire of the ships, where he hoped to envelop and overrun them.[18] His troops were divided into two main bodies between Kleen Keeten to the north and Groote Keeten to the south. Each wing faced inwards, towards the centre with its outside flank protected by the dunes on the seaward side and the centre held lightly by the *jaegers*, supported by a single battalion of line infantry.[19]

This plan was helped by the confused fashion in which the British landed. The troops had been fed into battle in small groups, far from the control of their officers, and Divisional Commander Major General Pulteney had little idea of what was occurring. His victorious troops crested the dunes only to be met by a hail of bullets from 'well supported vollies of musquetry, and a continued fire of light artillery'.[20] By this stage the British had lost all order and restraint, surging onwards towards the centre of the Batavian line pausing only to loot the body of the unfortunate Lieutenant Colonel Lucq. Dalhousie believed that his command had landed 'at the extreme right of the enemy's line' and that they 'fell back on its main position' to the south. So the British troops (of whom he said 'I did not see a single regiment formed except the 27th') seem to have gone as far as the summit of Zand-dike ridge and then followed the *jaegers* in a largely southerly direction, along the ridges. Dalhousie said that his men raced detachments from the guards to the top of the ridge: 'Covered from the sight of the enemy we reached it and found all clear and the Dutchmen retiring very slowly along the slope. Having breathed a moment, the troops ran on a little way, gave a loud cheer and their fire, which immediately hastened the retreat below us.'[21] Having effectively driven a wedge between the two wings of the Batavian force, the British were now approaching the centre from slightly to the north.

The Batavian centre was a strong position on a second line of dunes, centred around a telegraph signal post where an artillery piece had been placed supported by the 2nd Battalion of 5 Halve Brigade (2nd of 5th HB). The two other battalions 'of that body were placed with their right in the houses of Groote Keeten and their left against the sea.'[22] These troops were formed and ready to support the *jaegers* and, it is reported, were 'not at all intimidated' by their comrades' headlong retreat.[23] As the British reached their position Lieutenant Colonel Henbig led his men in a counterattack with fixed bayonets, but he was killed at the head of his battalion and as a result they lost heart and fell back with the British in hot pursuit.

Despite the apparent setbacks suffered by his troops, Daendels' plan appeared to be working. The disordered British were strung out among the sand dunes with their lead troops now battling for the telegraph post in the centre. However, just as the enemy appeared to be entering the jaws of his trap, Daendels' subordinate on the right, Major General Van Guericke, decided to intervene. Fearing that the retreat of the *jaegers* and 2nd of 5th HB would allow the enemy to cut his communication with the centre, and despite strict orders to the contrary, Van Guericke resolved to shore up the centre. To this end he personally led a battalion of 7th HB and his whole force of cavalry to stop the enemy from bursting through into the plain, where Daendels had planned to envelop them.[24]

Pulteney had been shot in the arm and led away from the battle by his surgeon so had no chance of controlling his men. Moore wrote in his diary that Major General Sir Eyre Coote's brigade had driven the enemy 'some distance rather hastily, and perhaps too far, as they at last met at the termination of the sand-hills in a plain a considerable corps of cavalry and infantry with cannon.'[25] Dalhousie recalled that the Batavian 'dragoons advanced, but the ground being uneven, they soon wheeled off and retired at a gallop, leaving their officer, who seemed indignant at their conduct and went back at a slow walk.'[26] At this point the headlong career of the British Army was checked. Major Maule (of the Queens) said they took heavy casualties from artillery and the appearance of cavalry, despite its apparent impotence, gave the dispersed infantrymen pause for thought.[27] Perhaps sensing that the battle was slipping away from him, Daendels ordered the attack.

It was now midday and although his troops would be restricted by the terrain, Daendels ordered Colonel Crass to attack the advancing British from the left with the two battalions of 5th HB, which had been stationed at Groote Keeten, and sent orders to Van Guericke to support this attack with one from the right. The attack was made on a narrow front as the nature of the ground did not permit battalions to be drawn up more than two abreast and was supported by two pieces of artillery. As Crass' battalions set off in a northerly direction towards the British left, Zuylen Van Nywelt's brigade came up from Callantsoog and was sent to support the attack. The errant *jaegers*, whom Daendels had rallied personally, were also committed and were placed 'upon the flank of the high downs of the Sand-dike'.[28]

The attack caught the disordered British on their exposed flank and sent them reeling back towards the beach. However, Abercromby had arrived and was starting to reassert command. Daendels said the attack of 5th HB forced the British back more than a league, though the anonymous commentator who published the Batavian general's report for an English audience claimed this was under orders so may be attributed, at least in part, to Abercromby redressing his line.[29] Nonetheless, all agreed that, as Maule wrote, it was a 'brilliant' charge and certainly it had Daendels thinking that he would be able to drive the British back to their boats.[30]

From the Batavian perspective, all now depended on Van Guericke following up this attack with one on the right. However, Van Guericke wasn't where he was supposed to be and owing to the large number of ditches between him and Daendels it took a long time for the messengers, who were travelling on horseback, to reach him. It also emerged that when he had come to cover the retreat of the *jaegers* from the centre, he had left the remainder of his troops without orders at Huisduinen and they were not in a position to launch an attack.[31] Improvising quickly, Daendels ordered him to 'attack vigorously' against the telegraph post, which had now been captured by the British who, according to Walsh, were using it for 'directing the fire of the armed vessels and gunboats'.[32] This attack was intended largely as a diversion to take the pressure off the two battalions of 5th HB, which (according to Daendels) were now suffering. This was because Abercromby, having firmly re-established control, had withdrawn the scattered units from combat to reform and had fed 23rd and 55th foot into the fray from Coote's reserve.[33] Unfortunately for Daendels, the ditches and dunes, which were hampering his communications, also prevented Van Guericke from pressing home his attack.[34]

With hope of any assistance from the right fading, Daendels was forced to concentrate on his left. The seemingly irrepressible Colonel Crass attempted to launch a cavalry charge through the dunes to take the pressure off his men, but the sand was so loose the horses sunk in it up to their girths and were unable to assist. Daendels complained that the ground prevented him from bringing up any more artillery (though Maule believed that most of the British casualties were caused by artillery), which would have added weight to his attack. As it was he had to make do with feeding fresh units into the fight in succession – the whole of 3 Halve Brigade together with 3rd of 1st HB and 3rd of 6th HB battalions.[35] After suffering two British attacks the 1st and 2nd battalions of 5th HB had broken off their own attack and, exhausted, had been forced to retreat. Now they had been reinforced, the attack was renewed. Dalhousie, rallying his exhausted troops behind the reserve, watched the final act unfold and witnessed 'a strong column of the enemy advanced on as wide a front as the flat between the ridge and the sandhills would admit of.'[36] But the British too were bringing up fresh troops (D'Oyly's guards brigade) and control of the dunes around Groote Keeten swung back and forth for another two hours.

All witnesses agreed that it had been a hard-fought battle; Abercromby reported that 'the contest was arduous, and the loss has been considerable'. Around five o'clock in the evening, a group of British sailors had been able to bring up two field guns which, combined with the fresh guardsmen of D'Oyly's brigade, mounted a final attack. Whereupon, it was observed that: 'The enemy forming a close column with some artillery in front, sustained the attack with some firmness, and retired in good order to a position about six miles distant.'[37] To use Abercromby's words: 'the enemy was fairly worn out'.[38] Daendels agreed, 'despite the valour which the troops and the officers displayed'. He saw no chance of his counterattack making permanent gains without increased artillery support or a diversion from the right so he pulled his units out of the fight and retired to Groote Keeten.[39]

There had been little action on the northern end of the battlefield and what fighting there was seems to have been somewhat half-hearted. A private soldier of 92nd foot, which formed part of Moore's command, observed that his unit was spotted by a mixed force of enemy troops. He remarked that:

'As soon as they observed our advance picquets, they left the road and made a circuit through the flat ground to their left; and when they were out of the reach of musketry they made pause and fired two field pieces at us, which did us no hurt, and they passed on and joined their own troops.'[40]

With the Batavian commander in this sector getting himself involved in the fighting around the telegraph post, the troops essentially did nothing all day. They were restricted in what they could do by command problems, the terrain and the potent threat of the fleet's guns but had they shown the same level of aggression as their comrades to the south, the British troops in this sector could also have suffered serious casualties and the success of the expedition may have been in serious jeopardy.

Despite success in the south and comparatively easy landing in the north, the position of the invasion force was still somewhat precarious. Moore wrote that:

'Our situation at this moment was unpromising. An enemy was on both our flanks, and we were in a position which, however favourably it had been represented on maps, proved extremely bad. Sir Ralph determined that at night I should attack the Helder. A part of the guards were to assist. It was evident that if we failed, immediate measures must be taken for re-embarkation.'[41]

The troops set off on their hazardous march to Helder as soon as it became dark. The private of 92nd foot wrote that, 'There is something impressive in a march under the cloud of night, in a strange land where we cannot tell the danger we are in, and have to move forward in solemn silence.'[42]

It was a tense situation but fortunately, since the garrison had withdrawn quietly after spiking the guns in the batteries, the town surrendered without a shot being fired and no night attack was necessary.[43]

So the first stage was complete. The initial contingent was ashore, they had successfully fought off a determined attempt to repel them and now, with Helder captured, they were in a position to establish a firm bridgehead. The Dutch had put up more resistance than the optimistic intelligence reports had predicted and Abercromby admitted that he was certainly not going to underestimate the threat that they posed: 'The force that opposed us yesterday was about 7,000 men, well clothed, well armed, and well disciplined. They may be said to have behaved better than we expected. They certainly at times pushed our people with spirit and perseverance, as they returned several times to the attack.'[44] The arrival the next day of a contingent of 5,000 men under General Don further stabilized the situation for Abercromby's army and he could now weigh up his options and consider his next move.

Chapter 6

The Vlieter Conspiracy –
the Capture of the Fleet

It was now the navy's turn. Although it does not appear to have figured in the initial planning, the proximity of the Dutch fleet at Texel (just north of Helder) seems to have been the major consideration when Abercromby and the admirals decided to land at Helder. This fleet, though much diminished after its defeat by Admiral Duncan at Camperdown (Camperduin) in 1797, remained a considerable threat to the British domination of the North Sea and indeed to the success of the expedition. Abercromby wrote that:

> '[I]t would tend more to the honour and advantage of his Majesty's arms and the real interest of Great Britain, to attack in the first instance the Helder and Texel Island and by that means open a communication with Holland, and at the same time either to destroy or render unserviceable the Dutch Fleet.'[1]

Admiral Mitchell concurred heartily and it couldn't have escaped his notice that the Batavian fleet included a number of fine ships, which would make a welcome addition to the navy's strength.

It was thought that the Batavian Navy were particularly sympathetic to the Orangist cause and from an early stage in their planning, the prince's party had hoped to ferment a mutiny in the fleet at Texel. To this end, Carel Ver Huell, an émigré naval officer who had left the Netherlands in 1795, had been instructed by the Prince of Orange to contact any former colleagues still serving with the fleet who might be open to joining them. Ver Huell opened correspondence with Theodorus Van Capellen and Aegidius Van Braam, two captains commanding ships of the line in the Helder squadron.[2] It is believed that Van Braam may have rejoined the navy specifically to act as an agent for the Orangists and he was heavily involved in the conspiracy, reporting regularly to his émigré contacts and the British (through Thomas Grenville in Berlin) on the state of the fleet and perhaps sowing the seeds of discontent.[3] Van Capellen was also an Orangist; he had been in touch with Bentinck back in July 1798 complaining that financial difficulties would soon force him to join the Batavian Navy and it must be assumed that he had been recruited at that point. His subsequent actions certainly point to his involvement.[4]

The British were receptive to the idea of aiding a mutiny and were already looking at the possibility of the mutineers acting in concert with Duncan's fleet before they had even really considered landing at Helder. Thomas Grenville wrote to his brother of the 'ready disposition which Van Braam has shewn to manage the junction of the Dutch fleet of the Texel with that of Lord Duncan, whenever he shall be assured of foreign troops being ready to assist the restoration of the Stadtholder.' It was a dangerous path for the naval officer to tread, as he could be considered a traitor by either side if he played his cards badly. Thomas told Lord Grenville he required specific assurances:

'[T]he only conditions which I understand him to insist upon are that he shall receive an order from the Stadtholder to take the step and that he shall be fully satisfied upon the point of the Dutch ships being treated by us as allies, and being not required to strike their flag or do any act of submission; he undertakes to control Storey, he assures the consent of the generality of the fleet.'[5]

Van Braam also requested some émigré officers to replace those in the fleet he couldn't trust. He also had to await assistance or a reason to leave Helder because 'some new batteries have been erected upon the Texel and the Helder, and he believes that those batteries, which have been erected to control the fleet, would completely destroy it if it declared itself in port.'

Consent was obtained from King George for the mutineers to be regarded as allies and orders were drawn up by the Prince of Orange, authorising Van Braam to act in concert with the Royal Navy. Plans were made for the mutiny to be put in motion: 'It is probable that by means of a fishing boat or through some other channel, Captain Van Braam will open communication with Lord Duncan, and will settle with him the signals to be made and the measures to be taken for the execution of this plan.'[6]

Even before the troops had landed, Admiral Duncan had sent Captain Winthorpe of the navy and Abercromby's secretary, Lieutenant Colonel Maitland, in the revenue cutter *Cobourg* with a flag of truce. They carried the naval commander's ultimatum to Dutch Admiral Samuel Story and the commander at Helder, Colonel Guilquin, calling on them to surrender and offering them 'a favourable opportunity of manifesting your zeal for your legitimate sovereign the Prince of Orange, by declaring for him.'[7] Story refused saying that to accept Duncan's proposal would make him 'forfeit the esteem of every honest man' and he reported the offer to his government in Amsterdam.[8] They in turn expressed their indignation and protested that the attempt (presumably by Maitland) to distribute the Prince of Orange's proclamation whilst under a flag of truce was 'perfidious' and contrary to the laws of war.[9] With their offer rebuffed, the British would now have to resort to direct action.

Once the British had captured Helder the fleet had made sail and headed away from the threat posed by the port's batteries so surely they would be more open to negotiate their surrender?[10] After Story's earlier refusal, Vice Admiral Mitchell (now commanding the naval contingent) was taking no chances and on the morning of 30 August, having sounded out a channel (for the Dutch had removed the buoys and landmarks), he formed his fleet for battle.[11] He wrote to the Admiralty that:

'I got the fleet under weigh at five o'clock, and immediately formed the line of battle, and prepared for battle. In running in, two of the line of battle ships, Ratvifan and America, and the Latona frigate, took the ground. We passed Helder point and Mars Diep, and continued our course along the Texel in the channel that leads to the Vleiter, the Dutch squadron lying at anchor in a line at the red buoy in the east-south-east course. The Latona frigate got off and joined me; but as the two line of battleships did not, I closed the line.'[12]

At around half past ten, Mitchell dispatched Captain Rennie of the *Victor* (who had been specially selected for the task by Admiral Duncan) with a summons to the Dutch admiral:

'I desire you will immediately hoist the flag of his serene highness the prince of orange. If you do, you will immediately be considered as friends of the king of Great Britain, my most gracious sovereign: otherwise, take the consequences. Painful it will be to me for the loss of blood it may occasion; but the guilt will be on your own head.'[13]

The Dutch had seen them coming and Admiral Story sent a boat with two Dutch captains (Van Capellen and another conspirator called De Jonge) under a flag of truce. Mitchell's report stated that:

'Captain Rennie very properly brought them on board; and from a conversation of a few minutes I was induced to anchor in a line, a short distance from the Dutch squadron, at their earnest request. They returned with my positive orders not to alter the position of the ships, nor do any thing whatsoever to them, and in one hour to submit, or take the consequences. In less than the time they returned with a verbal answer, that they submitted according to the summons and should consider themselves (the officers) on parole.'

It is unknown what measures the mutineers had put in place before the appearance of the expedition but for the rest of his life Story believed that he was undone by traitors. The sailors of the fleet had been quick to see the hopelessness of their situation, with the narrow channel restricting their ability to resist the superior Russo-British fleet and its heavier ships, but they may have already been swayed by Orangist propaganda, which was spread through the fleet by counter revolutionaries. It is reported that the sight of Orangist flags flying in the Helder and other settlements captured by the British had led to mutinous stirrings aboard several ships in the fleet. The previous day a group of mutineers, armed with pistols and cutlasses, had taken over the powder magazine aboard Story's own ship, the *Washington*, causing the rest of the crew to refuse to go below decks for fear they would be blown up in the night.[14] At this point, Story was informed that disturbances had broken out on several other ships and he was forced to go along with the surrender negotiations. He later wrote that this 'moment was the most painful to me that I ever experienced'.[15]

In his report to the Batavian minister of marine, Story was at pains to emphasize that he asked for a truce merely to gain time to quell the unrest and during the hour that Mitchell had set for his ultimatum, he had convened a council of war aboard his flagship, the *Washington*, which all the captains attended. However, it was at this point that it became apparent to Story that not only were the crews of many of the ships refusing to take defensive action, but a number of his captains were now openly expressing their allegiance to the former regime. Like the Batavian Army, a large proportion of Story's sailors were not Dutch but Germans and Scandinavians, yet they seemed to have embraced the idea of changing allegiance wholeheartedly; refusing orders and shouting '*Oranje boven!*' ['Orange top!'].[16] Aboard the flagship, the gunners ran to their guns, 'extracted the balls and threw them overboard, and also a great number of cartridges' so they could not fire on Mitchell's squadron.[17] Things cannot have been helped by Story's decision to send Van Braam, the Orangist agent, to reason with the mutineers. This seems an odd choice given that Lieutenant Colonel Maitland (serving once again as a negotiator and present onboard the *Washington*) specifically reported that Van Braam, together with captains Van Capellen and De Jonge, had already declared 'their attachment for the Stadtholder and the former government, and their disgust at the present government and their French connection', though perhaps these comments were made to Maitland in private.[18]

Story had been thoroughly undermined. There was clearly no way he could now fight and there was no way that he could win if he did, so he penned a defiant letter of surrender to his opponent:

'Neither your superiority, nor the threat that the spilling of human blood should be laid to my account, could prevent my shewing you to the last moment what I could do for my sovereign, whom I acknowledge to be no other than the Batavian people and its representatives, when your Prince's and the Orange flags have obtained their end. The traitors whom I commanded refused to fight; and nothing remains to me and my brave officers but vain rage and the dreadful reflection of our present situation: I therefore deliver over to you the fleet which I commanded. From this moment it is your obligation to provide for the safety of my officers and the few brave men who are on board the Batavian ships, as I declare myself and my officers are prisoners of war.'[19]

Story was at pains to stress that he was surrendering due to his untenable position rather than defecting to the allies. When he and his officers arrived on Mitchell's flagship the *Isis* on 2 September, they handed over their swords as vanquished foes.[20] It was a subtle but important distinction to make but it was a distinction that was lost on his government. Having struck their colours as a sign of surrender, the Batavian ships were now provided with Orangist colours, which had been bought by the British specifically for the occasion.[21] By running up these flags, the Dutch captains were signalling their intent to sail under the orders of the Prince of Orange, which in the eyes of the Batavian Directory was an act of treason for which they were all tried. Despite his protestations of innocence, Story was declared perjurious, without honour, infamous and banished for life on pain of death, as were Van Braam and Van Capellen.

Mitchell had little doubt as to the result had the Dutch decided to fight:

'I may say ... if I had brought them to action, I trust it would have added another laurel to the navy of England in this present war. The Dutch were astonished and thunderstruck at the approach of our squadron, never believing it possible that we could so soon have laid down the buoys and led down to them in line of battle, in a channel where they themselves go through but with one or two ships at a time.'[22]

The king himself later expressed the view that it may have been 'more brilliant' to have taken the ships by force of arms but 'not so agreeable to the upright conduct followed alone by this nation'.[23]

As it was the mutiny became wholesale. The removal of the captains under the terms of their parole had led to an escalation of violence. An officer was drowned, anyone found to be loyal to the republic was attacked and mutineers tore up the Batavian flag.[24] The British officers, whom Mitchell had sent to take control of the ships, had some difficulty restoring order. Eventually the crews were removed and combined with deserters, who had come over in some numbers since the fall of the Helder, to form the nucleus of a new Orangist army on the island of Texel. The ships were given British prize crews and were sailed off to Yarmouth. Only five particularly decrepit frigates were given Orangist crews and allowed to sail under the orders of the Prince of Orange.

It was a significant success. Without firing a shot, Mitchell had acquired the rump of the Batavian fleet and removed, at a stroke, the last significant threat to the Royal Navy in the North Sea (and indeed the expedition). Bunbury wrote: 'here was the English object of the expedition achieved; the Dutch fleet, arsenal, and stores were in our possession.' Although some in parliament may have felt the whole affair was 'corrupt and clandestine', England was jubilant and many (including Bunbury and Moore) later expressed the wish that the expedition had packed up and returned home at that point.[25]

Although much was made of this triumph in parliament, none of the political or strategic objectives of the expedition were met by the capture of the fleet. It was a fortunate occurrence but it was merely a bonus and the main prize was still untouched. In order to achieve the principal objective of the expedition, as envisaged by the ministers who planned it and their allies, the Netherlands had to be liberated and the resources of France diverted towards them. To achieve this, Abercromby would have to fight but he was showing little sign of being prepared to do so. Although he had beaten Daendels, consolidated his position and been reinforced, he just waited. Many commentators, both at the time and subsequently, have been critical of this inaction but, as we shall see, there are numerous factors to be considered in mitigation of this apparent error on the general's part.

Chapter 7

He Who Hesitates ... Abercromby's Dilemma

Abercromby was a naturally cautious man. He had not expected the landing to be a success and seemed surprised by the initial gains. In his report to Dundas he wrote:

'We have succeeded in an enterprise which, as far as I can be allowed to judge, was most precarious, and which, if I were to give an opinion even after success, ought not to have been risked. We are now to make the most of our success, and as soon as we shall be enabled to procure horses and wagons to carry forward our tents and little baggage, we shall endeavour to push on to Alkmaar, where the country becomes more cultivated and productive.'[1]

This was how war had been waged throughout the eighteenth century. Edward Walsh, a surgeon of 29th foot, wrote that 'the Dutch seem to have been astonished and panic-struck at the boldness and rapidity of our movements' and the numerous critics of Abercromby's strategy believe that he should have capitalized upon this.[2] It is unlikely that Napoleon, or indeed any of the revolutionary generals, would have remained on the beachhead in the face of defeated enemy waiting for carthorses. The Swiss military theorist Baron Jomini suggested that:

'Abercrombie could have taken advantage of his superior numbers to advance into the interior and use his resources to provoke an insurrection of the inhabitants. But although the reinforcements he had received brought the strength of his Corps to over 16,000 men he confined himself to making a few provisions for chasing Daendels from the position of Zyp.'[3]

This idea certainly has merit and it could be that with a more aggressive strategy, Abercromby would have quickly taken Amsterdam but that is not how most eighteenth-century armies waged war.[4] Abercromby had no idea what he was facing. He had no means of finding out what was ahead of him; the Orangist intelligence didn't seem to have covered the Helder area and he had no decent maps and no cavalry to conduct reconnaissance. Indeed he had written to Whitehall for 'three or four regiments of Light Dragoons to be sent to him urgently as the want of cavalry is severely felt.'[5] He knew there were enemy forces ahead of him but he couldn't be sure of their strength. His intelligence had told him that the Batavians were small in number and unlikely to fight him but his experience at Callantsoog had given him reason to doubt that assessment. He had also been assured that the French troops in Holland numbered no more than 5,000 but they seemed to be massing before him and he had no way of ascertaining their number. His troops were already suffering from a lack of food and fresh water and it would have been irresponsible of him to push forwards into an unknown country against an enemy of unknown strength. French armies of the period regularly marched without baggage and lived off the land but this had brought them no friends in the countries they ravaged and was a direct cause of the unrest threatening their conquests throughout Europe. This was not something that an army of liberation would be able to do.

It must be remembered that the expedition was not intended to conquer the Netherlands but to help the Dutch throw off the French yoke. The ministry, informed by Orangist agents, had led Abercromby to believe that the country was ripe for counter-revolution. He'd been told the troops wouldn't fire on the Orange flag, were only kept in the ranks by their republican officers and the British Army would set off a popular revolt. In fact early discussions in planning the expedition had urged caution at this point, for fear of setting off a spontaneous rising throughout the Netherlands before the expedition was in a position to support it.[6] Abercromby had never been entirely convinced by these claims and what he had seen since his landing had done little to overcome his doubts.

On landing, a series of proclamations was issued by Abercromby, the Prince of Orange and his son, the Hereditary Prince of Orange, informing the Dutch people of the benign intentions of the expedition and calling on them to 're-establish their ancient liberty'. The army, declared the Prince of Orange, 'do not come to you as enemies, but as friends and deliverers, in order to rescue you from the odious oppression under which you are held.' Past digressions would be forgiven and the Dutch were urged not to hesitate 'to meet and to assist your deliverers'. The army and navy were ordered to 'contribute to the re-establishment of the legal government' and promised rewards for doing so. Lastly, it was declared that those who continued in their 'adherence to the oppressors of their country' would be treated as 'decided and irreconcilable enemies'.[7] The reaction to these proclamations varied between indignation and indifference. Certainly there was no rush to overthrow the directory or even assist the expedition. Walsh recorded that 'the inhabitants of the part of the country in our possession displayed no cordiality in their attachment to the cause we maintained ... they proved cool and cautious in their friendship, but active and vindictive in their enmity.'[8]

The only sign of any discontent in the armed forces was the mutiny of Story's squadron in the navy and a fairly steady flow of deserters from the army. Abercromby was not greatly impressed by these men but intended 'forming a corps' from them under a Lieutenant Colonel Sontag ('who is very intelligent, and who has been to us most useful' and claimed a number of former Dutch officers were with him and that he was being advised by Baron de Heerdt).[9] Despite this glimmer of hope he remained cautious about the implications. 'It is impossible as yet to form any opinion on the disposition of the country,' he said.[10] Abercromby's pessimistic inclinations were not encouraged by subsequent events.

Major General Don was dispatched with terms of surrender on 31 August. Don was considered to be the best man for the job as he had already had some contact with 'the Prince of Orange's friends in those countries'. In fact Dundas had him in mind to command a force that would act in conjunction with the counter revolutionaries, the numbers of which Don anticipated would rise in Groningen and Friesland after Abercromby's force had departed.[11] Daendels however delayed him, referring him to Brune, who would not allow him to proceed to The Hague and declared that he 'would use his utmost endeavours to prevent any intercourse between the British Army and the Batavian Directory.'[12] The diplomatic mission could also now be considered a failure.

The landing at Helder, although not the point expected or hoped for by the Orangists, was the signal for an attempted counter-revolutionary coup. A motley force of émigrés, a few hundred at most, led by the Hereditary Prince of Orange and armed with sabres, a few muskets, pistols and hunting guns, slipped over the border at two points in the province of Overijssel.[13] The two points were widely separated but, if the operation had been successful, would have given the prince control of this important province and provided an entry point for any future intervention from Prussia. He called on the small town of Coevorden to surrender and advanced to the edge of Arnhem at the confluence of the rivers Ijssel and Rhine. The other group of these 'partisans' penetrated as far as Westervoort, on the left bank of the Ijssel, close to Arnhem. However, their efforts were in vain as 'the proclamation of the Prince of Orange did not excite the movement in the country that they had hoped for.' National Guards with artillery were dispatched from Arnhem and Oldenrad and attacked the Orangists at Westervoort Bridge, dispersing them easily. The prince, taking advantage of his newly acquired fleet, embarked at Emden with his officers and went to join the Duke of York's army, arriving at the island of Texel on 8 September.[14]

The arrival of the Prince of Orange at Abercromby's headquarters did little to convince him that the Dutch were ready to rise in support of the invasion:

'The Hereditary Prince of Orange arrived a few days ago; he has many projects to which I listen, but follow what to me appears for our interest. He has organised 2,500 sailors and deserters, with which he wished to join this army and has solicited levy money and pay for them.'[15]

Abercromby tucked the Dutch 'volunteers' out of the way on the island of Texel without really having much faith in their utility. 'They have some arms, and they may either be employed on the armed vessels in the Zuider Zee, or on the coasts of Friezeland in promoting revolution,' he wrote. By now he was convinced that there was little appetite in the country for a mass rising and his view was echoed by his Dutch adviser Van Heerdt who, wrote Abercromby, 'seems to think we build too much on the exertions of the Orange party.'[16] Even if there had been widespread support for the

Orangists in the country, few dared express it following the declaration of martial law by General Brune. The arrest of a respectable Orangist named Judith Van Dorth, in the wake of the Prince of Orange's attempted coup, showed the determination of the authorities to deal with dissent. Charged with inciting a riot and conspiring to murder a known republican, Judith was eventually shot by a firing squad. Although she subsequently became a martyr to the Orangist cause, her case and the general atmosphere generated by her death must have played a part in discouraging any potential counter-revolutionaries from declaring themselves openly.[17]

The idea that the Dutch would rise had, however, been central to the ministry's thinking throughout and Dundas had addressed the House of Commons on 26 September declaring that:

> 'The expedition to Holland was ... adopted by his Majesty's Ministers under such auspices as to justify a sanguine hope, that it would be attended with ultimate and complete success; that the event of it must depend upon the disposition of the inhabitants to second the efforts made to rescue them from the degrading oppression under which they groan.'[18]

Even at this stage there were those in parliament that doubted this position and their doubts were borne out by what was occurring in the Helder. Despite the ministry's enthusiasm for the concept of counter-revolution, to dwell on this aspect is to accept that the only purpose of the expedition was to cause a Dutch revolt. Whilst this would have been desirable, it was by no means the pivot of the campaign and an opportunity to strike a blow at France and divert attention from the Austro-Russian offensive in the Alps did not depend entirely upon the liberation of the Netherlands.

Besides his worries about the Dutch, Abercromby had other concerns. For one thing, his army had been camped on the landing beaches since their arrival and apart from the small garrison of the 'dirty disagreeable town of Helder' the majority of the troops simply had to live amongst the dunes. Digging holes and trenches in the sand provided little shelter from the cold winds and the incessant rain (which was to plague the entire expedition) meant those who had greatcoats resorted to sleeping in them on the sand.[19]

Major Finlay of the Royal Engineers, who had suffered a wound in a previous campaign which resulted in a wooden leg, wrote to his wife to say they 'had no beds but the sand, and no covering but our great coats and the sky. My leg has not been off for the last 3 nights.' He complained of being 'fatigued to a degree you can scarcely conceive' and it is unlikely that he was alone.[20]

However relief was at hand, for having been reinforced by Don's brigade on 28 August, Abercromby moved forwards on 1 September. It was, he said, 'a matter, as much of necessity as of choice'.[21]

The British now occupied a strong position following the Zype Canal (now called the Noord Hollandsch Kanal), roughly parallel with the coast from Krabbendam (inland from Petten) in the south to Oude Sluis in the north with outposts at Schagen, St Maarten and Eenigenburg.[22] With the assistance of the Engineers, the whole line – which followed a steep dyke with a 'fine gravel road along the top' raised above the marshy farmland, which predominates in this area – was strengthened with 'field works', redoubts and entrenchments.[23]

Abercromby felt that the right of his position was under the most threat and reinforced it with a couple of Moore's battalions, which formed the left of the position:

'I received an order in the evening of the 5th to march with the Royals and 92nd Regiments, and take post upon the left of the Guards in the first line, my right on Zype Sluys, my left on St. Martin and Brug. General Don's brigade was ordered to close their cantonments to the left to make room for me.'[24]

Moore was given the two battalions of the 20th Regiment of Foot (20th foot) in compensation for the other regiments of his brigade (14th, 49th and 79th, which held Oude Sluis on the left of the line). He left a detailed description of his position in his diary:

'A high dyke in front of the canal and generally within cannon shot of it, is now our line of defence instead of the canal though our cantonments are chiefly on the other side of the canal. Four bridges cross it, four more are being made with boats, and communications are being opened from the canal to the dyke. Our pickets are upon the dyke, and command an extensive view, besides which we occupy as outposts the villages in front of the dyke, viz. Schagen, St. Martin, Groenvelt, Haring's–Karspel, Ennigerburg, and Krabbendam.'[25]

A number of these outposts were very close to those of the enemy. Abercromby inspected the defences and consolidated his position by capturing villages that overlooked his position, but he had no intention of going onto the offensive. He was aware that his strategy would be unpopular at home and, in a letter to members of the government, he wrote: 'My determination to remain on the defensive until reinforced may not meet with the approbation of his Majesty's ministers or professional men, yet I am certain that I have acted right.'[26] Whatever the military implications of Abercromby's strategy at least his men were more comfortable. Dalhousie of the Queen's found a billet in the home of a bookseller, which he used to stock up on maps and Walsh wrote of the 'fine supply of excellent black cattle and sheep' and the comparatively comfortable accommodation in 'large and commodious farmhouses'.[27]

Nearly a fortnight later (11 September) Abercromby was still waiting for reinforcements. 'I long for our reinforcements,' he wrote. 'I know you will say why is Sir Ralph Abercromby so long inactive, but I am prepared for that. If no reinforcements arrive, and if I am no longer able to defend my position I must then fight.'[28] It was a remarkable prescient statement for, as he continued to strengthen his position, the Franco–Batavian forces prepared to attack him.

Since his retreat on August 27, Daendels had also been desperate for reinforcements. A single French battalion had joined him, only to receive orders to return to Belgium leaving him 'the melancholy conviction that he would not receive any reinforcements, and that it would not be in his power to prevent the enemy from penetrating his left.' He had therefore retired and ordered Krayenhoff to fortify the approaches to Amsterdam by land and sea.[29] Reinforcements had started to reach Daendels shortly afterwards and on 2 October, General Brune arrived to take charge. Although it was rumoured that the two men didn't get on, the fiery Frenchman's arrival meant that an attempt could be made to drive the invaders back into the sea.

The British were not entirely inactive. Abercromby had conducted a reconnaissance in force using Moore's brigade on October 8, which:

> '[T]ook possession of the village of Wannenhuizen, close to the enemy's outposts, and threatened an attack on Schorldam. Demonstrations were made from other quarters in order to cover a reconnaissance which Sir Ralph wished to make as far as Broech and St. Pankras. He was stopped at the village of Langdyke, in front of Haring's-Karspel, where a skirmish ensued between the 11th Light Dragoons and some of their light troops. At about 11 A.M. I retired from Wannenhuizen, and we all returned to our cantonments.'[30]

A clash was becoming inevitable but, with his fears about the clearly increasing forces before him, uncertainty about the Dutch and concerns about the suitability of the terrain for offensive action it was unlikely to be Abercromby who initiated it.[31]

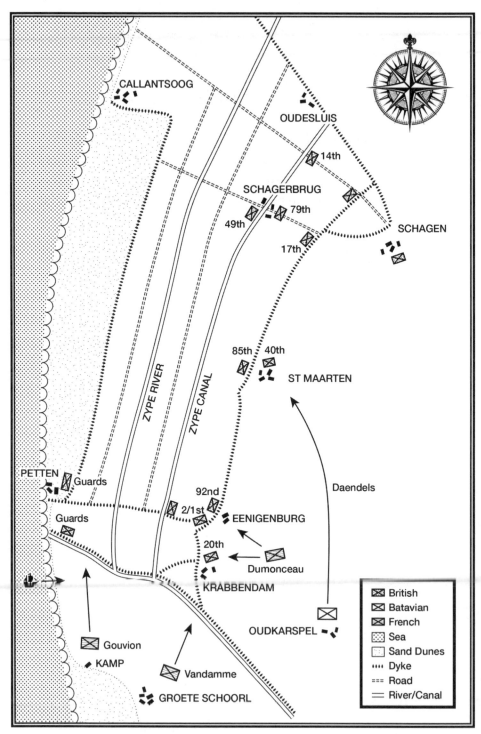

Map 3. The Battle of Krabbendam, showing the Franco–Batavian attack and the British position on the Zype Canal. (*Produced by John Harcourt*)

Chapter 8

Krabbendam – Brune Counterattacks

Τ he British position was a strong one founded on the dykes that backed the Zype, a formidable canal that ran parallel to the coast from Krabbendam to Oude Sluis. Entrenchments and redoubts had been constructed along the high dyke and along a smaller canal (now called the Groote Sloot) which ran in front of it. Abercromby had also established fortified outposts in the villages that commanded the roads and bridges crossing these waterways, and had given them strong garrisons backed up by a system of pickets and alarm posts along the dyke that would enable him to move reinforcements quickly to any threatened point. The southern end of the line was covered by yet another canal and dyke, which ran from Krabbendam to the sea near Petten, which was also fortified.

This southern end formed the left of Abercromby's line and was held by the most reliable troops in Abercromby's army: the two guards brigades. The most vulnerable point of the line, where it bent northwards at Krabbendam, however was entrusted to 20th foot under Lieutenant Colonel Smyth. The two battalions of this regiment were composed almost entirely of recruits from the militia who had yet to see any serious combat. It was a bold choice on Abercromby's part and shows the level of faith that he must have had in their commander. The Gordon Highlanders (92nd foot) and the 2nd Battalion of the 1st Regiment of Foot (Royal Scots) of Moore's brigade covered the line from Krabbendam to St Maarten, with the 40th Regiment of Foot (40th foot) under Colonel Spencer holding the village of St Maarten. The rest of Don's newly arrived division, who were also militiamen, were to the left of them with the end of the line held by the residue of Moore's command.[1]

The enemy had not been idle and all available troops had been rushed to the front. General de Brigade Gouvion, with two battalions of 42 Demi Brigade (42nd DB), one company of artillery and three squadrons of Chasseurs à Cheval (light cavalry), arrived first and took up position at

Haarlem and Beverwijk, covering the coast.[2] General Brune himself arrived to take charge of the defending forces on 2 September. He reorganized the Batavian force, splitting it in two (one division under Daendels and the other under Dumonceau) and rearranged them in French fashion: 'By order of the General in Chief they formed advanced guards composed each of two battalions of Jaegers and of companies of grenadiers formed in battalion.'[3] He also instructed them to reduce the large number of female camp followers and cut down on the immense train of baggage wagons that followed every battalion in the Batavian force, but it seems that this edict was ignored.[4]

He bought with him a Dutch division from Amsterdam, six battalions of French infantry and a substantial force of artillery under General de Brigade Seroux, which had been sent urgently from Belgium. 'Tired as these troops were by their forced march, Brune was anxious to drive the enemy off before they could be reinforced.'[5] With the arrival of Vandamme's division five days later, he felt he was strong enough to take the offensive and began immediately to make preparations for an attack on the British position on 10 September.

Brune's plan was to attack the right of the British position from the south towards Petten (starting from Schoorl) with his French troops under Vandamme. To their right Dumonceau's Dutch division was to march from Schoorldam along the canal to Krabbendam, take the bridge and hit the British line at the point at which it turned northward. On Dumonceau's right, a third column under Daendels was to assemble at St Pankras, advance north, capture Eenigenburg and break through the defence line along the Zype, where it would 'attack strongly on the left to support the central division.'[6]

The British were aware that the enemy was stirring against them and remained in a state of high alert. Those manning the outposts along the Zype were not permitted to lie down but had to sit up with their weapons to hand and regular cavalry patrols were sent out beyond the lines to observe the enemy.[7] On the evening of 9 September, there had been a clash when a small party of Light Dragoons attacked the Batavian *jaegers* at Oudkarspel, but they barricaded themselves in and fired at the dragoons at close range killing twelve and driving the rest off.[8] During the following night the outposts of 92nd foot at Eenigenburg became aware of movement from the enemy positions. The beating of drums was heard as well as the rumbling of wagons, indicating large numbers of troops in motion. A messenger was dispatched to wake General Moore. Moore was alarmed and at some time between three and four o'clock in the morning, he rode through the darkness to investigate this activity himself. At the same time, he dispatched a party of the 11th Light Dragoons (11/Dragoons) to the outpost at Haring's-Karspel 'with orders to patrol forward as soon as it was day.'[9] On reaching 92nd foot's position at Eenigenburg, their commander, Captain John Cameron, reported that all was now quiet so Moore set off after the dragoons.[10] He hadn't gone far when 'a dragoon overtook me with a message from Lieutenant-Colonel Smith, reporting that a considerable force was marching to attack Krabbendam.'[11]

Things had started well for Daendels. The aggressive Colonel Crass had set off at two in the morning with the advanced guard and by four they had made themselves masters of Haring's-Karspel and Drixhoorn. However, when Crass advanced towards Eenigenburg, which he had been ordered to capture, he found all the roads blocked by the 'division of Lieutenant-General Dumonceau and the Brigade of Major-General Bonhomme'.[12] As a result, Daendels was not able to make the attack upon Eenigenburg as had been ordered and attacked St Maarten instead. He called a quick halt to regroup and establish communications with the central division on his left and found the other part of his own command under General Barbou, who had arrived by a more circuitous route (via Oosterdijke) on his right. Despite a spirited defence by Colonel Spencer and 40th foot, Daendels reported that his attack was initially successful.[13] Supported by the fire of his light artillery, his grenadiers had captured a redoubt at the entrance to the village, silenced an artillery battery and were 'preparing to carry the rest of the position by main force' when the ubiquitous Colonel Crass reported that Bonhomme's troops on the left were retreating in some disorder, having been repulsed at Eenigenburg.[14] This would have left Daendels' men dangerously exposed on that side as they launched their attack, and as the movement affected the morale of his own men causing his *jaegers* to join the stampede to the rear, Daendels called a halt to rally his errant *jaegers* and reorder his attack columns. According to one report he had accomplished this by two o'clock and was ready to renew his attack when it became apparent that there had been no progress made at any point along the line. Not wanting to overextend himself, he rested on his laurels and did not look beyond maintaining his initial gains. Half an hour later he became aware that the fire had entirely ceased on the left and the enemy was feeding troops through Schagen and Walcoog against his right. At the same time he received orders from General Brune to retreat to his original positions. Supported by the brigade in the centre under General Bonhomme, Daendels reported that it was effected in 'the greatest order', despite a lively pursuit from 40th foot and the harassing fire of the enemy artillery, which set fire to the village of Drixhoorn with their shells.[15]

The central division of the Franco-Batavian attack was commanded by Lieutenant General Dumonceau who was tasked with attacking the defences between Krabbendam and Eenigenburg, with the removal of the position at Krabbendam being considered critical for the success of the attack. Unfortunately for him things went badly from the beginning. The Batavian engineer Krayenhoff attributed the division's misfortune to poor staff work on the part of Brune's French *aides-de-camp* (ADCs) who had ordered General Bonhomme's brigade to approach its objective along a road that did not exist.[16] As a result they were forced to take a route further to the right than had been planned thus impeding the progress of Daendels' troops on their way to Eenigenburg. This 'unforgivable mistake' was compounded by the time it took to assemble the division, which meant that Colonel Bruce's brigade was trying to move through Alkmaar at the same time the local farmers were bringing their produce to market; their carts blocking the gates and preventing the troops from getting through. Whilst admitting that the operation was planned in haste, the French claimed that the hold up was caused by the Batavian battalion at the head of the column sending its baggage and female followers to the rear. Whatever the reason for the delay, the central division was late in starting its movement and its line of march was disrupted. This disruption was compounded by the state of the roads, which forced Bonhomme to move his division to the right of his allotted line of march.[17] Hoping to make up lost time, Dumonceau changed his plan and decided that, as well as the attack he had been ordered to make against Krabbendam, he would launch an attack against Eenigenburg, which had originally been the objective assigned to Daendels.

The British commander, Moore, was pretty confident that Smyth could hold Krabbendam and had identified this part of the line as crucial to the security of his sector. He wrote that:

'I was more anxious about that part of the dyke which was in [the] rear of Haring's-Karspel and Ennigerburg, because a good road through those villages ran along it, and the impediments of the country made it extremely difficult for an enemy to advance except by roads ... I galloped towards that quarter which was the alarm post of the Royals and 92nd Regiments. I was confirmed in my opinion that an attack was intended to be made there, as it was now sufficiently light for me to distinguish large bodies of the enemy marching towards Haring's-Karspel. By this time the regiments were nearly at their alarm posts. The picquets from the villages were falling back, but Captain Anderson [whom Moore had sent to the outposts] had the presence of mind to get the different bridges on the canals lifted up. This gave them time to retire, and retarded the advance of the enemy.'[18]

Abercromby sent Moore instructions to join him at Krabbendam with one of his battalions but the major general declined as he felt strongly that his 'presence was indispensable where I was, and less necessary at Krabbendam, as he was there.'[19]

Dumonceau arrived with his forward units in front of the enemy positions at five o'clock in the morning, immediately attacked and overran the outpost at Tuitjenhorn and followed up as far as an artillery battery in front of Eenigenburg, which it then prepared to assault. He pushed a half battery of light artillery out in front of his brigade, which he flanked with *jaegers* and advanced his infantry in a dense column against the rear of Selschardik. They moved through the village and immediately suffered from the deadly fire which the British artillery was able to bring down upon them from its position on top of the Zype Dyke, and were able to bring deadly fire down on the column. The head of the column reached the entrance to Selschardik and then deployed on the plain beyond.[20] Under the covering fire of its light artillery, the column then charged towards the dyke 'with shouts and drums and bugles'.[21] The men from 92nd foot were waiting. The dyke had sheltered them from the fire of the approaching Batavians and as the attackers got to within fifty paces of the ditch, 92nd foot stood up on top of the dyke and fired 'a volley or two' which, combined with the fire of the field guns emplaced on the dyke, proved so galling that they were shaken, became 'a little disordered' and ran back the way they had come to shelter at the rear of the village.[22] Meanwhile, 92nd foot sat back down behind the dyke to shelter themselves from the fire of the Batavian artillery. 'The shot whistled over our heads, and fell, when its strength was spent, on the ground in our rear,' a soldier of the regiment later recalled.[23] As a result of the strength of this position, 92nd foot suffered only one man killed and three wounded in the entire battle, though Moore was wounded by a musket ball, which struck his finger but was deflected by his telescope, and thus failed to do him serious harm.[24]

At this point Daendels intervened, helping Bonhomme to rally his fleeing soldiers; but it seems their nerve was broken for the two generals were unable to bring their troops back into the line of fire. Bonhomme was therefore forced to take a stand, out of the reach of the guns, and await the results of the attacks to either side. Through the fire of the light artillery he was able to keep 92nd foot behind the dyke and by maintaining their position, his men provided support for Daendels' men who by this time were being counterattacked by the British.

Dumonceau's original objective had been Krabbendam and the lieutenant general was determined to take it, even though he had only a portion of his troops available. Without waiting for Colonel Bruce's brigade, which was still trying to get out of Alkmaar, Dumonceau personally led a small body of troops borrowed from Bonhomme's brigade in a headlong attack on Krabbendam. His *jaegers*, led by Adjutant General (Lieutenant Colonel) Vichery, quickly overran the entrenched positions covering the approach to the village and half a battery of light artillery was run up and placed on a dyke overlooking the position. The fire of the light artillery's 6–pounders kept the defenders' heads down for an hour, preventing them from retaking the outposts until Bruce's brigade finally arrived, allowing the attack to proceed.[25] The 3rd Battalion of *jaegers* attacked immediately 'with headlong fury' and carried the redoubt to the right of the village, which covered a lesser dyke.[26] They were followed by Bruce's infantry column, which fought its way into the village despite heavy fire from the men of 20th foot occupying the buildings, and hand-to-hand fighting broke out in the narrow village streets. It was too much for Smyth's militiamen who abandoned their post with some haste, allowing the Batavians to take control of the village and its vital bridge canal crossing. [27] According to one of Brune's ADCs, the *jaegers* pursued the broken enemy almost as far as the dyke, despite heavy fire from the positions on top of it. [28]

At this point the attack broke down. In his report to Minister of War Bernadotte, Brune claimed that the unit following the *jaegers* was 'seized by a terror inspired by their cowardly officers'. [29] The men began to flee, throwing away their weapons. This panic spread to the other troops, making them retreat and instantly losing Dumonceau all the ground he had gained. However, with threats and encouragement, in concert with Adjutant General Vichery and Chef de Brigade Clement (ADC to General Brune), he managed to rally his troops and bring them back before Krabbendam, where the enemy had already returned. [30] Smyth had rallied his men quickly and perhaps with reinforcements committed by Abercromby from the reserve (the British commander makes no mention in his report of his own role in the battle), he launched a counterattack, which drove the Batavians out of the positions they had taken and re-established British control of the area. Bunbury attributed the success to the quality of Smyth, who was shot in the thigh during the action, as well as 20th foot which he said 'was a regiment that never would be beaten.' [31] The fire of the Light Artillery prevented 20/foot from pressing their adversaries too closely but at three o'clock General Brune ordered a retreat to the initial positions. Brune later ranted that the retreat in Krabbendam 'robbed us of our chance of victory' and he had fourteen of the officers and men involved shot. [32]

The picture was similar on the left of the Franco–Batavian line. The column under General de Division Vandamme had begun its attack, as planned, on the southern end of the British position in the dark just before dawn. The experienced French units advanced with their accustomed ferocity, with grenadiers leading the column and a cloud of skirmishers in support. [33] Like the Batavian columns, Vandamme's command was split into two parts. The right wing was to join the left of Bonhomme's division in the attack on Krabbendam, assaulting the village from the south whilst the Batavians came in from the east. With two battalions of 42nd DB, Chef de Brigade Aubrée marched through Breelaan, over the bridge that led to the windmill at Krabbendam, to support Dumonceau's attack. The bridge was covered by the fire of two cannons but heedless of this, they rushed the battery, overwhelming it and obliging the artillerymen to abandon their guns. However, by the time they reached the village, Dumonceau's men had been thrown into panic and were in full retreat so their manoeuvre ground to a halt.[34]

The next unit along was the advanced guard under Adjutant General Rostollant, who also advanced with great élan, driving in the British outposts at Hargerweg and arriving at the foot of the dyke. Here however the advance was stopped. It seems that the French reconnaissance hadn't fully assessed the size of the canal; Brune's staff officer admitted that the operation was planned in too much haste to have made any provision for crossing what turned out to be a substantial obstacle. The locals, whose help they tried to enlist, were not forthcoming and they could find no way to cross the canal securely. Maddened by the continuous musketry and grapeshot from the top of the dyke, the grenadiers tried anyway and thirty were drowned: 'swept away by too much ardour', according to the ADC. A captain of 42e DB named Delenteigne threw himself into the water with sword clenched between his teeth to try and find a point where his men could cross. Although under heavy fire the brave captain tried several points along the canal but could find no suitable ford for his men and had to admit defeat.[35]

At the same time, Vandamme himself advanced out of Slaperdijk with two battalions (one each from 42 and 49 demi brigades). The dyke at this point was very high (roughly at a right angle to the Zype position), defended by a large battery in front and by two casements on the flanks, exposing the attacking troops to a crossfire and not allowing them to march in their accustomed dense column. The front ranks were scythed down by the destructive fire poured into them by the guards' battalions in their defensive positions. Bunbury wrote that they persevered with the attack despite their exposed position displaying 'reckless bravery', though they stood no chance of success.[36] General de Brigade David was shot through the neck whilst at the head of his grenadiers encouraging them forwards. Unconscious, he fell to the ground and a small group of his men ran to his aid, also suffering wounds as they attempted to remove him from the fire-swept plain. Their efforts were in vain as David expired moments later, just as the attack faltered and his men sought cover from the murderous volleys of the British guardsmen. They retired shortly afterwards having suffered heavy casualties.[37]

Finally, General de Brigade Gouvion commanded the part of Vandamme's division that was tasked with assaulting the extreme end of the British position closest to the sea. Its main objective was the village of Petten. Like most of the other brigades Gouvion's attack began well, capturing Camperduin and forcing its garrison to pull back to the dyke. They then advanced along a feature, which Brune's ADC called the 'white dyke', that ran parallel to the beach, hugging the slope to avoid the fire from the British position, which enfiladed his right flank. According to Brune's ADC they were approaching Petten, driving their enemy before them and were confident of taking their objective when they were recalled.[38] However, other sources claim that as they approached Petten, Gouvion's decision to advance along the edge of the beach proved to be disastrous, for favourable winds had allowed a small flotilla of naval vessels to operate close to the shore and these opened a heavy fire on his men.[39] These ships were probably the frigate *Shannon* 'and some of the gun brigs', which had been detailed by Mitchell 'to prevent the General's right flank being turned.'[40] Fully exposed to this deadly fire, they too took heavy casualties and were already retreating when they received Brune's order to fall back on Slaperdijk.[41]

The retreat was now general and by three o'clock the entire assault force was back in its starting positions. Despite Brune's claims to the contrary, the retreating attackers were pursued and harassed by troops of the reserve under Colonel MacDonald for some time which, reported Abercromby, 'quickened their retreat' and caused them to abandon an artillery piece, some baggage wagons and their bridging train. In his official report, Abercromby expressed his pleasure at the performance of his troops, writing: 'It is impossible for me to do justice to the good conduct of the troops.'[42] Brune also expressed satisfaction with his troops, putting a positive spin on the outcome of the battle:

'Our French division, only seven thousand men strong, has deployed
  with every imaginable valour and heroism, it was impossible to

distinguish the old soldiers from the conscripts, numbers of whom made up the whole group. General Vandamme, whose courage is well known to you, declares that he has never seen braver soldiers. The division remained the mistress of the field of battle and occupied the front of the dunes of Camp and Slapendyke.'[43]

However, it was clear that he had been beaten at all points and the activities of the Royal Navy had given him serious concerns for the security of his left flank. His report noted that they had landed forces behind his lines between Leyde and Haarlem and ransacked houses along the coast.[44] He was also less than pleased about the performance of his Batavian allies and reported to the Batavian Directory that: 'The day should have been decisive for us had all the corps done their duty alike.'[45] Still seething, he wrote to Bernadotte to say: 'In general, the Batavian divisions have not lived up to the promise of their firm appearance.'[46]

There was worse to come. That evening, as the Batavian soldiers began to disperse to their cantonments to get some food and go to sleep, alarm spread through their camp. A sergeant of *jaegers* ran amongst his comrades shouting that 'the English cavalry had got into the Langedyke and were murdering all they could find there.'[47] It is quite possible that 11/Dragoons were indeed patrolling aggressively in the area; we know that on 9 September they had probed the Batavian lines at that very point.[48] Whatever the truth of the rumour, its effect was electrifying. Daendels reported that because his troops were billeted in villages that were in a defile, it was impossible to see whether they really were under attack. The report spread terror amongst the troops who were 'fatigued, surprised, without arms, in a moment of repose, and dispersed in the houses.'[49] A large part of the division took to their heels and to Brune's particular disgust, carried their colours with them.[50] Daendels said 'they arrived like a torrent at Saint Pancrass, where luckily the Lieutenant General had established his headquarters. He immediately sent forward the battalion of the 5th Demi brigade [Halve Brigade] whose presence restored order.'[51] However, not all of them were stopped and some men got into the artillery park crying that the enemy was pursuing them. The artillery drivers in most armies were still civilian contractors and the Batavian drivers were no exception. They mounted up and fled towards

Haarlem leaving their guns behind them and spreading panic throughout the area. Eventually they were stopped between Alkmaar and Amsterdam by the Groningen National Guards.[52]

Brune, already incensed by the day's failure, was beside himself with fury. 'Send me forces, my dear Bernadotte, or I do not know how I shall take the combinations of cowardice and treason which surround us,' he wrote to the minister of war. 'I will write to Generals Daendels and Dumonceau asking them if they can answer positively for their divisions if I give them the order to shoot the perpetrators of these cowardly perfidies.'[53] He was particularly keen to punish the regimental standard bearer who had carried his flag in the midst of the rout. Daendels was convinced the whole thing was the result of treachery, believing that the sergeant of *jaegers* who started the panic had been paid by the 'disaffected', but he agreed with Brune that there should be reprisals and had the sergeant shot in front of his unit.[54]

The whole affair reflected badly on the morale of the Batavian troops and Abercromby reported that they were starting to desert in large numbers at every opportunity.[55] Perhaps there was a chance that the Dutch troops would come over to the allies after all. Brune's attempt to oust Abercromby from his comfortable position on the Zype had been a failure and whilst many attribute the plan to his offensive dynamism, evidence of the spirit and élan displayed by French commanders and their forces it is in fact a vindication of Abercromby's defensive strategy. Not only did the offensive reveal the strength of the forces that would have opposed him if he had attempted the march on Amsterdam many believe he should have made, it showed the ease with which such terrain could be defended. Brune's force had engaged two thirds of the British force at most and had never had any real chance of success. Here was a salutary lesson for the British when they went over to the offensive a few days later.

Chapter 9

The Grand Old Duke of York –
the Arrival of the Allied Commander

Abercromby felt that his decision to remain on the defensive had been vindicated to some extent by his repulse of Brune's attack yet he knew that he faced criticism at home. The general wrote to the secretary of state for war and said: 'It is possible that my determination to remain on the defensive until reinforced may not meet with the approbation of his Majesty's Ministers or of professional men, yet I am certain that I have acted right.'[1] He felt that his concerns about the difficult nature of the terrain had been borne out by the failure of the enemy attack. He also remained – despite the steady trickle of deserters crossing to the British lines – pessimistic about the chances of a general rising in favour of the Prince of Orange. 'I believe,' he wrote, 'that the Prince has been deceived in thinking that he has more friends than enemies in this country. If we can advance, everyone will be on our side, but there are few who will risk anything.'[2]

After the euphoria over the surrender of the Dutch fleet, relations with the navy may have also deteriorated. Vice Admiral Mitchell was an independent-minded man with his own ideas of how to go about achieving the expedition's aims and appeared to Abercromby to be ignoring his suggestions. This included the sensible suggestion that he should arm a fleet of shallow draft vessels to threaten Amsterdam.[3] Having previously complained to Dundas that he hadn't heard from the admiral at all for three days, on 11 September Abercromby wrote of his relief at the return of Mitchell's trusted subordinate, Captain Oughton, adding 'he is a man of sense and alone can manage him'.[4] It is fair to say that Abercromby had little faith in the success of the enterprise and looked forward with enthusiasm to the arrival of the reinforcements and the Duke of York, so he could hand over command.[5]

On 13 September, Abercromby's fervent wish was granted and the Duke of York at last set foot on the Helder to take command of the army. By now he was 36-years-old and the results of good living and five years behind a desk at Horse Guards were showing.[6] He had last commanded an army in the field during the disastrous Flanders campaign of 1794 and many were disparaging about his appointment.[7] Nonetheless it was felt that a prince of the blood would not only be the best person to deal with the Russians, but his part in the deliverance of Holland would enhance future relations with the Dutch.[8] Abercromby was greatly relieved as it appears that there may have already been stirrings of the disharmony that was to plague Anglo-Russian relations throughout the campaign. He expressed his doubts that the Russians would obey his orders and York himself wrote to the king soon after his arrival, excusing himself for not writing immediately on the grounds that he had found himself 'under the necessity of setting out almost immediately for this place, which is the headquarters of the army, in order to obviate anything unpleasant that might have happened had the Russian General joined Sir Ralph Abercromby's corps while I was not present.'[9]

As Abercromby had hoped, after a 'tedious passage of five days', York took immediate command and inspected the Russian contingent on the march. He observed that: 'The body of men are very fine and strong, though not remarkably tall; they are clothed exactly in the style the Prussians were in the time of Frederick the 2nd only that their clothing is green instead of blue.'[10] Then, accompanied by the Prince of Orange, he inspected the position that Abercromby had established on the Zype calling it 'astonishingly strong'. He also reported the reaction of the local people to their prince: 'I was rejoiced to see him so well received by the country people in all the villages through which we passed; it appeared to me really to come from the heart and not at all to be put on.'[11] Abercromby, however, was less impressed: 'The Hereditary Prince of Orange is here with us. He is modest and unassuming; his manners are not popular, and he does not yield readily to the friendships of his countrymen, whose sincerity he perhaps has good reason to suspect.'[12]

Perhaps overawed by the size of the force that had now disembarked, the Batavian Directory sent an emissary (Mr Mollerus, a former minister) to allied headquarters on 12 September. They claimed to have no knowledge of General Don's attempt to deliver terms to them and said they were prepared to treat with the House of Orange even if the expedition was ultimately unsuccessful. They claimed that 'their great dread was to live any longer under the tyranny exercised over them by the French.'[13] This was to be the only indication of their appetite for a change of regime throughout the entire campaign and nothing concrete came of the negotiations.

For the enemy, the lessons of 11 September were clear. General Brune had pulled his troops back to their original positions and began to dig in while he awaited the arrival of the reinforcements Bernadotte had assured him were hurrying from Belgium. Daendels was to cover the right of the position; his left was protected by the fields which were 'cut with an infinity of channels almost everywhere' but his right was an area of more open terrain and easy to turn.[14] Therefore he cut the bridges, which would allow the enemy to approach Niedorp and Verlaat, which were strongly entrenched. He also further strengthened the post at Oudkarspel, constructing redoubts in front of it and digging trenches on all sides of the village, which with Noord-scharwoude, Zuid-scharwoude and Broek formed the basis of his position.[15] Daendels reported that:

> 'These four villages form a narrow defile, which offers in no one part of its whole length a single spot where eight men can be drawn up in front. A deep canal covers it all along the right flank, but the enemy possessing all the roads which lead to that canal could easily turn this position.'

To prevent these villages being overwhelmed Daendels found it 'necessary to construct both numerous and difficult works.' In addition to cutting the bridges he dug up the roads along the dykes and built batteries to prevent the enemy from approaching his vulnerable right. 'In spite however of the zeal of the engineers, and the activity of the Lieutenant-General, these works unfortunately were not finished when the enemy attacked on the 19th of September.'[16]

Immediately to Daendels' left, Dumonceau's division occupied the area from Schoorldam to Oudkarspel. He fortified the bridge at Schoorldam but was concerned about Warmenhuizen. All along the line the positions of the two armies ran in close parallel, in some instances no more than sixty yards apart, and this village was particularly close to the British lines. Realizing its weakness and intending to fortify its perimeter, Dumonceau went to reconnoitre this position only to find the bridge cut and the British guards in possession. The next morning, before daybreak, he sent two companies of grenadiers and two of *jaegers*, under Captain Goudoever, who, under enemy fire, restored the bridge, chased the English from the village and established a garrison. Dumonceau then set to work fortifying this position.[17]

The French were stationed on the left of the Batavians. Vandamme's division, which had been reinforced with four battalions and four squadrons of cavalry, occupied the steep sandhills known as the heights of Camperduin.[18] These sand dunes are similar to the ones that overlook the landing beaches but are more extensive. Rising in places to a height of 300 foot, they stretch from Groet right down the coast and are covered by thick pine forest, especially around Bergen.[19] Abercromby's ADC, Bunbury, left this somewhat poetic description of the French position:

'The dunes between Bergen and the sea present a formidable barrier of defence, from two to four miles wide, some hundreds of feet in height, and broken and twisted in the most irregular forms, like huge waves in an ocean stirred by tempests. Along their crests, and overhanging the road from Petten to Bergen, were posted the advanced guards and light detachments of the French, overlooking our lines.'[20]

This position straddled the main route to the important town of Alkmaar and was centred on the large village of Bergen. General de Division Vandamme had 'raised some redoubts and batteries both at Slaperdijk and on the left at Schorel.' He had also fortified Koedijk and Bergen and 'was assured of his defence by two works each side of the canal'. In order to maintain communications between the three divisions of the army, Vandamme placed a bridge of boats on the Groote Sloot and had the road between Avenhorn and Alkmaar patrolled by the 10th Light Dragoons (10/Dragoons). It was also reported that, somehow, hearing of a plan to occupy Hoorn 'with the intention of threatening our right and carrying away the naval stores' Brune sent 200 Batavian infantry to forestall this move.[21]

In the British camp, the arrival of the Russians had raised expectations that offensive operations would commence shortly and having inspected the troops and the position, the Duke of York began to draw up his plan. Major Maule of the Queen's summed up the mood within the army:

'From this moment, everyone looked forward for offensive operations. The opulent cities of Holland already opened themselves to our view. I was fortunate in being present when the Russian division arrived at the lines. The head of the column, composed chiefly of grenadiers, defiled past the Commander in Chief at midday; and were well appointed, and made a fine and imposing appearance.... The appearance of such an ally naturally gave rise to high expectations.'[22]

There were numerous difficulties facing York but primary amongst these were the strength of the enemy position and the nature of the landscape itself. Although the republicans had not completed their preparations, it was clear that the advance would be obstructed, roads and bridges destroyed and multiple obstacles placed in their way. The enemy had thrown up a number of earthworks and, as Bunbury reported, clearly had 'an abundance of artillery' with which to defend their position.[23] This would make an assault hard enough by itself but there was the added difficulty of the terrain. The whole area was low lying and marshy and as York himself described: 'a plain intersected every three or four hundred yards by broad deep wet ditches and canals'.[24] This would seriously impede the advance of an eighteenth-century army, which required wide, flat areas to deploy its long firing lines and the dunes would give a major advantage to the defenders. Nonetheless, the enemy had already been sent reinforcements and York could assume that more would be on the way so an attack had to be launched as soon as possible.

Perhaps in view of the poor results of his campaign in Flanders in 1795, the Duke of York was instructed to place his plans before a council of war composed of the senior allied commanders. This arrangement invited criticism from most commentators but was common in coalition armies at the time and was, in this instance, made necessary by the political nature of the campaign. After consultation with his council of war, York decided upon an attack by widely separated columns which commentators such as Alison and Jomini attributed to 'the nature of the ground', which 'precluded the employment of large masses'.[25] Given the reason for the defeat at Tourcoing in 1794 had been the failure of the column under Austrian General Clerfayt to support the Duke of York's column, it is surprising that York would have adopted such a plan.[26] It also seems odd, given his personal experience of this kind of warfare, that he didn't make more provision for maintaining communication between the columns, particularly bearing in mind the difficult terrain in which they were to operate.

The attack was intended to drive the enemy from their positions and open the way to Amsterdam.[27] To that end, the army divided into two parts, the right of which was divided into several columns, the composition of which York detailed in his official report:

'The Columns upon the right, the First commanded by Lieutenant-General D'Hermann, consisting of:

The 7th Light Dragoons, Twelve Battalions of Russians, and Major-General Manners' Brigade;

The Second, commanded by Lieutenant-General Dundas, consisting of:

Two squadrons of the 11th Light Dragoons, Two brigades of Foot Guards, and Major-General His Highness Prince William's Brigade;

The Third Column, commanded by Lieutenant-General Sir James Pulteney, consisting of:

Two Squadrons of the 11th Light Dragoons, Major-General Don's Brigade, Major General Coote's Brigade; marched from the positions they occupied at Daybreak of the morning of the 19th.[28]

The object of the first column was to drive the Enemy from the heights of Camper Duyne, the villages under these heights, and finally to take possession of Bergen: the second was to force the Enemy's position at Walmenhuysen and Schoreldam, and to co-operate with the Column under Lieutenant-General D'Hermann: and the Third to take possession of Ouds Carspel at the Head of the Lange Dyke, a great Road leading to Alkmaar.'[29]

The column on the left was commanded by Abercromby and consisted of two squadrons of the 18th Light Dragoons, the Combined Grenadier Battalion, the Combined Light Infantry Battalion, 23rd and 55th foot under MacDonald and the brigades of the Earl of Chatham, Moore and the Earl of Cavan. In his dispatch, York said this column was 'destined to turn the Enemy's right on the Zuyder Zee' but his actual orders make clear that there was more to it than that.[30] The reason for detaching so large a force was not to make an intervention on the right flank of Brune's force – as many believed at the time and have done since – but rather to march behind it, cutting it off and striking straight at Amsterdam. York calculated that he had enough troops to beat Brune in a straightforward, frontal assault, and if successful, Abercromby's force would prevent them from simply falling back to another defensive position. It was a bold plan and if it had worked it is likely that the Franco-Batavian army would have been destroyed and the capital taken.

It was also an elaborate plan, and relied on all the columns achieving their objectives and keeping to the timetable so the enemy could not concentrate on each column in turn and defeat them in detail. Although there has been much criticism of this plan as a compromise created by the council of war, it was devised by York alone and the other commanders went along with it, making only minor changes. In his letter to Dundas, Abercromby wrote:

'The plan of attack was, I am persuaded, the best that could be devised; it was laid by H.R. Highness before General Hermann, myself, and General Dundas, and it met with our united approbation, General Hermann declared that it contained all his ideas, and I heard no difference of opinion on the subject.'[31]

York himself echoed Abercromby's words in his own report: 'The Council approved the plan unanimously and Herman (the Russian Commander) added that it was exactly what he would have proposed himself.'[32] It was, however, a plan that was far from foolproof and was seen as flawed even by those executing it. Bunbury believed that the allies should either have launched an all out frontal attack with their whole force or a series of feints while the main attack rolled up the enemy line from Hoorn on the right.

'However,' he said, 'the Council of War resolved on the adoption of a plan which afforded neither the advantage of superior numbers, nor that of the time necessary for the effect of a movement on the side of Hoorn.'[33] General Moore also felt that the attack was hurried and the detachment of Abercromby's force 'ill imagined'. He added that the subordinate commanders had not been sufficiently briefed and had been unable to liaise with one another.[34]

Despite the misgivings of those involved, and those commenting on the battle with hindsight, York must have felt his plan gave his army the best chance of achieving a swift and decisive victory that would silence the critics back in Britain and hopefully ignite the long awaited counter-revolution in the Netherlands. He must have gone to bed at his Schagerbrug headquarters on the night of 18 September confident that the morning would bring him victory.

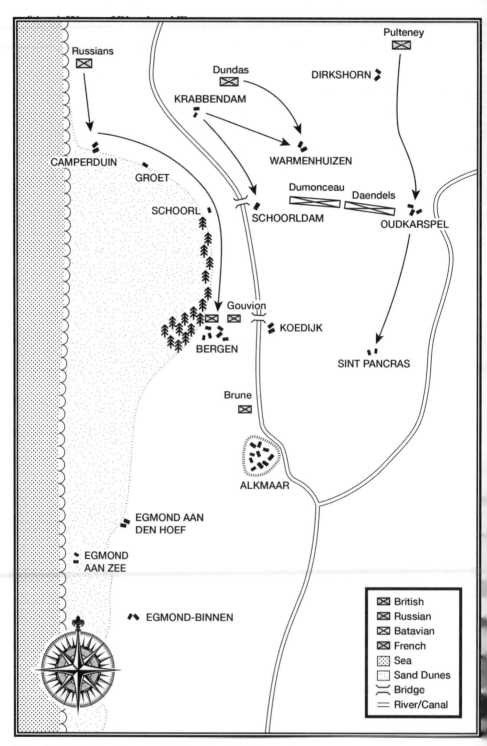

Map 4. The Battle of Bergen. (*Produced by John Harcourt*)

Chapter 10

Bergen – the Russian Attack

The Russian assault on the village of Bergen began in the very early hours of 19 September 1799. Assigned the position of honour on the right of the line, the Russian attack was supposed to be synchronized with the advance of British columns in the centre and on the left but, perhaps understandably, after having been cooped up on their troopships for weeks, the Russians were impatient to prove themselves.[1] They were tired from their long journey and hungry having not taken to the rations of salted pork and rye bread that the British had supplied. In addition, they had only been able to drink vodka because their water supplies had been polluted with salt water as a result of the rough seas they had endured. To make matters worse, their excitement and anxiety about the forthcoming battle had rendered them unable to sleep.[2]

The attack had been scheduled for dawn but at about half past two in the morning, news reached the Russian commander Lieutenant General Herman that the *jaegers* and grenadiers commanded by his subordinate, Major General Schutorff, had already begun to attack the French outposts on the right.[3] As the sound of firing became increasingly audible through the fog, it appeared that the fighting was intensifying and Herman, deciding that his right must be supported, ordered a general advance.

The twelve battalions of Russians set off in good order with their grenadiers leading the way along the Slaperdijk, a narrow causeway raised above the waterlogged fields, and soon reached the first of a series of positions the French had hastily prepared to impede their progress. With 'a great shout which was repeated by the whole of the Russian troops' Herman's column surged forward and proceeded to direct a heavy but ragged fire upon the enemy position and quickly overwhelmed it. According to Captain Herbert Taylor, who was attached to Herman's staff as liaison officer, resistance from the position was light but the Russians sustained heavy casualties as a result of their own wild volleys. Taylor claimed that the Russian commander was aware of this: 'I observed to General Hermann that the troops in the rear must have fired upon those in front which he admitted was more than probable.'[4]

Despite their casualties the Russians pressed onwards but the difficult terrain led them to crowd together on the narrow causeway. In the darkness their ranks became disordered, their units intermingled and their officers began to lose control of the men. High winds and heavy rain muffled sounds, making it impossible to hear orders shouted or the beating of the drums.[5] Nevertheless they soon reached a second redoubt and although its defenders put up more of a fight in order to save the 4-pounder cannon which had been placed there, it too was quickly swallowed up by the Russian tide.[6] Again the Russians took heavy casualties and again it seemed that in the dark and confusion many of them were self-inflicted. Schutorff's ragged band, which had begun the attack, advanced along the dunes to the right of the main column and Taylor believed that they too were firing at Herman's men causing yet more casualties.[7]

General Herman now led his fraying column into Groet in person and the village quickly fell. The situation was becoming increasingly chaotic with the shot 'flying in every direction' and the Russians constantly shouting for artillery support, even though it was too dark to discern any targets. Herman himself was coming under fire. His horse had been wounded as he led the attack and he complained that Taylor's red coat was drawing enemy fire so he left him and moved off to the 'sand hills on the right'.[8]

Meanwhile, the Russian second line had come up but rather than being kept in reserve as Taylor, quite rightly, felt it should, they 'joined the first and mixed with it'. By this point any order in the Russian ranks had broken down. Taylor remonstrated with the Russian officers he was able to communicate with (for he spoke no Russian) in an attempt to get them to reorder their troops and stop them firing at their comrades. Although they recognized the wisdom of his advice, they could not act upon it as they were unable to identify their units and had apparently no control over their men who ignored their calls to cease firing.[9]

In this anarchic frenzy, the Russians pressed on to the village of Schoorl where they at last encountered some sustained resistance. Brune had tasked Adjutant General Rostollant with the defence of this sector and he formed a body of men in front of the village of Schoorl, with its right at the bridge of Schoorldam and its left in the dunes. He placed his light artillery (two 4-pounders) on the left in advance of his front covering the exits from Groet. On his right he had a battery of two 12-pounders and another two 4-pounders at the Schoorldam bridge. In this position he 'awaited the enemy with resolution' and met them with a devastating volley of musketry and grapeshot, delivered at point-blank range. The bodies of the Russian dead covered the ground right up to the muzzles of the French guns. They continued to press their attack, extending the right of their line into the dunes to outflank the French defences, which together with pressure in the vicinity of the Schoorldam bridge made Rostollant feel his position was untenable and so he withdrew towards Bergen.[10]

Elated, the victorious Russians now moved towards Bergen along a narrow, enclosed road which, explained Taylor, 'lay through houses and narrow enclosures of very thick underwood, with a ridge of sand hills close upon the right.'[11] Taylor became extremely concerned about the enemy troops to the left and again attempted to get the Russian officers to counter this threat:

'The fire from the left was very heavy, and we could at times distinguish the French troops in the openings. I pointed out to several officers of the grenadier battalion forming the advanced guard the necessity of extending a little to their left, in order to cover that flank as they advanced, and to establish a communication with the English troops whose fire we begun to perceive considerably to the left.'[12]

However, once again, the Russian officers were unable to exercise any control without the presence of any senior commanders and the confused mass ploughed on towards Bergen. Taylor emphasized the threat and the volume of fire still coming from their left and was concerned that (from his perspective at least) the Russians seemed to be doing little about it.[13] Throughout this advance, Taylor said the Russians fired indiscriminately in all directions and continued to take casualties from the fire of their own troops in the sandhills on their right.

Although they had been surprised by the rapidity and impetuosity of the Russian advance, the French had not been idle. Gouvion, the French commander in Bergen had been unaware of the Russian attack until it was almost upon him (apparently strong winds had masked the sounds of battle) so had little time to prepare. He placed two battalions of 54 Demi Brigade in front of Bergen, one battalion of 42e DB in front of the chateau, half of 3 Demi Brigade and the grenadiers of 72 Demi Brigade (72e DB) guarded the interior of the village and the other half moved to the left of Bergen to maintain communication with Egmond. In order to prevent the enemy from penetrating into the plain on the right of the village, 2 Demi Brigade marched to the redoubt at the Sangoet windmill, and the light artillery, supported by 16ᵉ and 5ᵉ Chasseurs, placed themselves to the right of Bergen to sweep the road to Schoorl.[14]

As the Russians neared Bergen, the woods lining the road thinned out on the left allowing Taylor to see the villages of Koedijk and Schoorldam and 'the whole country beyond it as far as the Lange Dyke'. Gouvion had established his battery of 'several pieces of cannon' at the windmill (about 400 to 500 yards from the avenue) with a body of cavalry and infantry drawn up alongside. Taylor said:

> 'As we advanced through the avenue to this opening, the fire of musquetry from both our flanks and the village in our front was extremely severe, and we were also exposed to the fire of the battery upon the left. The troops however, proceeded, and reached the opening, but here they were checked by the fire of the French Artillery which was now directed against the head of the column, and by the appearance of their cavalry and infantry drawn up upon the left. The troops were crowded together in a most confused mass, and were very clamorous for artillery which was at length brought up with great difficulty, as the horses were hardly able to move.'[15]

This artillery checked the advance of the French infantry but the Russians continued to take heavy casualties from all directions as they milled about in a confused mass. The situation was saved by the appearance of Major General Essen who 'immediately ordered the troops to halt and form' and brought up artillery to provide cover on the left and to fire at Bergen. A battalion of grenadiers was also deployed to guard the left but, noted Taylor:

'No precaution was taken at that time to secure the right.' At this point General Herman reappeared with reinforcements from the rear. However, the grenadiers Essen had placed on the left were forced back to the avenue by the fire of the French forces and, recounted Taylor later: 'we again fell into the same confused mass from which we had for a moment been extricated.' Herman and Essen were now unable to reassert their authority and get their troops back into order. Taylor said that Herman 'repeatedly told me he no longer had any authority over the troops, and they would not obey him.'[16] Nevertheless, the momentum of the advance was such that Bergen was taken and Herman was able to assert some control again.

Whilst the Russians rallied their troops and set up their defences in Bergen, French Commander in Chief Brune had been made aware of the situation and was putting things in place for his counterstroke. The Batavian division under Dumonceau was brought up from the reserve and General Bonhomme was ordered to cross the bridge of boats at Koedijk with two battalions and the Hussars of the Central Division to attack and capture Schoorldam. This would not only support the French centre but it would cut the Russians off from the support of the British column, which was now making its presence felt at Schoorldam. Finally he sent to Bergen two battalions of 49 Demi Brigade (49e DB) led by Brigadier Bardet, with orders to General Vandamme to attack the enemy and chase them from the position.[17] Vandamme, who went on to have a successful, if controversial, career under Napoleon was already an experienced commander at this stage of his career and he commanded the best of the French contingent. As soon as he arrived in front of Bergen Vandamme prepared his troops for the attack: he gave the right to Gouvion and entrusted his left to Rostollant, undertaking the direction of the centre himself.[18] Adjutant General Rostollant took two battalions and plunged into the woods to the left of Bergen. Here he joined forces with the men from the outposts who had been dislodged by Herman's initial advance and waited for his moment.

At half past eight, Vandamme began his attack. Walsh claimed the Russians had dispersed to loot Bergen but not only had they been rallied, they were well placed to resist the counterattack.[19] The French attackers suffered terrible casualties as they were fired on by Russian troops in the houses and on a low hill in front of the church, causing them to be forced back several times. However, Gouvion's appearance on the right surprised the Russians outside the village, who were presumably still in disorder, and may, as Bunbury claimed, have been 'straggling after plunder in the villages'.[20] Whatever the cause of their disorder, they were overturned and the French were able to attack Bergen from this side as well. Vandamme personally led a desperate bayonet charge into the centre of the village and most of the Russians, their artillery now out of ammunition, broke and ran leaving their cannons behind. As they abandoned Bergen the Russian column split up and most men fled in 'an indescribable disorder' back the way they had come. They suffered terrible casualties, including divisional commander Lieutenant General Jerepsoff, who was numbered amongst the dead. The fate of the others was no kinder; closely pursued by General Gouvion's men these unfortunates fell back into the woods where Rostollant and his troops were lying in wait. There were few survivors: seven standards, the remaining artillery, its horses and caissons and more than 100 men were captured.[21]

Bunbury believed this was the turning point of the battle: 'If there had been a reserve, fresh and in good order, the battle was won. But there was nothing but one mass of confused men. Such people were not to expect victory over the active and intelligent Frenchmen on their own ground.'[22] General Herman tried to rally the remains of Jerepsoff's division, which had retreated into the dunes, but they were too closely pursued and despite their 'courage and great intrepidity' were dispersed each time they regrouped. 'Finally, fully abandoned in the dunes and having had all his horses killed he had no choice but to implore clemency from his vanquishers and became their prisoner.'[23] The allied commander, the Duke of York, believed that with Herman's surrender all chance of rallying the Russians was gone as he was popular with his men and they lost all heart 'upon his being taken'.[24] However, in such a chaotic situation it would be unlikely that the loss of a leader would have been widely known and by this stage there was little hope of stemming the tide. Major General Essen rallied around 3,000 men at Schoorl but they too were overcome 'by the courage and ardour of the French' and streamed back towards the villages they had set out from that dark foggy morning.[25]

The Russians were finished as a fighting force that day. They may have been worn out from their initial exertions as the march from their landing point the previous day had left some of them exhausted, thus indicating their level of fitness after weeks on board transport ships wasn't what it should have been.[26] They may also have been demoralized by the unfamiliar terrain in which they had to operate and the heavy casualties they had sustained. Additionally, they may have just become too disordered by the advance for discipline to be restored. Certainly their performance, particularly in respect of their discipline, was subject to a great deal of criticism from their allies who made no secret about who they blamed for the failure of the attack.[27]

Complete defeat on the allied right was prevented by the actions of a British brigade under Major General Manners. This brigade had been attached to Herman's command but had fought its own battle up to this point, isolated in the dunes. Taylor claimed that it was dispatched after he reported the situation to York but 14-year-old Edward Gomm, serving in his first battle as a lieutenant in the 9th Regiment of Foot (9th foot), painted a different picture. The two battalions of 9th foot had made a four-hour march through the night to join the Russians in front of Schoorl at two o'clock in the morning. They had slowly followed the Russians in their advance, being joined on the way by their commander, Major General Manners and a battalion of the 56th Regiment of Foot. The brigade then continued to act as a reserve for the Russians covering their line of retreat.[28]

Initially they had been sent to mop up any resistance in the sandhills around Schoorl after it had been taken by the Russians, but they could find no sign of the enemy and were left behind as the Russians careered towards Bergen. At this point the enemy reappeared and 'opened a very heavy fire of musketry and grape upon' them as they emerged onto the plain beyond Schoorl. A fierce fight broke out which, according to Gomm, lasted around two hours and in the course of which he received a glancing blow from a bullet near his left eye. The British made ground but owing to the plethora of drainage ditches, which were too wide to leap and had to be waded, this was accomplished slowly and in a somewhat irregular manner. Eventually, enough of the British soldiers were able to wade through these ditches to form up outside Schoorldam, which had been reoccupied by the enemy after the Russians had passed through. The village was taken again at bayonet point and the enemy, which was reportedly 'unwilling to stand the charge…retreated very precipitously through Schoorldam.' This was as far

as Manners' men got, however, for the effects of the night march and the
lengthy fire fight were beginning to show. Gomm said 'most of the troops
were scarcely able to walk' so the brigade was halted to reform. The extensive
sandhills in this area made it easy for large bodies of men to manoeuvre
unseen and lie hidden from their enemies. The French were particularly
adept at using this terrain to their advantage when on the defensive and the
troops at Schoorl, which Gomm's comrades had failed to find that morning,
were still in the surrounding woods and sandhills and were threatening to
cut off their retreat. Therefore, the weary British turned about, trudged
back and engaged their elusive enemies in another heavy fire fight. [29]

Meanwhile the Russians had been evicted from Bergen and the survivors
now streamed back towards Schoorl where Manners' fortunate presence
prevented the Russians from being overrun. In spite of colliding with the
fleeing Russians, the brigade rallied and launched an attack on the village of
Schoorl. The French were apparently convinced that they had encountered
a formidable body of troops: 'The French troops already fatigued from
fighting yielded to the number and freshness of these troops and retreated
to the dunes and Heereweg and Bergen, followed closely by the enemy.'[30]
Manners was reinforced by the three battalions of Russians who had been
with British General Dundas' brigade, D'Oyly's guards brigade and by
35th foot under Prince William of Gloucester.[31] These troops retook Schoorl
and Schoorldam and attempted to reignite the offensive by turning the
French left. 'General Vandamme, being aware of this manoeuvre, refused
his right wing and elongated his position in the plain and shortened it in the
dunes, thus threatening a sudden attack on the enemy's very extended front
and cutting them off on the left.'[32] Thwarted and low on ammunition, the
British retired to their starting points, pursued by enemy cavalry who cut
down stragglers and took a number of prisoners.[33] Manners' brigade hadn't
been able to turn the tide but they had prevented the rout of the Russian
column from becoming a catastrophe, though York was to later complain
somewhat peevishly that 'almost the whole of the poor fellows whom we
have lost fell in covering their retreat.'[34]

The whole incident was to have serious effect on the relationship
between the allies. Although York claimed to have treated the whole affair
with diplomatic kid gloves; praising the Russians' 'spirit and gallantry' and

'intrepidity' in the face of 'formidable resistance' in his official dispatch even here he made no secret of his opinion. In person, where perhaps he should have brought the full force of his diplomatic skills to bear, he was positively rude. Bunbury reported that after Bergen 'the Duke of York took up a violent contempt, as well as dislike of the Russians. He ridiculed them at his table, and talked of them disparagingly and too loudly.'[35]

It was not just the army's commander that had a poor opinion of them; most of the British accounts of the Battle of Bergen feature horror stories about pillaging and rampant indiscipline on the part of the Russians. Bunbury levelled a charge of wholesale looting: 'Every house had been plundered, the lock blown off the door with a shot or forced with the butt of a musket.'[36] Indeed, a soldier from Manners' brigade claimed to have witnessed such thefts: 'I saw some of them with cheeses and butter and all badly wounded, and in particular one man had an eight days clock on his back.'[37] The French also made a point of highlighting the 'very great excesses in the villages they occupied during the action. The poor Batavian peasants have been massacred and burnt in their houses including women and children; several villages are still on fire.'[38] Whether these excesses occurred or not, they are indicative of the regard in which the Russians were now held by their allies, despite their great courage in the battle.[39]

The Russians for their part were humiliated and angry. They had achieved their objectives despite heavy casualties and took great offence at the criticism levelled at them. Herman's successor, Major General Essen, wrote to the tsar blaming the British for the loss of the villages his troops had fought so hard for. The British, he said, started too late and did not support their allies as they had promised.[40] The Russians also complained that the British hadn't lived up to their side of the agreement in terms of supplies, particularly the provision of horses.[41] Coupled with the loss of the popular and accommodating General Herman the whole affair was to cast a shadow over allied relations for the rest of the campaign. General Essen was a proud and obstinate man and objected in the strongest terms to the Duke of York's version of events. As the campaign progressed he became increasingly difficult to deal with.[42] With Anglo-Russian relations already in disarray this was a far from auspicious start to York's offensive.

Chapter 11

The Other Columns – the British at Bergen

As the Russians began their headlong career towards Bergen, the other columns of York's army formed up in the darkness to play their part in the duke's plan. Immediately to the left of the Russian column, Lieutenant General Dundas' column commenced its attack on Warmenhuizen just after daybreak.[1] The three battalions of Russians, which Herman had insisted were detached from his division, advanced from Krabbendam, while the 1st Regiment of Foot Guards set off from Tuitjenhorn. The guards attacked the east side of the village, while Major General Sedmoratsky's troops rushed in from the west, the two contingents arriving at their target almost simultaneously. Like all the villages which made up the republican frontline, Warmenhuizen was heavily fortified with three cannons dug in defending the approaches. Nevertheless, the attack from both sides took the defenders by surprise and the village quickly fell, with its 500-man garrison becoming prisoners.[2] The gallantry of the Russians in this attack was singled out for particular praise in York's official report.[3]

As soon as Warmenhuizen was taken, the victorious troops marched on joining the Guards Grenadier Battalion, which had already been sent to the left in order to link up with Herman's Russian column. To accomplish this they would have to capture the village of Schoorldam and to cross the broad Alkmaar canal, but the roads had been dug up, which meant the troops had to move through the fields on either side. However, these fields were crossed by numerous ditches, some of which were so wide that bridges had to be thrown across them. So despite the urging of the Duke of York, who personally accompanied the troops, it was nine o'clock before they reached the outskirts of Schoorldam.[4] This apparent tardiness was later criticized by the Russians, even though they were well aware of the difficulties presented by the terrain and indeed admitted that it had forced them to keep to the roads allowing the French to outflank them.[5]

The village of Schoorldam was also heavily fortified and was attacked in an almost identical fashion to Warmenhuizen, the flanking force being provided on this occasion by Manners' brigade, who were following in the wake of the Russian column and were on the left bank of the Alkmaar canal. Once again the village fell quickly to this two-pronged attack and its sizeable garrison joined its comrades from Warmenhuizen in captivity. The republicans had destroyed the bridge over the canal and it was an hour before the British were able to repair it and pass over to support the Russians. However, they were too late, for by this time the Russians had been pushed back from Bergen and the Duke of York had the 'mortification' to personally witness their headlong retreat.[6] The British maintained their position in Schoorldam throughout the remainder of the action, despite the increasingly heavy fire that was directed against them by the enemy troops.[7]

While the bulk of his troops had been assaulting Warmenhuizen and Schoorldam under the direction of the Duke of York, Dundas had moved with the remainder of his division – comprising the Guards Grenadier Battalion, the 3rd/Guards and the 2nd Battalion of the 5th Regiment of Foot (2nd of 5th foot) – to establish communications with Lieutenant General Pulteney's division on the left. Dundas soon observed that Pulteney's men were experiencing some difficulties and detached the 3rd/Guards and 2nd of 5th foot to assist.[8]

Lieutenant General Pulteney commanded the third, left flank, column of the attack force and had been tasked with the capture of Oudkarspel. This column had also set off at daybreak, heading along the 'high causeway leading to Alkmaar', control of which would be vital for future operations. Two significant geographical features restricted the area of operations; the Alkmaar canal on the right flank and on the other side 'a low stripe of mud and a broad wet ditch'.[9] The column was around 5,000 men strong and was supported by three gunboats manned by the navy, each carrying a 12-pound carronade, which had been deployed on the canal by Captain Popham and 'kept pace with the head of the column'.[10]

Pulteney accompanied Don's brigade, who approached their target from Dirkshorn to the northwest and advanced along the causeway, detaching the 2nd Battalion of 17th foot (2nd of 17th foot) along the way to begin a flanking move to the left. The column quickly overcame the outposts, which were in the process of being relieved, but there the advance stalled.[11] Major General Don described the situation:

'The head of the village was strongly fortified with a double row of entrenchments, containing 8 or 10 guns, and a canal, a short distance from this entrenchment, the bridge over which the enemy had broken down, but there was still room to pass over it singly. In front of the canal, and very close to the entrenchments, was a dyke, which afforded a good position, and appeared absolutely necessary to take.'[12]

The enemy opened a storm of fire on the attacking British. Under the direction of Adjutant General Du Rutte and Colonel Crass, the Batavian infantry fired volleys of musketry from their redoubts and the artillery opened up with a murderous salvo of grapeshot from a distance of thirty paces. This fire, said Daendels, caused the attacking column to 'retire in the greatest disorder'. According to Daendels this first attack was particularly costly as 'the enemy lost a great number of men, and amongst them Captain O'Donnall, and another, who were wounded and taken prisoners.'[13] On the Batavian side, Adjutant General De Rutte, was slightly wounded and he and Colonel Crass 'had their clothes pierced by several shot.'[14]

Things were no better to the east of the village where Coote's brigade had found the bridge broken down and the approach covered by an entrenched battery of heavy guns and howitzers. Colonel Dalhousie of the Queen's recounted:

'The General's orders were to carry this battery, if possible, and to get into the village of Oude Karspel. The 85th proceeded to Oude Miew Dorp to cover our flank, the four light companies and the 27th were sent down the Leeman Weg, leading direct on the battery, and the Queen's and the 29th moved along the dykes under General Coote until they reached the corner where the battery was open to us. Our two 6-pounders and the howitzer opened fire immediately, but the heavier metal in the battery soon silenced us and showed the impossibility to execute our orders from the side of the broad and deep canal. We lay all forenoon under the sloping bank of the dyke, the light companies scoured the woods to our left and took some prisoners. We now and then threw a shell from the howitzer into the battery.'[15]

The British on the right quickly rallied and Major General Don immediately directed part of the 1st Battalion 17th foot, the 1st Battalion 40th foot and three companies of light infantry, to cross the canal under the command of Colonel Spencer of 40th foot and take the dyke in front of the enemy's position.[16] This position protected the British from the enemy's fire and according to Daendels, they were able to mount artillery on it (though this isn't mentioned in any British accounts) and return the Batavians' fire on equal terms. Don reported that the Batavians 'made several attempts to dislodge these troops, but were constantly repulsed.' The dyke negated the advantage the entrenchments had given the defenders and now they took heavy casualties, particularly amongst the artillerymen in the redoubts, though the fight continued and Daendels reported that his gunners dismounted two British guns and 'blew up their ammunition wagons.'[17]

All this time, 2nd of 17th foot had been working their way, by a different route, to a point close to the village to the left of the remainder of the brigade. Here the enemy had constructed another redoubt in a meadow from which they launched 'several fruitless attempts to drive back that battalion and to turn our left flank.'[18] With 2nd of 17th foot standing firm in their position in the face of these attacks it negated the threat to the left.

Although his left was now secure, Pulteney was unable to get through to Coote's brigade, who were pinned down on the east side. It was now about ten o'clock and Daendels had been made aware of the British successes at Warmenhuizen and Schoorldam as well as the wounding of his comrade Dumonceau. As the enemy seemed to have suspended their attack, he went in person to direct reinforcements from his reserve at Sint Pancras to support Dumonceau's beleaguered division. Fearing that the enemy might also be approaching his right, Daendels also sent a battalion to cover the villages of Purmerend and Monnikendam where work was still in progress on the defences. It was at this point that the battalions, which Dundas had detached, made their appearance on Pulteney's right and were able find a way across the ditches (which Daendels had thought impassable as the local peasants had informed him that they were at least seven foot deep). Approaching unseen through dense woodland these troops were now able to outflank the Batavian defences on the west of Oudkarspel.[19] Although their position was now compromised by the British outflanking movement, Crass and Du Rutte felt that they were better off remaining behind the defences of Oudkarspel than attempting a retreat in difficult terrain in the face of the enemy.

With the enemy now distracted by pressure on both flanks, Pulteney resolved to launch another attack from the dyke position. Following the failure of the previous attack and the destruction of the British cannons it had gone quiet on the left. The shattered cannons remained on the dyke and even the flanking column had disappeared; it seemed to the Batavians that the British had retreated. Requesting support from Daendels to fall on the flanking column, Du Rutte launched a sally from his position to retake the dyke but to his dismay he found the British were merely preparing for an attack from behind the embankment and now surged out from behind it, attacking him 'with vigour'.[20] To compound the Batavian's discomfort, the flanking column also now reappeared. The men had merely been lying down in the corn to mitigate the effects of the enemy's artillery and stood up to attack the grenadiers that Daendels had sent to oust them.

Daendels reported that:

'On both sides the enemy approached us within the distance of 30 yards, in spite of the discharge of grape shot from our artillery, which swept away whole platoons at once; but our grenadiers finding that they were fired upon all sides, fell back in disorder out of the entrenchments and impeded the direction of the cannon, which were compelled to slacken their fire. To complete the misfortune, the carriage of one of the guns took fire just at this moment, in the redoubt, and blew up nearly all our artillerymen.'[21]

The guards of the flanking column followed the fleeing grenadiers into the village. Taking advantage of the general disorder they surprised and overthrew the defenders and, in the words of Daendels, 'by this bold and unexpected effort made themselves masters of our entrenchments.'

Coote, pinned down on the other side of the village, had up to this point been restricted to a desultory bombardment of the enemy's positions with his artillery. But after seeing the success of the troops on his right, and hearing their cheers above the musketry, he took the opportunity to attack the battery that had been causing him so much trouble. He pushed forwards the light companies of Queen's and 29th foot and captured the battery whose occupants had now fled as Don's brigade surged through the centre of the village behind them. Managing to get hold of a couple of small boats, Coote was now able to ferry the rest of his brigade across the canal and enter Oudkarspel.[22]

The Batavian General Beinen described the chaos that ensued:

'The English continued their pursuit, firing blindly into the bunched-up mass and advanced with fixed bayonets. The retreat of the Batavians developed into a flight. Daendels himself was dragged along, lost his horse and escaped capture only by a trumpeter offering his own. The idea of making a stand had to be given up; the troops standing in reserve were unable to hold up the fleeing troops, and themselves joined in the flight. The flight became general.'[23]

The Batavians retreated along the Langedyke closely pursued by the victorious British as far as Sint Pancras and 'upwards of 700 prisoners, 14 guns and a great quantity of ammunition' were taken.[24]

Oudkarspel was occupied by Coote's brigade and Major Maule later recalled the scene which greeted them:

'The village, which we entered, presented a sad spectacle of the horrors of war. Numbers were found in the houses, as well as in the streets, extended upon the ground pierced with balls and otherwise severely wounded. Artillery and ammunition-waggons, with their ill-fated horses dreadfully lacerated by cannon-shot, with their drivers laying dead beside them, filled the streets at various points.'[25]

The brigade took up defensive positions around the village and by eleven o'clock the Queen's were bivouacked alongside a windmill where, having been in motion since two o'clock that morning, those that were not on duty succumbed to their fatigue. However, the retreat of the Russians led to a general withdrawal from all points and by midnight the regiment was on the march back to Schagen. Maule recalled with some distress the plight of the wounded who had been left on the field around the redoubt since the attack that morning and whose moans could now be heard on all sides in the darkness. Several of the regimental surgeons were dispatched to their aid and remained with their charges as the brigade marched on and were later captured by the returning Batavians.[26] In the distance, heavy firing could still be heard from the direction of Bergen and the flames of burning villages lit the night sky. By now the weather, which had been poor all day, took a turn for the worse. The retreating British were lashed by heavy rains and 'tempestuous' winds, which carried the cries of the wounded to further distress the troops, already disheartened by having thrown away their hard earned gains. The Queen's finally limped into Schagen as the clock struck four.

Meanwhile to the right of Pulteney's division, Dundas' men had also been ordered to fall back. The troops were reportedly so tired that they obeyed the orders to retreat without question and the Duke of York became aware that the vital post of Krabbendam had been abandoned. Bunbury was dispatched immediately to organize a defending force from any troops that happened to be in the vicinity:

'But such was discomfiture, and such the want of good handling of the troops during this retreat of the 19th September, that battalion after battalion passed through the village and entered the lines, without finding any general officer to give an order or a thought to the important object of keeping hold of Krabbendam. I rode till, at a short distance within the lines, I found one of the battalions of the 1st Guards, under the command of Colonel Maitland, resting on their arms in column on the muddy road. I delivered the Duke's orders to the Colonel, and begged he would not lose a moment in returning with me to Krabbendam, for the French were close at hand. He told me that his battalion was tired out; that they had been hotly engaged many hours, had lost a large proportion of officers and men, and that their ammunition was nearly spent. I insisted; and urged the danger, and the fatal consequences which might ensue. Maitland ... still demurred. He

Duke of York. (*Royal Collection Trust / All Rights Reserved*)

The landing at Cabrit 1808 (National Maritime Museum)

General Abercromby. (*National Portrait Gallery*)

General Brune. (*Rijksmuseum Amsterdam*)

General Daendels.
(*Rijksmuseum Amsterdam*)

The capture of General Herman. (*Rijksmuseum Amsterdam*)

The dunes north of the landing beaches. (*Author's image*)

Waterlogged landscape south of Helder. (*Author's image*)

Beach at Schoorl. (*Author's image*)

Sea of dunes. (*Author's image*)

Woods around Bergen. (*Author's image*)

Zype Canal and dyke. (*Author's image*)

assured me his men were quite worn out; and he appeared to have lost the powers of his mind under fatigue of body and anxiety.'[27]

At this point one of Maitland's grenadiers called out from the ranks: 'Give us some more cartridges and we will see what can be done.' With this indication of the willingness of the men to fight on, Bunbury recounted, the guards 'marched for Krabbendam; and I galloped to find and bring to them a supply of ammunition.' With this vital post secured, the British fell back to their starting positions and their enemies moved up with renewed confidence to retake their abandoned positions.[28]

Far out on the left, Abercromby's column had begun its wide flanking march towards Hoorn at eight o'clock the night before the battle was due to start. 'The distance as the crow flies did not exceed thirteen miles, but was increased to more than twenty by the deviations of the road, which, moreover, was in an extremely bad condition.'[29] As a defensive measure the Batavians had broken up the road that was to carry the flanking force on its march, so the plan to capture Hoorn quickly was already under threat. As both Moore and Bunbury, who accompanied the column, later pointed out, the time allotted by York was insufficient for them to capture Hoorn and march on Purmerend, even if conditions were favourable.[30] On the night of 18 September conditions were anything but favourable. Private Surtees, at the time serving in the combined Light Infantry Battalion, was also a participant in the march and left this account of the conditions:

'We moved off as it became dark, but such was the state of the roads that it became the most trying and distressing march that I believe ever troops undertook; the roads were literally knee deep in mud in most places, while every now and then they were rendered nearly impassable, both by the enemy having broken down the bridges over the innumerable canals and dikes which intersect this country, and these canals in many places having overflowed their banks.'[31]

Surtees said the dense march formation further delayed the column when meeting obstacles and he talked of men falling into canals, mistaking them in the dark for smooth roads.[32] As a result of this energy–sapping, demoralizing march the troops were quite worn out by the time they reached Hoorn and in their fatigued state, prone to panic. As Bunbury recounted:

> 'When the advanced party arrived at the very gate of Hoorn, without being fired at or challenged, some staff officers (I being one) who had been sent to the front by Abercromby, knocked for admittance. No answer was returned; the knocking was repeated, and a loud hail to the gatekeeper was given. In the meantime the wearied infantry had grounded their arms, and stood leaning beneath the pelting rain, and more than half asleep, on their muskets. At length a sentinel was roused from his slumbers: he peeped over the gate, and dimly discerning a crowd of horsemen, he shouted an alarm: the guard waked up, and hastened noisily to draw more bolts and chains, while their drum was beaten to awaken the Burghers. Our officers cried loudly, "Open your gates, or they shall be blown down by our cannons!" and to enforce the effect of this threat, the dragoons were ordered to open to the right and left, so as to let the two guns be run up to the front. Instead of giving the word of command quietly, the leading officer shouted, "Back, back, make way for the guns!" "Back, back," was loudly repeated by the dragoon officers. Our jaded infantry were roused from their unconscious slumbers by the sudden clatter of the horses on the pavement, the rattling of the cannon wheels, and this unhappy cry of "back, back". In an instant the 23rd and 55th broke like a flock of sheep, plunging into the deep mud at the sides of the causeway, and dreaming for some minutes that they had been surprised by a sortie of cavalry!'[33]

Bunbury felt 'far from sure, that if there had been 500 dashing fellows ready to rush recklessly out of the portals of Hoorn, they might not have dispersed our 11,000 men.'[34] Nonetheless Hoorn surrendered without a shot being fired. Abercromby, however, now felt that his exhausted troops were not capable of pressing on to Purmerend as directed in York's instructions and ordered a halt for the night.[35]

Once again Abercromby's actions, or lack of them, have been the subject of criticism from historians but York's instructions were pretty vague and certainly conditional on the success of the other columns. The actual order reads:

> 'This column … will push forwards with all possible expedition for Purmerend. In an operation so extensive and in a country not accurately known it is impossible to enter into detail. If the attack on the right proves successful, Sir Ralph Abercromby risques nothing in pushing every advantage to the utmost.'[36]

There can be no doubt that the troops were exhausted and, with the weather conditions continuing to be atrocious, Abercromby felt he should await news of the other columns.[37] There is some confusion as to the time the column reached Hoorn (Moore says one o'clock, Bunbury says between three and four) so it is unclear how long the troops had been able to rest before they should have set off again. A quick reconnaissance showed Abercromby that although the main road to Purmerend was intact, all the others had been broken up and the bridges destroyed, which would have meant moving his 15,000 men along a single road at a snail's pace. This impediment would have meant that even with six hours rest the column would have been unlikely to reach its objective in time to have any impact on the battle and would have been vulnerable to counterattack. Military theorist Jomini considered it 'fortunate' that Abercromby could not continue as nothing would prevent Brune from crushing him before York was in a position to support him.[38]

Abercromby's report after the battle stated that: 'The state of the roads, the fatigue of the troops, the broken nature of the ground, above all, the uncertainty of events on the right made (an advance) impossible.'[39] Anxious not to risk anything without further orders, he sent Bunbury 'to apprize the Duke of York of the state of affairs on the side of Hoorn; but though I was well mounted, and took short cuts across the marshes, I did not join his Royal Highness till the Russians were in full retreat.'[40]

So, once again Abercromby waited on events. At midday Lord Bentinck, acting as one of York's aides, brought a letter informing him that Warmenhuizen had been taken and that the Russians and guards were advancing on Schoorldam but that there was no other news. This was not enough to persuade Abercromby to move. As Moore put it: 'everything remained still in doubt [so] no resolution could be taken.' Abercromby sent Moore to reconnoitre the area and prepared to remain in Hoorn. However, about four hours later a second letter was received (this time carried by Captain Fitzgerald) which informed the cautious Scot that 'the Russians had now been repulsed and it was necessary for Sir Ralph Abercromby to march immediately with his corps and join the Duke.'[41]

Orders were given for the column to turn round and, like the others, return to its starting point. The British had been well received by the local inhabitants 'who came out of the town in their holiday clothes, with orange cockades in their hats.'[42] Moore said that in view of the 'great goodwill' they had shown, Abercromby felt obliged to leave the townsfolk with some protection from possible reprisals and accordingly the 55th Regiment of Foot (55th foot) remained behind when the column returned.[43]

The return march was, if possible, more arduous than the advance had been and was witness to some indiscipline, particularly amongst the former militiamen. One of their officers recalled that:

'We had not started our return above half an hour when the rain fell in torrents, making the road, which was scarce passable, one mass of mud. Our newly enlisted heroes did not like this at all; many of them fell out in the dark; and we had to make several halts to pick up the stragglers. We could hear the words now and then "D_d [damned] bad sort of soldiering this! – I wish the man had his ten guineas again!" and other phrases of discontent. However, they were obliged to bundle along, half asleep and half awake.'[44]

So ended the Battle of Bergen and perhaps with it the only real chance of bringing the campaign to a swift and successful conclusion. The troops themselves were particularly disgruntled at being withdrawn from positions they had fought so hard to wrest from a determined enemy and the recriminations flew thick and fast. As we have already seen, many blamed the Russians while others criticized Abercromby, implying that he was dilatory. York's biographer, Burne, referred to his 'abject failure' and placed all the blame upon his lack of preparation.[45] The attack on Hoorn however, was not intended to be an essential part of the battle plan. York felt that the other columns were of sufficient strength to overcome the enemy alone and the left hand column was intended only to deliver the *coup de grace* to make the result decisive. In retrospect, Lord Chatham (Pitt's brother and commander of one of the brigades in Abercromby's column) believed that the plan may have been overambitious but felt that it was right to take the opportunity to beat the French outright:

> 'Perhaps the business was made rather too sure of; but one is almost unwilling to lament, that the whole force had not been employed in the attack of ye enemy, as undoubtedly the move made towards Horn, was under all the obstacles which this country every step presents to our advance, the most judicious that could have been, with a view to improving our success, had it happily occurred, by a rapid march upon Amsterdam.'[46]

Moore disagreed believing that: 'The detaching of Sir Ralph with so large a body of men so late as the evening before the general attack was ill imagined. Such a body taking advantage of the first successes of the Russians might have decided the day. It should have been detached, if at all, at least ten days earlier.'[47]

Others blamed the council of war. Secretary at War Lord Windham wrote of the battle's failure:

'After all was the plan of attack good? I cannot but suspect that it was not. I do not mean that the Duke of York is to be blamed, or that anyone could be blamed for acting on a system sanctioned by so many great authorities.'[48]

However, the plan was largely York's with only minor alterations being suggested by the council. Whilst it seems that, as Chatham said, an attempt had to be made to defeat the French decisively, Moore's point that the whole operation was 'hurried' must be conceded. The plan may have been the best chance for success but it was over-elaborate with insufficient time given for preparation and execution and the fault for that must lie with the Duke of York.

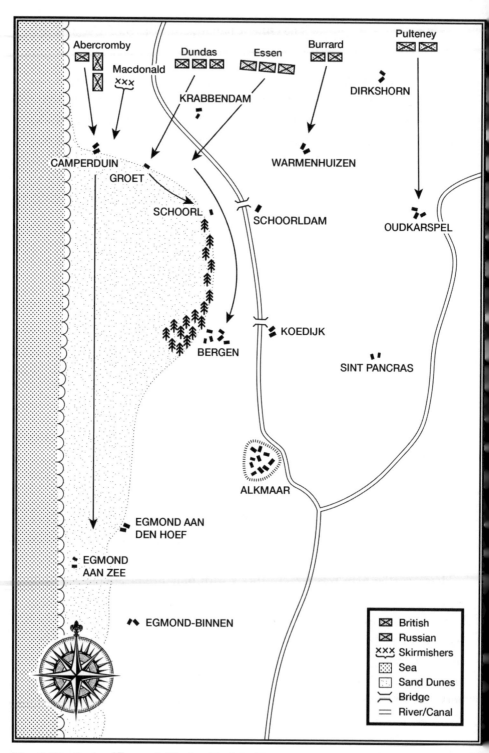

Map 5. The Battle of Egmond. (*Produced by John Harcourt*)

Chapter 12

The Battle of Egmond/Alkmaar –
2 October 1799

The defeat at Bergen was a setback for the allies but all was not lost. The Duke of York was not discouraged; having been reinforced by a fresh brigade of Russians and another regiment of British cavalry, he began preparations for a fresh offensive.[1] However, some have questioned York's wisdom in trying a different version of a plan that had failed so spectacularly already. The Franco-Batavian position had proved itself immensely strong, had been further fortified and its defenders reinforced by fresh troops from France. Surely another frontal assault was doomed to fail?[2] Certainly alternatives were suggested, both at the time and by later commentators. Admiral Mitchell had created a small flotilla of gunboats and shallow draft bomb-ketches, which had been harassing Dutch towns along the Zuider Zee, and the French historian Gachot believed that a column of troops landed by this squadron at Hoorn could have reached Alkmaar 'in the rear of the French in a few hours'.[3] However, these craft did not have the capacity to transport thousands of troops and their equipment, and the Zuider Zee was too shallow to accommodate the transport ships that had been used in the initial landing. The option to send troops to back a promised Orangist coup in Friesland was also rejected as little had been seen to suggest that there was any substance to Orangist claims of support.[4]

The only remaining option was another frontal assault, so York had to draw up a plan that would take into account the lessons of the previous attempt and provide the expedition with the best chance for a decisive victory. Once again the invaders would have to contend with the Helder's difficult terrain and persistently appalling weather and once again York would have to consult his fellow commanders in constructing his scheme. The British generals were in broad agreement with his ideas. Moore bemoaned the evacuation of Oudkarspel after its costly capture on 19 September but felt that an attack was the only option: 'Our situation is such as to make battle necessary. No diversion can be of use to us. We must beat the French or give up the point.'[5]

The Russians were less easily convinced. The amiable but reckless General Herman had been replaced by Major General Essen, who was a commander of an entirely different hue. Prickly from the start, Essen had been badly shaken by his experience on 19 September, when he had tried to hold together the remains of the disintegrating Russian force as it had streamed in disorder from Bergen. Now he bombarded York with demands for clarification of orders and British support for his division. Although Essen was clearly ill-disposed towards his allies, relations with the Russian commander cannot have been helped by York's behaviour towards him and his staff.[6] It is perhaps telling that so much of their correspondence seems to have been conducted by letter. Essen had instilled in his troops the need to maintain their formation and discipline during the march and it was said that they 'burned with anxiety to wash out the stain which their disasters … had cast on the Imperial eagles.'[7] York did eventually agree to divert Dundas' two brigades to guard the Russian flank and although some have argued that this weakened the thrust on Bergen, it did prevent a possible repeat of the issue on 19 September, of the Russians being outflanked from the dunes.[8]

With the Russians apparently placated, York drew up a plan that would enable his army to overcome the difficulties presented by the terrain, strike a decisive blow against the enemy and hopefully open the way to Amsterdam. The enemy position was by now exceptionally strong. The natural advantages presented to the defender by the dykes, ditches, dense woods and sandhills of the Helder area had been enhanced by entrenchments, gun emplacements, obstacles and fortified villages. The roads had been dug up to slow the movement of the invaders, particularly their artillery, and Daendels, at least, considered his position on the republican right to be 'impregnable'.[9] Walsh described the position:

'The country between Alkmaar and Egmont is partly a plain, and partly sand-hills. In this situation, therefore, an army would be protected in front by broad canals and high dykes or embankments of great solidity, running in parallel directions across the country; its wings would be covered by the two seas, and its centre by a large and strong fortified town.'[10]

Once again the army was divided into four principal columns. The first, on the right, was commanded by Abercromby and was intended to march along the beach (thus negating the ability of the ditches and dykes to retard its advance) to attack Egmond aan Zee 'with a view to turning the enemy's left flank'. The second column was composed of Russian troops under the awkward Major General Essen. York described its role:

'[T]he greater portion marched by the Slaper Dyke through the villages of Groete and Schorel upon Bergen, by the road which all the way skirts the foot of the sandhills of Camperdown, about three hundred foot high, presenting a steep face to the country much wooded, but from their summit more gradually sloping towards the sea. Part of this column, under Major-General Sedmoratsky, debouched from the Zuyper Sluys, and were destined to cover the left flank of the remainder of the Russian troops moving under the sand hills, to co-operate with the brigade of Major-General Burrard in the attack of Schoreldam, and to combine their attack on Bergen with the troops upon their right.'[11]

The third column was under Lieutenant General Dundas and had been assigned the task of supporting the Russians. Coote's brigade was to clear the road to Groet and then detach 'the required number of troops' into the dunes to cover the Russian right, whereas Lord Chatham's was to follow the Russians whilst also covering their right and join them for the attack upon Bergen. Major General Burrard, commanding the 2nd Guards Brigade, set off from Tuitjenhorn and Krabbendam, marched along the left of the Alkmaar canal, where Popham's seven gunboats had been launched in support, and joined Sedmoratsky's attack on Schoorldam. Burrard was also to maintain contact with the fourth column, led by Lieutenant General Pulteney, which was to cover the left flank as far as the Zuider Zee and 'was destined to threaten the enemy's right and to take advantage of every favourable circumstance that should offer.'[12]

Bunbury, serving as ADC to Abercromby, felt that 'The plan of operations was complicated; and considering that these involved and intricate movements were to be executed by raw troops in a country where communications were difficult and uncertain, it is not surprising that many blunders and disappointments ensued.'[13] General Moore was more optimistic and wrote: 'I have not a doubt that, if the Russians do their duty, we shall prove completely successful.'[14] As it was, the attack was delayed because of the appalling weather, which drove the sea so far up the beach that there was insufficient room for the column to deploy.[15] Dripping staff officers sent the assembled troops back to their quarters and Moore, having developed a fever, took to his bed with a 'tartar emetic'.[16]

On the evening of 1 October it was decided that the weather had improved sufficiently for the attack to be mounted. The regiments were ordered to cook one day's provisions and instructions regarding the timing and order of march were issued.[17] After days of waiting, the troops received their orders with some relief as Surtees recalled:

'We were of course, all life and glee on receiving the information and the usual quantity of provisions having been issued, and every other preparation made in the night, we moved off by the same road by which we had usually advanced to our alarm post.'[18]

The troops left their quarters and formed up at three o'clock in the morning. After waiting for low tide, Abercromby's column began its advance at six o'clock under the watchful eye of the Duke of York, who stood on a low hill near Petten, surrounded by his staff to watch the column move off.[19] Because of the limited space on the beach, the formation was especially dense:

'The infantry were directed to move in a column of companies from the right at half distance; the artillery upon the right of the column, opposite the proper intervals. The cavalry were also upon the right. Colonel McDonald, with the reserve, a battalion of Grenadiers and one of Light Infantry, and 300 Russian Yagers, had orders, after driving the small picquet of the enemy from the height of Camperduyn, to move in the sand-hills upon the left of the column and to flank it during the march. The column itself was to move upon the beach.'[20]

The beach, like that at Callantsoog, was bordered with high sandhills and the left of the French position began at the edge of those hills.[21] Abercromby's column moved along the flat beach but the reserve, which was intended to protect his left, had to advance along the dunes, making it difficult for them to maintain their formation and to communicate with the main column.

MacDonald's brigade, although referred to as the reserve, acted as a kind of advanced guard for the entire army and got to work immediately attacking a redoubt in front of the village of Camperduin.[22] The artillery emplaced on Camperduin Hill began to fire as soon as the light infantrymen came within range but for once the terrain favoured the attackers and, being lower down in the dunes than the French cannon, the shot passed harmlessly over their heads. Surtees, who was amongst them, said that he couldn't even see the barrage over the heads of the men in front of him.[23] The position was held by the 3rd Battalion of 60 Demi Brigade (60e DB), who quickly fell back before MacDonald's men, yielding the village and the heights above it.[24] This sudden attack caused General de Division Gouvion, who commanded this sector, to fear that his flank was to be turned, so he sent General Aubrée with three battalions (two of 49e DB and one of 48e DB) into the dunes to shadow the enemy column along the beach.[25] MacDonald meanwhile, 'instead of keeping to his right, inclined from Camperduyn to his left and joined General Coote's brigade and the column of Russians.'[26] This column was separated from Abercromby's by at least four miles of sandhills so MacDonald's departure exposed the left flank of the column.

Its left now uncovered, Abercromby's column continued along the beach where, unimpeded by the deep sand of the dunes or the waterlogged fields and ditches encountered by the other columns, it made good progress. The horse artillery, which preceded these troops, fired upon the enemy whenever they appeared and took a heavy toll upon them. An anonymous private of 92nd foot recalled that this made for some gruesome sights along the beach:

'We had four pieces of cannon in front, which fired upon the enemy, who retired along the beach as we advanced. I passed close by a man, who had been struck with a cannon ball upon the knee joint, and left a ligament of skin on each side of it, which held the leg suspended to the thigh. A little further, I passed a man who lay stretched upon his back, dead; his eyes and countenance, had something in them particularly dreadful ... I was so struck with this man's ghastly appearance, that I thought to myself, "Were I a poet, I would choose, as my subject, the horrors of war, that I might persuade mankind not to engage in it."'[27]

The enemy (presumably Aubrée's men) began to appear in numbers among the dunes overlooking the beach, which caused some unease amongst the British generals. Moore later complained that by this point 'Colonel McDonald's corps was not seen nor were there any tidings of it to be heard for a considerable time, when a note from him to Sir Ralph mentioned him being at Groet, a village upon the opposite side of the sand-hills.'[28] Moore was livid and blamed MacDonald personally for this divergence from the plan. Whatever Abercromby thought about the actions of his protégé, he knew what had to be done.[29] Weakening his main thrust, Abercromby detached part of Moore's brigade to take MacDonald's role and enter the dunes to cover the left. This decision was not made a moment too soon for Moore wrote:

'About this time their Light Infantry and Hussars began to skirmish with my advanced guard. I had scarcely formed the 25th and 79th Regiments when they were attacked. I gave orders to the commanding officers to prepare their men to charge as soon as I should give the signal, which I did when I thought the enemy sufficiently near. These two regiments advanced with great boldness, and drove the enemy for a considerable distance, not, however, without loss. I was wounded in the thigh, but not so as to be disabled from doing my duty.'[30]

Despite this bold action, the skirmishing intensified, the private of 92nd foot recalled:

'There was a great deal of bloodshed in the interior of the sandhills, by the continued skirmishing, and detached attacks upon particular points. These sand hills were admirably adapted for this mode of warfare; the enemy would have been much more easily driven out of trenches; for the sand hills were the same as a succession of trenches, so that when the enemy saw our troops advancing, they continued to fire upon us until they saw we were just near enough to allow them time safely to retire to the next range of hills.'[31]

As soon as the British readied themselves to attack a range of dunes, the French would pull back while maintaining a harassing fire and soon more units were sucked into the running skirmish. The Royals and 49th foot were ordered out to support 25th and 79th foot and then the Grenadier Battalion of the Guards were also sent in.[32] This running battle continued for several hours until the column eventually reached a point two miles in front of Egmond, where the French had drawn up two lines of fishing boats on the beach as a makeshift barricade, with gaps for troops to pass through.[33] Here the attackers encountered fresh enemy units, which moved to counterattack Moore's now somewhat battered brigade 'with considerable intrepidity'.[34] These troops were 90 Demi Brigade (90e DB), freshly raised in Lille and only recently rushed to Holland. Their commander Grillot and his officers led them to the attack but he was seriously wounded and the conscripts soon found themselves outnumbered. The troops from 90e DB continued to skirmish until three o'clock when their ammunition began to run low and, no longer able to resist, they broke and ran.[35] However the British barely noticed, for while this was occurring General de Brigade Aubrée, whom Brune had sent to guard the coastal approaches to Bergen, had seen that only 92nd foot, some guards and the cavalry remained on the beach and so launched a dense column to attack them. However, it seems that he had overlooked the horse artillery for, as his brigade approached, the cavalry screen moved aside and they were subjected to a lively fire at close range. Realizing his mistake, Aubrée quickly stopped his column and redeployed his men in the shelter of the dunes facing the shore. But it was too late; the artillery had caused such disorder amongst his men that he had to move them further into the dunes to rally.

By now a considerable part of Abercromby's division were fighting as skirmishers in the dunes. Whether this was intentional or was forced upon them by their piecemeal deployment and the uneven ground is unclear. Either way the French saw them as a 'swarm of skirmishers' and Aubrée formed his men into platoon groups and charged each group in turn to shift them from the dunes. The tactic worked and the British fell back pursued by the men of 72e DB. Some of the British skirmishers were thrown back onto the beach and a 'galling fire' began to fall on the units still on the beach.[36] The cavalry, who had suffered little so far, now moved further away, actually entering the surf to get out of range. The infantry however suffered casualties from this fire, with several officers and men being wounded including Abercromby's son.[37] Three companies of 92nd foot were sent into the dunes to support 25th foot who were being put under great pressure by Aubrée's men. But, as Moore recounted, these men advanced 'incautiously into so hot a fire, they suffered prodigiously, and the whole began to give way.'[38] To make matters worse, Mercier, the commander of the French unit with whom they were struggling, perceived this movement as an attempt to turn his flank and gathered a group of 'braves' to mount a counterattack. Moore, now on foot having lost his horse, tried to rally his men in person and sent his ADC, Captain Anderson, for the rest of 92nd foot but it was too late, for Mercier's braves 'advanced briskly' and forced them back onto the dunes. The melee was intense. Mercier was hit by a single ball, which passed through both thighs wounding him fatally, and Moore, on the point of being surrounded, turned to run back to the beach when he was 'knocked down by a shot which entered behind my ear and came out at my cheek under my left eye.'[39] Moore thought his wound was fatal but he was helped up by his soldiers and 'conveyed back to my quarters' ten miles away. His quick thinking in ordering up 92nd foot had saved the day, for the remaining six companies had charged the enemy 'with great spirit'. Led by their colonel, the Marquis of Huntly, who was shot in the shoulder 'whilst animating his men to the charge', they repulsed Mercier's braves 'with slaughter and allowed their comrades to rally behind them and also return to the fray.'[40]

Although their leader had been slain and their counterattack thrown back, the braves of 72e DB could take some satisfaction in the knowledge that they had given the rest of Aubrée's brigade a breathing space, allowing them to fall back in good order on the position already occupied by 90e DB.

Meanwhile, 92nd foot were drawn into the confused battle in the dunes. An anonymous private of the regiment, marching with the foremost company, later recalled:

> 'We marched forward, and passed a number of the enemy's troops, and came to a place where there was a more than ordinary opening, and the sand rose pretty high, in the form of a semicircle; into this opening we wheeled, and were instantly exposed to a fire upon both our flanks and front. This staggered us, and we began to fire upon the enemy, in place of pushing instantly forward to that part of the height that was on our right, driving the enemy from it, and taking up a position there; from which we could have done them more harm, and not have been so much exposed ourselves. We continued to stand still and fire for a few seconds, and then began to move forward, firing as we advanced.'[41]

This diversion into the dunes effectively ended the progress of Abercromby's column towards Egmond as all his units except the cavalry and artillery were now skirmishing in the dunes. The fighting continued for some time, becoming increasingly fierce and desperate as the units became dispersed in the dunes:

> '[T]he action soon became on both sides quite irregular; for the sand hills separated us into parties, so that the one party frequently did not see what the other was doing, and in some instances parties of our troops came suddenly upon parties of the enemy. In one instance, one of our parties having climbed to the top of a sand ridge found that a party of the enemy was just beneath, and instantly rushed down the ridge upon them but the side of the ridge was so steep and soft that the effort to prevent themselves from falling, prevented them from making regular use of their arms. They were involuntarily precipitated amongst the enemy ... neither party were able to make use of the bayonet; but they struck at each other with the butts of their firelocks, and some individuals were fighting with their fists.'[42]

At about the same time as 92nd foot charged, MacDonald's reserve brigade reappeared and immediately attacked on the left. As the sun began to set the French, now massively outnumbered, finally gave up the ground that they had fought so hard for and retired towards Beverwyk.[43] The battle however was not over, for this last effort on the part of the British had cut the enemy's lines of communication between Bergen and Egmond on the coast. Seeing this, General Brune resolved to make a vigorous effort to re-establish this important communication before the end of the day. He ordered General Daendels to send two battalions of infantry, a squadron of dragoons and his company of light artillery 'in great haste' from Alkmaar to Egmond aan Zee, under General de Brigade Durette. At the same time, Major General Bonhomme had also detached a squadron of hussars to Egmond aan Zee and Commander of the Artillery, General de Brigade Saint-Martin, ordered a number of guns to be deployed on the beach. Brune himself took post in Bergen and sent Vandamme to Egmond aan Zee with orders to 'vigorously attack the enemy's right' in the hope that this would force them to move away from his lines of communication.[44]

When Vandamme arrived at Egmond aan Zee he found that General Saint-Martin had deployed his artillery and its fire had stopped the enemy above the exit of the coastal road, where generals Boudet and Fuzier were still holding out. Observing this temporary lull, Vandamme immediately gathered all the cavalry that had arrived at Egmond aan Zee and, having ordered the artillery to stop firing, he personally led them through the gap in the lines of fishing boats and charged the unsuspecting British.

Meanwhile, Abercromby had decided that his troops were too exhausted to attack Egmond itself and it seemed that the action was over. He ordered Henry, Lord Paget, commander of the cavalry, to send forward a troop of horse artillery to cover the position while his infantry regrouped and took up positions for the night. The cavalry, who had seen little action during the day, withdrew into the dunes, where they could not be seen from the beach, and dismounted to rest their horses. The gunners were deploying in the growing darkness when, to their astonishment, a horde of enemy cavalry burst through the gaps between the fishing boats and surrounded them. The guns would have been captured but for Lord Paget and a group of about a dozen officers who happened to still be on horseback, chatting nearby. These officers, quickly followed by a smaller group of sergeants and troopers from the 7th Light Dragoons, charged the enemy horsemen and, surprised at the unexpected intervention, were checked long enough for more dragoons to mount and join the melee.[45] Vandamme's cavalry were repulsed but, realizing they were only facing a handful of men, they 'rallied and advanced again' as a troop of the 15th Light Dragoons came up, joined those already engaged, charged and drove them off half a mile. Some even rode into the sea to escape.[46] According to Bunbury, 'most of the Chasseurs, were killed or taken' and French sources claimed that at this point Abercromby launched his final assault to seize the strategically vital entrance to the coastal road.[47] Having achieved this, the French said Abercromby was prevented from advancing further by the fire of Saint-Martin's artillery and Vandamme's infantry from behind the fishing boats. Conversely, British sources implied that this had already occurred, that Abercromby considered it too late to attempt further action and that the infantry of both sides had suspended their skirmishing 'as it were by mutual consent' to watch the cavalry melee.[48] Whatever the true sequence of events, the battle was now effectively over, though the two forces continued to exchange cannon and musket fire until darkness finally brought the day's fighting to an end.

Chapter 13

Egmond – Battle of the Dunes

Colonel MacDonald commanded an ad hoc brigade comprised of a battalion each of the combined grenadier and light infantry companies of the militia regiments, together with 23rd and 55th foot. This brigade was designated the reserve but as Walsh declared, the term in this instance 'appears to have been a misnomer, as that corps never failed to lead the attack in every action in which it were engaged.'[1] We are told that MacDonald was a 'very wild warrior' and that having encountered the enemy he followed them into the sandhills and forgot his orders as 'he got excited, followed them up, met with more, entangled himself in the waves of those great sand-downs … had a battle to himself.'[2]

MacDonald was supposed to have followed Abercromby's column as it marched along the beach, protecting its flank from attack from the dunes. Perhaps MacDonald believed that he was following the spirit of his orders by pursuing the *tirailleurs* through the dunes. Perhaps he was unaware of how far he had strayed from his objective in the heat of the action and the confusion of the dunes. Perhaps he simply had insufficient control over his inexperienced soldiers. Whatever the reason for his error it certainly had an adverse effect upon the outcome of the battle, ensuring that Abercromby's weakened column, which detached forces to guard its own flank in his absence, was unable to achieve its objective. It would be wrong however to assume that MacDonald had played no active part in the battle, for his brigade fought continuously from the very start until its bitter end.

The terrain in which MacDonald's men were to operate was extremely difficult. An anonymous lieutenant, probably serving with the combined grenadier battalion, left his account of the actions of MacDonald's brigade. He described in some detail the sandy landscape in which they were operating:

'[I]n occasional spots would be found small level plains of sand
surrounded on all sides by these many-shaped hillocks. The line of
hills as it sloped towards the level country was partly covered with long
slips of scrubby wood or coppice; affording shelter for such troops
as the enemy might please to keep in concealment. Through all this
region it was impractical to bring up Artillery, even the Hussar horses
of the French that were opposed to us were frequently up to their
shoulders in the loose sand, and the difficulty of even moving infantry
in any shape was very great.'[3]

The brigade moved deeper into the dunes, led by the Light Battalion with
whom Surtees was serving:

'[W]e now approached the bottom of this sandy eminence, when my
company was ordered to unfix bayonets, (for we had previously primed
and loaded,) and dash on at double quick time till we came in contact
with the enemy. No time was left for reflection now, the immediate
duty we had to perform occupied all our attention fully.'[4]

The company were immediately engaged by enemy skirmishers who fired at
them and fell back through the dunes with the Light Battalion in full pursuit.
They were joined by the Grenadier Battalion and it must be assumed that even
if he was aware of the direction that his command was moving, MacDonald
could have done little to stop it at this point. The whole division plunged
into the dunes; the soft, undulating ground disordering their formations
and turning them into a mob.[5] The lieutenant caustically likened his men to
a flock of sheep, saying they could only be formed into a semblance of order
by the promise of a charge, at which they would scramble up the dunes
towards the enemy who invariably gave way. The lieutenant expressed his
surprise that the French would give way before such a 'scrambling attack'
and believed it to be indicative of their poor quality.[6]

Whilst this may have been the case, given what we know about French
manpower during the campaign, it seems that their tactics were perfectly
apt in this situation. Massively outnumbered, the barely-trained conscripts
were able to hold up MacDonald's whole brigade for most of the day and

distract them from their planned objective. The French skirmishers had no intention of standing to contest the wild charges of the militiamen for they were simply not in a position to do so. They formed up on the crests of the dunes and fired down on the approaching masses until they began to climb the dunes, whereupon they would fall back to the next height. Surtees believed that this was evidence of their superior training as 'riflemen' with 'their balls doing much more execution than ours', but this is just a matter of perception.[7] The French were small in number, operating out of necessity in skirmish formation, and invariably firing from cover.[8] In the course of the entire day, Surtees' battalion had only four men killed and sixty-one wounded, despite being engaged almost continuously.[9] Nonetheless it was an effective tactic; a fact which even the lieutenant was forced to admit:

'Indifferent as they were, they stood much in the way of our progress: the sand-hills, fringed with their glazed cocked-hats, had to be fought for, one by one, so that it took up to twelve hours to cover our distance of ten miles, the fire of the infantry not ceasing till seven in the evening.'[10]

MacDonald's brigade aggressively pursued the retreating French, moving steadily to their left through the dunes, until it came into contact with the Russians who were advancing with extreme caution towards Bergen. At this point they met with stiffer resistance. The French commander Brune, accompanied by the newly promoted General de Brigade Rostollant, had been observing their progress through the dunes and had decided to redress his line to form a single united front. Bergen now formed the central hub of his position and maintained his communications with the Batavians to the right. The left was flanked by the sea and ran through the dunes along the vital coastal road, which the French referred to as the *chemin des Coquilles*. Changing his order of battle in the face of the enemy was a tricky business and captains Roseau and Lejeune from his staff were killed whilst putting these changes into operation.[11]

Lieutenant General Dundas, author of the army's controversial drill book, had been allotted a 'difficult part' in the plan. His division was to support the Russians and maintain contact with the left but, according to Bunbury, he executed this part with 'great judgement and coolness, though thwarted and embarrassed by a variety of cross occurrences.'[12] Coote's brigade, consisting of the Queen's and the 27th, 29th and 85th regiments of foot formed the vanguard of Dundas' column and set off as soon as MacDonald had cleared the road to the sandhills on their right.[13] Almost immediately however, there was friction between Coote and Essen, on his right, as Coote himself reported:

'General Essen, commander of the Russians, would not however move from the Slaper Dyke until I had cleared the way for him by turning a three gun battery at the end of the dyke, and instead of sending one battalion of mine into the sand hills, he would not march until four battalions were placed there to cover his right flank. In short, though contrary to the general disposition and arrangement of His Royal Highness, I was obliged to comply or the Russians would not move.'[14]

Once the prickly Essen had been placated, his troops moved forwards in an immense column towards their objective, the village of Schoorl. Here they drew 'in a line parallel to the feet of the Sand-Hills, and proceeded to attack the enemy's lines in front of Schorel.'[15] The French maintained a strong position between Schoorl and Schoorldam, covered by artillery batteries in entrenched positions and on the Koe Dyke to the rear. General de Brigade Simon had placed his grenadiers at the entrance to Schoorl, which he had garrisoned with the 3rd Battalion of 60e DB, and light infantry on the flanks.[16] Coote's brigade attacked the French *tirailleurs* in the hills above Schoorl, who retreated in some haste pursued by the triumphant British.[17] Having been informed of this movement and foreseeing disaster if Coote's men got around the flanks of the position, Vandamme sent urgent reinforcements to cover Simon's retreat. The two battalions of 42e DB arrived just in time, entering Schoorl from one side as the attackers came in from the other, and a lively combat ensued in which Adjutant General Maison was gravely wounded leading the relief force. The pressure on the position from Coote, MacDonald and the Russians combined was too much for the French and they were forced from the village, only pausing to set fire to the houses to impede their pursuers.[18]

While the Russians were assaulting Schoorl, Burrard's 2nd Guards Brigade had worked their way round to Schoorldam on the left via Warmenhuizen and, supported by the fire of Popham's gunboats, attacked that village. Here, one Citizen Varé held command but, seeing that the position on his left had been vacated, he felt that his was untenable and crossed the canal with his demi brigade, mirroring Simon's withdrawal towards Bergen.[19] Following their retreat, Burrard and the gunboats continued with their attack and attempted to dislodge the enemy entrenched on the Koe Dyke but they remained occupied with this task for the rest of the day.

The Russians had by this point reached Bergen, the scene of their defeat a few days earlier, and Essen was determined that no similar misfortune was to befall his command on this occasion. Keeping his troops under strict control he advanced towards the position with extreme caution while, on his left, his subordinate General Sedmoratsky tried to outflank the French position. This advance was overlooked by the troops of both MacDonald's and Coote's brigades who were now in the hills above Bergen. Surtees (who was with the former) observed that the Russians 'were most distressingly retarded by the innumerable canals or ditches, by which the country was so intersected, and which were generally impassable by fording.' The ditches enclosed the fields to such an extent that the Russians, having fought their way to one side of an enclosure, could find no way out of it and 'they were obliged to retrace their steps, and get out the same way by which they had entered, the enemy all this while pouring into them a close and destructive fire.' Surtees said that although this must have tried their patience the Russians 'bore it with great steadiness'.[20]

Eventually Sedmoratsky was able to form his men alongside Essen's but they moved no further for the rest of the day. The Russians unleashed tremendous volleys of musketry against the village and their guns exchanged fire with the French artillery, which British observers reported was 'strong and well served', far superior to the Russian's 'ill-served' guns. Yet no attempt was made to take Bergen.[21] It could be that Essen was awaiting some sign that Abercromby had succeeded on the right but, as we have seen, that would not be forthcoming. He may have feared that to advance further would expose his men to envelopment as on the previous occasion. Whatever the reason he refused to budge, creating a further low point in the already strained Anglo-

Russian relations. The failure to take Bergen a second time greatly reduced the chances of a victory.

The French took advantage of the breathing space provided by Essen's inaction to consolidate their position. As Brune had already put a plan in motion to withdraw his outlying units to form a continuous line from Bergen to the sea, he now ordered a counterattack and rushed reinforcements to Bergen from Alkmaar. Although the bayonet charge led in person by generals Barbou and Simon was ultimately unsuccessful, it forced the allies to concede ground that they had taken in the woods and dunes around Bergen and enabled 42 and 54 demi brigades to enter Bergen and bolster its defence.

In an attempt to retrieve the situation, the Duke of York ordered Dundas to deploy his entire command to the right of the Russians:

'I therefore directed Lieutenant-General Dundas to march Major-General Lord Chatham's Brigade from the plain into the sandhills to the right of Major-General Coote's, leaving one battalion (the 31st) to move close under the Hills parallel with the left of Major-General Coote's Brigade. This movement was admirably executed; and Major-General Lord Chatham's Brigade having arrived at some distance behind the 85th regiment, and outflanking it by about two battalions, the line was formed and the whole was ordered to advance at a brisk pace to gain the heights about three quarters of a mile distant, across a scrubby wood, and then by a gradual ascent to the summit of the sand hills: the 85th regiment at the same time charged, and drove the enemy before them, who being thus taken in the flank and rear, retired precipitately towards his right, and took post on the summit of the heights which hang over Bergen, whilst the remainder of Major-General Coote's brigade having also moved forward, joined the left of Lord Chatham's.'[22]

This well-executed manoeuvre put the British in a position to outflank their enemy and to finally throw them out of the sandhills to the left of Bergen. The French were forced to shelter in the pine woods around the village where they were able to rally but 85th foot now dominated the heights and occupied the pass in the dunes that led to Bergen (the *chemin des Coquilles*). So determined were the French to drive 85th foot from their position that they launched several furious attacks against them but failed to dislodge them. Switching to their left, the French, led by General Gouvion, attempted to force a similar pass held by 27th foot). They too were attacked by 'a considerable body issuing from the woods' but 27th foot counterattacked with a 'spirited charge' and drove them back to whence they had come.[23]

It was now three o'clock in the afternoon and Dundas' column was in complete possession of the range of sandhills between Bergen and the sea, where they were in contact with MacDonald's brigade. The French made one final attempt to remove the British from their lines of communication along the *chemin des Coquilles* and, having rallied in Bergen, they attacked MacDonald. His troops had advanced so far that they were close enough to Bergen to be taking fire from its batteries (which, according to Surtees did them little harm due to their extended formation) and were now 'warmly engaged' with the French who occupied a ridge of sandhills that ran in a perpendicular direction.[24] If they continued to occupy this position they would have posed a threat to Dundas' right so it was 'absolutely necessary to dislodge him'. Dundas moved up 29th foot to counter this move, closing the gap between his men and MacDonald's reserve and blocking the road from Bergen to Egmond. A general charge was ordered, which Walsh, a medical officer in 29th foot probably witnessed at first hand:

> '[T]his charge was bravely led on by the 29th regiment, and briskly
> followed up by the whole line; and, notwithstanding the ascent was
> to be gained amidst a terrible discharge of musquetry, cannon, and
> howitzers, the position was carried, and the enemy effectually repelled,
> from his last position on the Sand-Hills.'[25]

Pulteney's division had played little part in the battle. Tasked with occupying the Batavians on the allied left, they had merely threatened to attack Oudkarspel, preventing Daendels from seriously assisting the Bergen position. This threat was apparently quite convincing, as Daendels believed that his troops had beaten off three attempts to storm these entrenchments:

'The dike having been levelled, we were covered by great inundations, which rendered the same approaches that had been so favourable for the attack of the 19th of September, totally impracticable. The superior fire of our artillery arrested all the efforts of the enemy. Unable to reach our position either in front or on the left, they succeeded about five o'clock P.M. in pointing some heavy pieces of ordnance, and some mortars, against it, which played till night-fall.'[26]

Certainly these attacks cannot have been very serious as the casualty reports for the divisions under Pulteney's command list no more than half a dozen fatalities. Throughout the day, Daendels was only able to send a trickle of reinforcements to the French on his left so this part of the plan was especially successful.[27] According to French accounts, towards the end of the day Pulteney was even able to detach Prince William's division to attack the right of Bergen. However, the French say he was driven off by their artillery.[28]

The battle had ground to a halt. Abercromby's column, reported Moore, was 'too much jaded for further efforts'. The men secured their position and lay on their arms in the dunes, alongside their elderly commander who, according to Moore, 'had exposed himself much during the day, and he passed, poor man, a very miserable night upon the sand-hills suffering both from cold and anxiety of mind. He had two horses killed under him.'[29]

Moore (who also lost a horse during the battle) blamed the column's predicament entirely upon MacDonald, whose failure to cover the flank of the column weakened it and slowed its progress. Moore's brigade 'in particular was rendered completely useless, so that instead of arriving early at our point with a column fresh and ready to act, Sir Ralph was forced to stop short of it, not having 2000 men who had not been in action.'[30]

The French were seriously concerned about the situation at Bergen. With the British in control of the *chemin des Coquilles* there was a great danger that the central division would be cut off and forced to surrender. Or it would be obliged to make a disorderly retreat from which, with the allies occupying their lines of communication, they would be unable to regroup and 'act with sufficient concert to stop the progress of the Allies.'[31] Brune wrote to the minister of war: 'The battle of the day before yesterday lasted from five in the morning until eight in the evening. At ten o'clock they were still firing musket shots.' The ground, he said, had been vigorously disputed but with night falling the enemy had 'cut the communications between Bergen and Egmont and threatened to cut from Alkmaar to Bergen.'

Like the British the French troops were exhausted:

'The fatigue of the soldiers and I do not know of their dispositions but I have not seen much military spirit, made me see that if the enemy, who had superiority in numbers, were to attack us the next day, this weariness could occasion a real reverse.'[32]

Therefore the French retreated, leaving the British victors on the field, lying exposed amongst the dunes, cold and wet yet tormented by thirst. The private of 92nd foot wrote of his great thirst but said it was assuaged by soldiers digging temporary wells in the sand. Having filled their canteens the men 'went to look among the dead and wounded, for a comrade, of whom we could get no certain account.' They did not find their comrade but were 'greatly affected' by the 'spectacle of the dead, the dying and the wounded' who were unrecognizable in their agony. 'The groaning of the wounded was very afflicting; for they were mostly bad cases.' The private helped carry them to shelter and alleviate their discomfort:

'The universal cry of these poor men was for water. I supplied them as far as I was able, both enemies and friends; and amongst the rest one of our own officers who was most severely wounded. I had to hold him up and put the canteen to his mouth, for he was unable to help himself, he died during the night.'[33]

The anonymous lieutenant also recalled that the troops were plagued by thirst. Their exertions and the morning's relative warmth had led them to drain their canteens which, coupled with the salt from their rations, meant that by the evening they were 'obliged to lie down in all the agony of extreme thirst.' For once the Helder weather was a blessing:

'We had not, however, been long in a recumbent position, when the rain began to descend in torrents; a visit of this kind, after such a day of fatigue, would have been regarded, under other circumstances, as a matter of small comfort, it was now looked on as a blessing; many lay with their mouths open to catch some drops of the descending shower, and when their clothes and blankets became saturated with the wet, they were wrung out into their hats and the water was drunk with avidity.'[34]

Having survived the night, the allies observed with great relief that in the morning the French and Batavians continued their retrograde movements, evacuating their strongly fortified posts at Oudkarspel and along the Langen Dyke:

'His long protracted columns, accompanied by numerous field artillery, were plainly discerned defiling for an extent of several miles, along the chaussee heading to Alkmaar, and even beyond that town. Other divisions were seen in retreat on the line of the sea shore. The army of the Duke moved forward at daybreak. My regiment at mid-day were quartered in a large Chateau or palace, situated in a spacious wood not far distant from Alkmaar.'[35]

They continued to occupy Bergen but that too was evacuated around midday of 3 October when 85th foot filed in to take control. Abercromby entered Egmond aan Zee, and Major General Burrard finally occupied Alkmaar in the evening, which had also been abandoned by the French. York wrote:

'The exhausted state of the troops, from the almost unparalleled difficulties and fatigues which they had to encounter, prevented me from taking that advantage of the enemy's retreat … which, in any other country and under any other circumstances, would have been the consequences of the operations of the army upon the 2nd.'[36]

York could, and did, claim that the Battle of Egmond was a victory but it certainly wasn't the decisive blow that he had hoped for. Almost no part of the complex plan had succeeded. The indiscipline of his troops and possibly some subordinate commanders had robbed him of the control he needed on a tactical level and his failure, once again, to deal his enemy a knockout blow meant he had gained little strategically.

Maule summed up the position in his memoirs:

'Although the enemy had yielded the field of battle, the country beyond that field, with the exception of the town, was totally in his power. The same difficulties existed. The country, even to the walls of Amsterdam, presented the same obstacles, and without very considerable reinforcements, amounting in numbers perhaps to the strength of the existing army, the conquest of North Holland would be impracticable, and the object of the expedition consequently fail.'[37]

In addition to his strategic problems, York also faced continuing and worsening difficulties with the long-term aims of the campaign. The Russians had not had a good day and many were to blame them for the failure to turn the victory into a decisive one. Although not present at the battle, this anonymous commentator perhaps summed up the views of many British participants: 'This would almost infallibly have happened if the Russians had retained in this affair any portion of that ardour which they had shewn in that of the 19th, and had continued to push forward after the capture of Groet and Schorel.'[38] This view is even echoed in the account of the Batavian engineer Krayenhoff, who went to the trouble of questioning local inhabitants about the performance of the Russians in this battle and reported their notable lack of aggression.[39] General Coote, already annoyed by Essen, complained that the Russians had failed to assist him in any way and that those attached to him were actively uncooperative: 'I had a company of yaegers with me; they all lay down, officers and all, and declared that they had no more ammunition. I, suspecting them, opened their pouches and found them nearly all full, and their arms in perfect order.'[40]

In addition to their lack of co-operation on the battlefield there were further accounts of the Russians engaging in wholesale looting. The anonymous lieutenant wrote that whilst rounding up British looters he found 'in one house that had been gutted by a party of Russians, another party of their countrymen made their appearance, and finding nothing left but a harmless Dutch clock ticking behind the door, they took it down, pulled it to pieces, and divided the works.' The lieutenant felt that this behaviour was detrimental to the plan of raising the Dutch people to support the invasion: 'the wholesale plunder practised by our allies was small inducement to Mynheer to stir himself in our favour.'[41] In this view he was not alone. Count Bentinck-Rhoon, a member of a prominent Anglo-Dutch family and one of the Prince of Orange's staff, wrote to Lord Grenville on the subject:

> 'The Russians are not at the peak of discipline and order and leave wherever they go, traces of their passage and occupation. In some ways they may be excused because they are not treated as the English. They were offered meat for the troops but General Herman (who was captured) refused, so they take what they can; and it seems that it would be very good, since they are in the pay of England, if the Duke of York received an order to treat them the same as the English, because then they could also have the same discipline as the rest of the English Army, and be punished for any disorder; this is most essential as they will ruin the country if they continue like this, diminishing the good effect of the conduct of the English army upon the minds of the inhabitants.'[42]

If the aim of the invasion was twofold – the defeat of the republican forces and the encouragement of a popular counter-revolution – then the victory had moved York's army no further towards either and the behaviour of his allies was becoming a liability.

Chapter 14

Naval Operations

The navy had played an active role in the early stages of the expedition but Naval Commander Admiral Duncan had fallen ill and played only a minor role in the whole affair, returning to Yarmouth on 1 September, leaving his subordinate Vice Admiral Mitchell in charge.[1] The heavy weather had made it difficult to keep the invasion fleet together and Mitchell worked hard to maintain the cohesion of his disparate force of converted merchant ships, customs cutters and Russian warships as well as his own command and keep the Batavian Navy at bay. As soon as the invasion fleet entered Dutch waters the threat of attack from the Batavian ships was ever present and Mitchell had moved quickly to neutralize that threat by first bottling up the Batavian Navy and then forcing their surrender. Whilst he may have been personally disappointed that there had been no great sea battle, which would have led to personal glory for him as well as granted him and his men substantial prize money for any of the Batavian ships captured, the government were ecstatic at the result and he achieved the greatest success of the campaign. His superior Admiral Duncan thought it the greatest success of the war.[2]

However, some parts of the Batavian Navy remained at large and on 12 September Mitchell reported a clash between two of his ships and two Batavian ships of 'superior force'. Captain Porlock of the sloop the *Arrow* and Captain Bolton of the *Wolverine* came across a pair of warships flying the Batavian colours 'in the narrow passage leading from the Fly Island towards Harlingen'. Captain Porlock reported that 'I made the signal to engage the enemy', engaging the brig with Bolton first and then moving to take on the larger ship alone. 'Captain Bolton anchored his ship in the most masterly and gallant manner I could have wished, which was on his weather quarter, at a quarter of a cable distance, and so as to have enabled me, had it been necessary to give the enemy a broadside in passing.'[3] A warning shot was sufficient and the enemy brig, now potentially caught between the fire of two ships, hauled down his colours in surrender. However, Porlock was now sailing against the wind and as he approached the larger ship, she was able to fire a full broadside at the *Arrow* for twenty minutes before he could bring his guns to bear. Porlock's report stated that 'this annoyed us very much, and cut us up a good deal in the hull, sails, and rigging' but he was eventually able to close with the Batavian ship (*De Draak*; armed with sixteen 18-pounder guns, two 'long English' 32-pounders and six 50-pound howitzers) and after a battle that was described as 'smart, but short' the Batavian ship also struck her colours. Despite the howitzers having used ammunition know as Langridge Shot (a tin case full of iron bars used to damage a ship's rigging) Porlock reported only one fatality. However, he was unable to ascertain his enemy's casualties as he considered the ship unseaworthy and destroyed her.[4] They took another ship (the *Dolphin*) on their way back to the island, which hoisted Orange colours on their approach and accepted the surrender of the island in the name of the Prince of Orange.

As well as this activity on the Zuider Zee, General Brune also complained that English vessels appeared on the coast to worry the Franco-Batavian rear, near Haarlem. He reported that they landed numerous men who pillaged and devastated the houses and property of many unfortunate peasants.[5] So even though their main focus was the captured fleet, the navy were active in advancing the aims of the expedition through this period.

The navy were very pleased with themselves but General Abercromby was not impressed. He called repeatedly for Mitchell to fit out gunboats and arm the local, shallow drafted, *schuyts* (local flat-bottomed sail barges) and send them into the Zuider Zee to threaten Amsterdam, but on 4 September he complained that he hadn't heard from Mitchell for three days.[6] It seemed to Abercromby that, although there was still a great deal of hard fighting ahead, his naval colleague thought the expedition was won, or at least that his part in it was over. Mitchell however, had other concerns. For instance, the troopships carrying the reinforcements for the expedition, including the Russians, needed escorting. Additionally, there were still Batavian ships in the area and the Admiralty was afraid they could pose a threat to the troopships or join the French fleet at Brest.[7] Further ships were sent to escort the Russians and the *Inflexible* arrived on 12 September with the second contingent of Russians. However, the navy were very much afraid of the disruption that enemy shipping could cause. In fact Mitchell said that protecting the convoys and supervising the disembarkation 'has been the reason also of my not going from hence until I had his Royal Highness's instructions to co-operate with the army as far as wind, tides, and depth of water will allow me.'[8]

Whether he was stung into action by Abercromby's criticism or his preparations took longer than the soldier had appreciated, Mitchell was in action on the Zuider Zee two days after York's arrival. He shifted his flag (and his bunk) from the *Isis* to a smaller ship, the *Babet* and, having lightened her enough to get into the shallow water, set off with a small flotilla of similarly lightened ships to stir up the coastal towns and villages.[9] The first point he reached was Enkhuizen, on a peninsular between Den Helder and Hoorn, where his flotilla anchored and was met by a boat full of men in Orange cockades. He went onshore and later wrote that 'we were received by all the inhabitants with every testimony of joy at their deliverance from their former tyrannical government, and in their highest degree expressive of their loyalty and attachment to the House of Orange.'[10] Mitchell reinstated the old burgomasters [town mayors] and was feted by the townsfolk who also cut down the republican tree of liberty in the town square. The town of Medemblik, a little further north, soon followed suit.

Whether this was proof, at last, of support for Grenville's hoped-for counter-revolution or just an understandably canny reaction to the appearance of a small fleet outside their undefended town remained to be seen. Mitchell was convinced of their honesty and believed that the appearance of his flotilla 'had the most wonderful and happy effect, and given the greatest confidence to those well disposed to the House of Orange.'[11] Others were less convinced. Walsh wrote that:

> '[A]ll these changes were effected with as much apathy and indifference on the part of the inhabitants as a scene shifter would feel in converting, before the astonished spectators, a wood into a city ... how far their sincerity, in their professions of allegiance was to be trusted, could only be judged of by their subsequent conduct.'[12]

However, happy to have a mission that suited his temperament, Mitchell set off for his next target filled with a crusading zeal: 'I shall not lose a moment's time in moving forward, when the wind and tide will permit, as far as lays in my power, what is finally intrusted to my charge.'[13]

As well as spreading the gospel of counter-revolution throughout the Helder region and keeping the enemy guessing as to the expedition's next move, the navy had sent additional ships, such as the *Inflexible*, and Captain Popham. Popham's orders instructed him specifically to 'bring into the interior the gunboats and other armed vessels to co-operate in any plan of attack' as well as assist with bridge building and 'facilitate our movements in a variety of instances'.[14] It wasn't long before he was in action. His first three gunboats, each mounting a 12-pounder carronade, were launched into the Alkmaar canal in support of Dundas' column on 19 September, inspiring the Duke of York to write that he felt 'much indebted to the spirited conduct' of this naval detachment and its commander who 'acted with considerable effect'.[15]

Meanwhile, Mitchell's shallow sea flotilla had been engaged in a war of the small boats. He sent another small force across the Zuider Zee to probe the towns on the opposite shore: 'I have detached Captain Boorder, in the *Espeigle*, with the *Speedwell*, to scour the coast from Steveren to Lemmer.' Prior to his departure, Boorder had been able to report to Mitchell that the inhabitants of Steveren and 'most of the neighbourhood towns' had hoisted the Orange flag and agreed to the same terms as Enkhuizen and Medemblik. 'I have likewise detached the *Dart*, with two gun Brigs, to cut off communication with Amsterdam, and the towns of East Friesland, that have not returned to their allegiance.'[16]

One of those neighbourhood towns was Lemmer and a week after the disaster at Bergen it had, perhaps understandably, still not embraced the Orangist counter-revolution. The town was fortified and garrisoned with about 1,000 soldiers but on 27 September a naval squadron was dispatched to attack it. The force was commanded by Captain William Bolton of the *Wolverine* and comprised his 14-gun sloop, *Haughty*, *Piercer* and *L'Espeigle* as well as two schuyts, requisitioned and armed by Captain Boorder of *L'Espeigle* and the launch from flagship the *Isis*[17] These vessels would have been of almost negligible value in the great naval battles of the time, such as Camperdown and Trafalgar, but here on the shallow Zuider Zee they represented a formidable force.

Bolton anchored his force six miles from Lemmer and the next morning sent an officer into the town under a flag of truce asking it to surrender. An exchange of terse notes followed, with Town Commandant Van Groutten attempting to stall while Bolton became increasingly bombastic, threatening to bombard the town and bury his soldiers 'in its ruins' if they did not raise the Orange flag within half an hour. The ultimatum was ignored and as the garrison used the time to establish a battery of 18-pounders on the north end of the pier, Bolton ordered the attack.[18]

Despite the advice of a well-disposed Dutch pilot, Bolton pushed his ship through the shallow muddy waters until it ran aground 'within a musquet-shot of the shore'. The improvised gunboats were also sailed very close to the shore, which immediately provoked the garrison to fire upon them, ignoring the superfluous flag of truce. This heavy bombardment 'was returned, from every part of the squadron' and the fight went on for nearly an hour before the garrison decided they had had enough and 'flew from their quarters', abandoning the town to the British.

The following morning the enemy returned but Bolton had been supervising his ships being towed off the sand banks, on which they had been stranded during the attack, and observed them approaching. He sent word to Boorder, who was defending their prize, and after a brief skirmish the attackers were repelled on all sides. As it was almost entirely surrounded by water, the town proved easy to defend against an overland attack. Bolton confidently predicted that if the expedition was able to send assistance to this area in time it 'would cause the whole province to throw off the French yoke.'[19]

However, the assistance they required would not be forthcoming. Despite stripping marines and sailors from the ships of the fleet that were too large to operate in the shallow waters of the Zuider Zee, it soon became apparent that Mitchell would need the army's help if he were to hold on to the towns that he was liberating. Just as Abercromby had complained about Mitchell's lack of activity, now Mitchell complained about the lack of co-operation from his opposite number. On 30 September he wrote angrily to Lord Spencer at the Admiralty that despite 'several communications with his Royal Highness upon our further co-operation towards my given object, Amsterdam; but out of *the forty thousand* of the army I have not as yet prevailed upon his Royal Highness to give any assistance.'[20]

From the navy's perspective, they were certainly playing their part and at the Battle of Egmond on 2 October Popham's gunboats were once again in action. He reported to the Admiralty that 'three of our gun-boats were sunk. They fired from 80 to 100 rounds each. The flotilla consisted of four carrying 24-pounders, and three carrying 18-pounders.'[21] York's dispatch after the battle reported that the gunboats worked in conjunction with Burrard's brigade attacking Schoorldam and bombarding enemy positions on the Koe Dyke.[22] In addition to this direct co-operation with the army, Mitchell's fleet were swiftly eroding the republican control of the Zuider Zee and threatening their communications. In the aftermath of the initial landing, Daendels had ordered his engineer Krayenhoff to fortify the approaches to Amsterdam by land and sea: 'he caused to be constructed on the lower coasts the batteries necessary for the defence of the Pampus, and requested officers of the navy to station their boats and other armed vessels.'[23] The British now came into conflict with these vessels and on 6 October, Captain Patrick Campbell of the *Dart*, commanding four 'armed vessels', attacked and captured 'four of the enemy's gun boats, each mounting four guns'.[24] Mitchell's miniature fleet roved along the Dutch coast with impunity attacking the enemy's shipping wherever they found it. When, on 8 October, Captain Winthorpe of the *Circe* observed a couple of enemy ships (a sloop and a schooner) anchored under the protection of the batteries at Delfzijl, in the Ems estuary, he did not hesitate to attack them. Although the guns of the battery were primed and ready, Winthorpe was able to board the enemy ships with his sailors and marines using the ships' boats and made off with his prizes without a single casualty.[25]

The Batavian Navy were now almost entirely devoid of ships and the Batavians were unable to prevent Mitchell from landing where he pleased. However, York's refusal to divert any men to assist him meant that he was unable to effectively defend those towns that he had liberated. He wrote again to Lord Spencer on 10 October, expressing his frustration and bewilderment at the strategic situation:

'To tell your Lordship the truth, I have ever since the 19th had my doubts of success. The falling back on that day with such an army, because the right wing of the army, composed of Russians, and those not all engaged I believe, staggered my ideas of a soldier indeed; and that the left wing under Sir Ralph Abercromby, comprising a force of 15,000 men, should without opposition in moving forward ... about 20 miles and took quietly the possession of the large town of Hoorn, a few miles distant from this place, and evacuate the same day are matters that I cannot understand. ... In company I constantly urged a force to be kept on the army's left to co-operate with me but no men could be spared; the loss now shows itself, and all my brilliant prospects are now at an end; if the left had kept possession of Hoorn from the 19th, I'll venture to say that ... we should have been in Amsterdam long ago.'[26]

It wasn't long before operations were launched to bring the errant towns back within the republican fold. On 11 October a force of around 700 men attacked Lemmer (possibly the original garrison), which was held by the force of sailors and marines that had captured it the previous week. Their commander, Captain Boorder, reported that the initial attack was made by a force of around thirty who attempted to storm the battery at the northern edge of the town. They were caught in a crossfire, were quickly surrounded by 'tars' armed with boarding pikes and 'immediately lay down their arms'. No sooner had these unfortunates been locked away than the rest of the force, which Boorder estimated at 670, attacked. 'Our little army did wonders,' wrote Boorder, 'for with sailors and marines our force was only 157. We fought them for four hours and a half, when the enemy gave way in all directions: I immediately ordered the marines to pursue them.' However, the fleeing enemy broke down a bridge, which curtailed the pursuit and enabled them to escape with their colours and two cannon.[27] The republican forces suffered heavy casualties but the lack of reinforcements meant that Boorder's position was increasingly vulnerable.

The following day Mitchell evacuated his small fiefdom, which he called the regency. Frustrated by the lack of support from York, he felt that his forces were insufficient to oppose the counterstroke that he knew must be coming and that the best way to keep the people and their towns safe from 'the vengeance of our enemies' was to leave. Certainly that is what he wrote in his parting letter to the men he had appointed to run Enkhuizen. He added that he hoped 'that members of your provisional regency, established at my express orders, will not suffer the least molestation; but should I hear that any of them have been injured, I shall return with my fleet to bombard the town until not one stone remains on another.'[28]

Krayenhoff expressed his disbelief that the fleet had not simply sailed up to Amsterdam's vulnerable coastal edge and disgorged troops into the city from this almost undefended side.[29] He acknowledged the need to assemble the fleet of shallow draft vessels but believed that this was accomplished with little urgency. It may be that, as he suggested, the navy were so entirely focused on the capture of the Batavian fleet that they had given little thought to their next move and had made no preparations for it. However, Krayenhoff assumed that the army and navy were working harmoniously together towards a common goal while this was blatantly not the case. Mitchell did little to co-operate with the army before York arrived and then York did little to co-operate with the navy. Each service was focused on the needs of its part of the mission without being able to see the benefits of co-operating on a wider strategy.

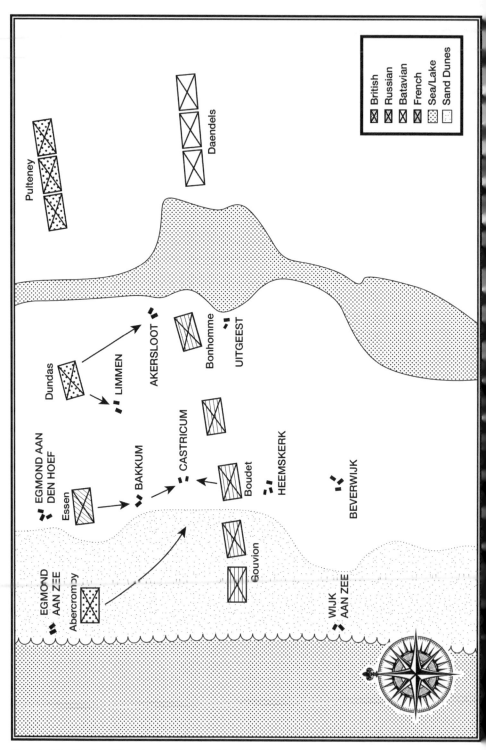

Map 6. The Battle of Castricum. (*Produced by John Harcourt*)

Chapter 15

The Battle of Castricum – Brune's Triumph

A lthough Egmond had not been the knockout blow that York had hoped for, he felt he was in a good position and began to make plans to move against Haarlem in order to close in on Amsterdam. His army occupied a position between the sea and the canal, with Abercromby on the right at Egmond aan Zee, the Russians under Essen at Egmond aan den Hoef and Egmond Binnen, and left under Dundas occupying the area between Alkmaar and Heiloo. Beyond the canal, Pulteney's command was spread from Alkmaar to Schermerhorn and Prince William of Gloucester occupied Hoorn on the Zuider Zee.[1]

Opposite them, now reinforced by six further battalions from Belgium, the French had worked without rest to fortify and strengthen their position. Their left, under Vandamme, consisted of the divisions of Gouvion and Boudet; the first of which was in a position from the beach at Wijk aan Zee, through the dunes to Heemskirkerduin, and the second in the village of Uitgeest. The right, consisting of Dumonceau's Batavian division (led by Bonhomme in his absence), was actually mostly behind the left. They occupied a position from Beverwijk to Akersloot following the edge of the Langmeer Lake. The advanced guard, under the orders of Pacthod, held Akersloot, Limmen and Bakkum. Daendels was opposite Pulteney and Fuzier formed the reserve at Beverwijk.[2]

Unbeknownst to their enemies the French troops were starving. As well as having to work through the night, digging trenches and building redoubts, their supply lines had been disrupted by their retrograde movement on 2 October and 10,000 loaves of bread and 14,000 rations of meat had fallen into enemy hands at Alkmaar. Brune blamed this on the continuing problem of the Dutch baggage train. He wrote to the French representative in Amsterdam complaining that the commissioner in charge of supply had been unable to remove the rations as all the carts and barges were being used by the women and impedimenta that the Batavians continued to bring with them on campaign, despite his repeated orders to the contrary. Not only had the rations been captured but the commissioner had been told to keep the next allocation at Amsterdam to await further instructions, which Brune either forgot to issue or the edict failed to reach him. Amidst cries of treason, the army (which had been well supplied by the Batavians up to this point) were left to starve rather than upset the local populace with widespread requisitions.[3] Despite their gnawing hunger, the republican troops occupied their positions on the night of 5/6 October and awaited the enemy's next move.

That move was not long in coming but was not intended to be a general attack. To stop the enemy from strengthening their position any further and to manoeuvre his troops into the best possible position to launch his planned drive to Haarlem, York had ordered a series of limited raids on the French outposts for dawn on 6 October.[4]

The attack was preceded by a couple of days of reorganisation on York's part. Lord Chatham wrote to his mother on 4 October telling her that he had 'moved in the course of yesterday to reinforce Sir R. Abercromby' and that the enemy had then evacuated Egmond aan Zee, allowing them to march in.[5] Moore said that Abercromby had been left 'several days separated and unconnected with the left' but it seems that Chatham's brigade had been sent to correct this. Christopher Hely-Hutchinson placed his brother John's (formerly Cavan's) brigade and D'Oyly's with Abercromby as well.[6] As Chatham was formerly under Dundas with Prince William's brigade (which were sent to Hoorn) as well as Manners' brigade, Dundas must have been reinforced. Manners' brigade did not seem to have seen any action so were presumably on the allied left opposite Daendels, as was Don's. Therefore Manners may have replaced Hely-Hutchinson/Cavan's 4th Brigade under Pulteney's command.[7] Moore's brigade had been in the thick of the action at Egmond so may have been pulled out of the frontline as they didn't appear to be involved in the ensuing battle. Certainly, 92nd foot were in Alkmaar and remained there throughout the day.[8]

The weather, which had been problematic throughout the campaign, was poor. Maule recalled that 'the morning loured; it seemed to presage an ill-fated change. A deep mist prevented the view of either friend or enemy.'[9]

This would prove a problem later but for now orders were issued to units in the advanced posts to push forwards. The combined Grenadier Battalion of MacDonald's brigade had been sent out the previous night and as they lay on the sand dunes they could see, to their surprise, the Russians advancing in a great column against the French line, apparently without support.[10] Shortly afterwards the Light Battalion were ordered to march from Egmond Binnen to relieve the grenadiers. Private Surtees was amongst them: 'We advanced by the sea-shore but had not gone far before we saw and heard unequivocal signs that we should have something more than outpost duty to perform; the fact is, the enemy was rapidly advancing.'[11]

Moving up the beach and into the sand dunes, the enemy Surtees saw may have been General Simon's brigade who were dispatched by Gouvion, the commander of the French left, at some time between seven and eight in the morning.[12] This brigade were sent to observe the advance of MacDonald's men from the heights in the centre of the dunes and to maintain communications with the brigade of General Boudet on their right.

In front of Alkmaar, Burrard's brigade of guards had set off at around seven in the morning, supported by Coote's brigade. Spearheaded by three companies of the 3rd/Guards and one of the Coldstream Guards, led by Colonel Clephane, they rapidly overwhelmed the lightly-held post of Limmen and marched on to Akersloot. Here the speed of the advance surprised Batavian Commander Colonel Nicolson, who was barely able to get his garrison to their posts when the assault began. The, by now, experienced Batavians of the 1st Halve Brigade stood their ground but the freshly arrived French took to their heels and, apart from their officers and a few hardier souls, 'became shameful fugitives' whom no efforts could persuade to return. The post stood for a short while before the Batavians withdrew towards Uitgeest, cutting the bridges and destroying the roads as they went. Clephane, having taken 200 prisoners, occupied the village as ordered, his limited objective secured.[13]

In the allied centre the Russians under Essen had been tasked with the capture of Bakkum. Advancing in dense columns from Egmond aan den Hoef and Egmond Binnen, they quickly took their objective. However, finding it was overlooked by a range of sandhills, they pushed on to secure them as well. This they also achieved with ease but rather than rest on their laurels they rushed onwards in defiance of their orders and entered Castricum. Here they met with determined resistance from General Pacthod who, with the men of 49 and 90 demi brigades and a Batavian battalion (2nd of 1st halve brigade) under Major Achenbach, withstood their furious assault for some time.[14]

Brune, meanwhile had arrived on the scene and, observing MacDonald's brigade moving up the beach, believed that this was a manoeuvre intended to outflank Pacthod in Castricum, so he ordered General Gouvion to send his division into the dunes and onto the beach to hold them off. At the same time, he ordered General Boudet to form his division in line near Noorddorp to march at once against the Russians. Pacthod also believed he was about to be outflanked by the Russians, who were now beginning to lap around the edges of Castricum, and so pulled his increasingly isolated force out of Castricum into the dunes behind the village. Here, with the 8th Regiment of Light Artillery commanded by Colonel Leroux covering the approaches, he was able to hold the Russians at bay until Vandamme and Boudet joined him with five battalions of fresh troops. Now suitably reinforced, the French immediately engaged the Russians from their position in the dunes.

Meanwhile on the beach, Gouvion, aware of the attack on Boudet, had been expecting an attack for at least an hour and perceived the arrival of MacDonald's Light Battalion as the threat he had been waiting for. Gouvion had placed General Aubrée's brigade on the beach with orders to attack the enemy as soon as they appeared, and held two battalions of 72e DB and the 5e Chasseurs à Cheval in reserve. Surtees, serving with the Light Battalion, wrote that the French cavalry (a new threat to the inexperienced militiamen) rode into the sea so that they could get a good look at the British position, which was obscured by a large sandhill. Seeing that the British were a small force, Aubrée sent forward his Light Artillery commanded by Captain Couturier, supported by a battalion and a half of 98 Demi Brigade (98e DB) and the 16e Chasseurs à Cheval and launched his attack.[15] The blow fell first on the Grenadier Battalion but Surtees and his comrades soon joined the battle. Surtees believed that the Light Battalion were outnumbered four to one and said that they attempted to adopt a *ruse de guerre* to make the enemy believe that they were stronger. But it failed and the French attacked 'with the most desperate fury, and in overwhelming numbers'. The inexperience of the militiamen proved their undoing for, as the fighting became fiercer, it became increasingly apparent that they were outnumbered:

'I regret to say, our young troops fell into considerable disorder and confusion. This giving the enemy greater confidence, of course he availed himself of it, and attacked us with redoubled impetuosity; and I lament to say, our dismayed and disheartened young soldiers fell from one degree of confusion to another … and what was at first a rather regular retreat, became at last a disorderly flight.'[16]

The Grenadier Battalion experienced similar difficulties and an officer serving with them believed that the apparent instability of the Russian units had an adverse effect upon his own men:

'It was somewhat trying to young and unformed soldiers to see this broken and ill-shapen mass approach, like a migration of land-crabs, and followed up by an elated and noisy enemy; but to do our big fellows justice, they did not quail at the sight, but covering themselves in the sand, they showed fight. They were at least conversant with the mysteries of priming and loading, and rattled away in very good style. But when from the approach of the enemy in such force it was found necessary to retire, there was no small difficulty in keeping them in hand, and preventing what ought to have been an orderly retreat of piquets becoming a disorderly rout.'[17]

The two composite militia battalions were now driven three or four miles back to Egmond Binnen, where they had started from, running along the beach in total disorder, desperately trying to keep ahead of their pursuers.

Fortunately not all of MacDonald's men were raw militiamen and 23rd and 55th foot were quickly dispatched to their rescue:

'We perceived some regiments advancing to our succour; among them was the 23rd, which advanced in line, and showed so good and steady a front as quite delighted us. We could also perceive to our left, that

the Russians had become engaged with the force in front of them, and
were holding it at bay.'[18]

The advance of the veteran battalions gave new hope to the routed and
broken militiamen and they rallied behind 23rd foot and rejoined the fray.
After a couple of volleys the British advanced upon their tormentors who
now themselves broke and were pursued back to the point at which the
action had commenced.

This movement threatened to cut Gouvion's communications with Simon
in the interior of the dunes and turn the right flank of 98e DB. So, leaving
six companies of 72e DB to guard the beach, Gouvion led the remainder
of his reserves through the Grande Gorge and into the dunes to retrieve
the situation. Combining his troops with Simon's brigade he charged at the
four battalions of MacDonald's brigade, who were now drawn up on a large
plain in the interior of dunes called the Wogelwater. Gouvion encouraged
his men by his example of bravery and *sangfroid*. Leading from the front
he entertained his advancing troops with 'military jokes' and 'bawdy airs,
to which the soldiers repeated the refrains and the firing of the two parties
provided the accompaniment.'[19]

Headed by the grenadiers of 72e DB, Gouvion's men swept through the
dunes and onto the plain at speed. There the grenadiers subjected the British
to some effective platoon firing while their comrades moved to envelop the
four battalions. Such was the speed of the attack that MacDonald's men
were pushed off the dunes once more and communications between the
two French brigades were restored. At this point it seems that the British
were reinforced by Hely-Hutchinson's brigade for the fortunes of battle now
swung back in their favour. The French fell back to the Heights of Justice
near Bakkum, pursued by British Light Dragoons who had taken advantage
of this retrograde movement to charge the companies of 72e DB on the
beach, forcing them to adopt a formation with their backs to the dunes.
In this position, 'supported by several oblique fires' they forced the Light
Dragoons to abandon their attempt to turn the retreat into a rout. With
neither side being able to gain an advantage, the battle in this sector now
settled down to an exchange of fire, which continued long after dark with
each side firing at the muzzle flashes of the other.[20]

In the meantime, the action, which had only been intended to be an adjustment of the allied line, had become general across most of the front. The unexpected advance of the Russians had exposed their flank and seeing this, Abercromby sensed danger and responded to Essen's demand for assistance dispatching a strong column towards Castricum. Christopher Hely-Hutchinson was serving with his brother John, who commanded Cavan's brigade following his wound. He recalled that:

'The Russians, with Colonel McDonald's Brigade, advanced rather too far upon the enemy, who came down on them in great force, our brigade, with that of Lord Chatham's, and General D'Oyly's, advanced to their support we advanced along the sand hills, with orders to support General D'Oyly who was on our left. In doing this we fell in with McDonald's Brigade, who were at the moment retreating in some confusion.'[21]

As we have seen, MacDonald's brigade soon rallied and, supported by this column now moving through the dunes on their left, had rejoined the battle.

The advance of MacDonald and the approach of Abercromby's column relieved the pressure on the exhausted Russians and gave them fresh heart, allowing them to renew their attack on both sides of Castricum. To the east, Sedmoratsky's troops pushed towards Bonhomme's Batavians whose position was centred on the village of Uitgeest. Brune however was unconcerned by this development as he knew this area was waterlogged and heavily dissected by ditches, which would greatly retard their march. On the west side Brune called up a battalion of 42e DB and two of the Batavian 6th Halve Brigade. Lining up these units in the dunes he launched them against the flank of the Russians with bayonets fixed. The effect was immediate. Already exhausted by hours of fighting, the Russians had thought the tide was turning in their favour but the ardour of these fresh troops was too much for them and they broke, fleeing in disorder into the fields behind Castricum.[22]

The collapse of the Russian right exposed Castricum and Brune seized his opportunity. Without a moment's hesitation he sent Pacthod at the head of a makeshift column drawn from 42 and 49 demi brigades with orders to attack the village. Accompanied by generals Vandamme, Boudet, Fuzier and

Malher, he then personally led a further three battalions to support their attack. The battle was fierce but the Russian grenadiers, who held Castricum, eventually gave way when their cannons, which had swept the entrances to the village, were overrun. The melee swirled through the village, with small knots of grenadiers fighting man to man with their furious attackers, but they were overwhelmed and retreated down the road to Limmen and through the dunes towards Bakkum at some speed.[23]

At the same time as Brune's well-timed counterstroke, Abercromby's column was marching to support the Russians. D'Oyly's brigade of guards had turned inwards to try to prevent the outflanking of the Russians to the west of Castricum but, by doing this, had exposed their own flank to the French who seized upon this tempting target with alacrity. As the French tried to turn the guards' right flank they were attacked by Hely-Hutchinson whose brigade charged them with bayonets fixed and another seesaw battle commenced. The brigade were to repeat this action three times before night fell, eventually driving off their opponents despite their 'considerable force' and dispersing them amongst the sandhills. In the course of this melee, Hely-Hutchinson was 'shot ... through the right thigh, rather high up' but the wound was not considered dangerous and his brother moved him to Helder for treatment.[24]

Chatham's brigade meanwhile had followed Hely-Hutchinson and D'Oyly and were coming up behind the Russian right when it broke. The Russians fled through the intervals in Chatham's line to the rear where, according to the grenadier lieutenant, they 'made no attempt to rally'.[25] The pursuing French infantry had fallen behind so the cavalry, led by General Barbou, took up the chase. Perhaps unable to fire because the fleeing Russians obscured their target, or being unaware of their danger owing to the heavy mist that still obscured the battlefield, the 'three battalions of the 4th principally sustained the shock of the enemy's horse by which they suffered severely.'[26] Around this time, and possibly in the course of this combat, Lord Chatham was wounded in the neck by a musket ball, which 'took off the epaulette from his shoulder, and forced away part of his coat and waistcoat' and he was carried from the field.[27] The cavalry presumably only caught a flank of Chatham's brigade for they carried on, led by 10/Dragoons, pursuing the fugitives to the foot of the dunes. The dragoons sped on, intent on their victims and paying little heed to their surroundings when they fell into a perfectly prepared ambush.

The Russians were trapped with the high dunes to their left and in front of them a canal over which the bridges had been cut. But just when all seemed lost, a couple of squadrons of British Light Dragoons, drawn from the 7th and 11th regiments and led by Lord Paget, crashed into the left flank of the imprudent Frenchmen as they passed the entrance of a gorge in the dunes where these troops had been concealed. The sudden appearance of the Light Dragoons completely demoralized the French Dragoons and after a brief clash in which one of their officers, Brigadier Goddard, received numerous sabre cuts to the head, they were thrown back, galloping through their own infantry who joined them in a disorderly retreat to Castricum. Having done their job, Paget's Light Dragoons pursued no further than the Heights of Castricum, which allowed Barbou to rally his shaken horsemen.[28]

Sedmoratsky's men, struggling through the flooded fields to the east of Castricum, had also been forced to retire by Brune's assault on the town in the centre of their position and they were pursued by Pacthod towards Limmen. On the outskirts of the village the Russians cut the bridge over the Schulpvaart stream and carefully covered the crossing with two artillery pieces, the fire of which stopped Pacthod's men in their tracks. He could pursue no further and contented himself by sniping at them with his *tirailleurs*. At this point there was a brief lull in the fighting while both sides reorganized their lines and committed what reserves they had available. Hely-Hutchinson's ferocious attack on what had become the centre of the republican line, together with Paget's cavalry charge, had eased the pressure on the Russians to the extent that by about five o'clock they felt able to renew the contest. Sedmoratsky re-established the bridge over the Schulpvaart and sallied out of Limmen. Although evening was setting in the fighting was then rekindled along the entire line.[29]

The French were by now spread out in skirmish order in disparate groups through the dunes. Overwhelmed by fatigue, they hadn't eaten, were running short of ammunition and were dispirited by the continual rain. Small wonder then that the now rested Russian troops overwhelmed them and threw them back to the heights around Castricum where generals Boudet and Fuzier were able to rally them to some degree and hold the Russians at bay, though they continued to advance all around.[30]

For the French this was the crisis point of the battle. They clung to the dunes only tenuously and their morale was sinking. British cavalry had moved down the beach, succeeded in outflanking the French position and now looked to be preparing for an attack on the left of Boudet's infantry on the plain. Brune, sensing that the situation was becoming critical, took immediate action to remedy it. Putting himself at the head of the now rallied 10/Dragoons, the 4th Chasseurs à Cheval and a regiment of Batavian Hussars, he put them into battle order and waited in what remained of the daylight for the perfect moment to launch a charge. Seeing his chance, he ordered them forwards and, led by the Batavian Hussars under Colonel Quaita, they fell on the British cavalry in column, sabres flashing and forced them to retire. Seizing on this momentary advantage, Vandamme rallied several groups of 'braves' from the 42 and 49 demi brigades to attack the enemy infantry and, according to Brune's ADC, repulsed them some distance. Brune had averted the crisis, for either as a result of his actions or because they were responding to orders, the British fell back.

Maule recalled that his unit (Queen's with Dundas) were given orders to pull back at this point and were closely trailed by French *tirailleurs*, and light artillery: 'These last, were hurried through the mud and water, in which we stood, with incredible alacrity. The French gunners accustomed a long time in Germany and Italy to pursue, plied us with rare assiduity.'[31] Chatham's brigade, badly mauled by the French cavalry and lacking leadership since Chatham's wounding and the death of Lieutenant Colonel Dickson (chief of the 2nd Battalion, 4th Regiment of Foot), were surprised in the dunes by a battalion of 42e DB under Colonel Aubrée. Noting the superior size of the other party, Aubrée thought he would be obliged to surrender but, taking advantage of the poor visibility, decided he would try a bluff. It worked. Convinced they were surrounded by a superior force, part of the British brigade was induced to lay down their arms and surrender. The Russians had been unable to make it to Castricum a second time and now returned to Limmen while the British regrouped at Bakkum. Both sides were running low on ammunition and the fire fight slowly diminished until only a light fusillade could be maintained which was kept up until nightfall.[32]

Meanwhile, the left wing of the Anglo-Russian army commanded by Pulteney and based at Alkmaar had not made the slightest move throughout the day. In a position defended by a ring of ditches from Schermer to Schemerhorn, they opposed the Batavian division of General Daendels, who occupied a line from Purmerend to Monnikendam. Daendels seems to have been puzzled by their inaction but convinced himself that it was all part of a plot to undermine his army.

General Don had attempted to contact the Batavian Directory on 31 August but had been deflected by the French commander and sent packing without having made contact. However, the Directory had subsequently dispatched an emissary to make some preliminary diplomatic moves so it was now supposed that the victory of 2 October, together with the capture of Alkmaar, would give greater weight to Don's mission. He was therefore dispatched again under a white flag of truce to contact the Directory. The republicans believed that the units of the left wing were waiting for Don's mission to take effect so they could overcome the Batavian division without firing a shot. This was not the allied intention; there was simply no need for this part of the army to seek a better position for York's planned action but Don's mission was again a failure.[33] The republicans claimed that:

'The object of his mission was to paralyse the movements of this division so that elements of the enemy's left could be detached to participate in the combat; it was for this purpose that he carried a proclamation aimed at exciting a revolt against the French.'[34]

When he presented himself at the Batavian outposts Daendels sent Don straight to Brune who had him arrested and sent to the fortress at Lille as a prisoner. The French later tried to exchange him for the Irish rebel Napper Tandy, but this was refused and he remained incarcerated until 1802.

Although they played no part in the battle, the mere presence of Pulteney's division also prevented Daendels from participating. Apart from the transfer of the 2nd Cavalry and 2nd Light Dragoons to Beverwijk to reinforce the reserve, Daendels' only involvement in the battle was to pay a visit to Brune, leaving his division in the care of major generals Van Zuylen and Van Nyevelt.[35]

What was the Duke of York doing all this time? In his diary, Moore made a point of mentioning that the action had been precipitated by the Russians and a patrol by his nemesis, Colonel MacDonald and related this tale of York's reaction:

'Lieutenant-Colonel Kempt, who went from Sir Ralph to the Duke with the report, found him at dinner with several of the general officers. He told him that Colonel McDonald and the Russians were attacked, and that Sir Ralph believed the enemy to be meditating a general attack. No notice seemed to be taken of what he said, and Colonel Kempt was invited to sit down.'[36]

According to Bunbury (who was 'crippled by a rheumatic seizure' having slept in 'a pool of water on the night of the 2nd') having finished dinner, York finally took an interest in the day's events:

'[T]he Duke of York in Alkmaar was wondering what had fallen out, and what had become of his army. Though the rain poured down in torrents, the musketry was incessant, aide-de-camp after aide-de-camp was sent forth to make out what were the causes and objects of this off-hand engagement, and I was carried up and perched on the top of the tall steeple of Alkmaar, with a spy glass, to try to ascertain for the Duke what was the direction, and where were the main points of the fight.'[37]

Whereas the French thought the British attack was planned, the British believed that the French response was not and that they were merely reacting. Both were incorrect, for the account of Brune's ADC shows that the French general had very quickly planned and put into execution his response, apparently uninhibited by the confusion and poor visibility. Both sides claimed victory but whilst they had made gains and remained on the field, the British had suffered grievous losses.[38]

Chapter 16

Capitulation

It was to the army's surprise and disappointment that a retreat was ordered on 7 October. Losses had been high and the army were now a long way from their, somewhat depleted, supply depots. Prisoners taken during the battle had revealed that the enemy had been reinforced by five demi brigades (around 6,000 men) and more were expected, so York convened a council of war on the evening after the battle to discuss his strategic options. It had been their unanimous decision that the army should return to their former defensive positions on Zype.[1]

The Queen's retreated along the seashore at dawn, the deep sand making movement difficult. Baggage horses struggled to keep up with the retreating troops, many collapsed in the dunes under their heavy burdens and were scooped up by the pursuing enemy cavalry along with several hundred human stragglers. According to Walsh, these stragglers included about 300 women camp followers who were released three days later having been well treated.[2]

The rain was relentless and the retreat over broken muddy roads soon descended into disorder. Dalhousie recalled that he had to hail his brother (an officer serving under him) at regular intervals and eventually pass a cord between the saddles of their horses in order to stay together. By the time the Queen's reached the old headquarters at Schagen, there were barely fifty men still marching with the colours. Dalhousie summed up the feeling throughout the army when he observed the 'despondence and discontent on every face, all our work gone for nothing'.[3]

One of Dalhousie's officers, Maule, recalled:

'The weather and elements seemed to conspire against us, and continued hostile during the whole retreat. A powerful corps of cavalry hung upon our rear. These very troops had, a few hours before, covered the retreat of their own columns. No sooner, however, did they perceive the unexpected retrograde movement of the combined army, than they instantly changed their route.

'It must be confessed, the French generals and soldiers conduct themselves on such occasions with a vigour and alacrity unparalleled, without heeding fatigues, dangers, or privations; they take advantage and avail themselves with astonishing rapidity of the weakness, the errors or the misfortunes of their opponents.'[4]

The retreat continued throughout the day leaving Maule and his comrades 'weary almost to death by these continued marches, want of food, and the very worst of weather' until they finally reached Schagen Brug. The armies now resumed their former positions either side of the Zype and, emboldened by reinforcements and the retreat of their enemy, the French began to probe the defences.

The most serious attack fell upon the outlying posts of Winkel and Dirkshorn, which were defended by the brigade commanded by York's young cousin, Prince William of Gloucester. On the morning of 10 October, two columns of Batavian troops led by Daendels marched from Hoorn with orders to attack the village of Winkel. The force, consisting of four battalions of infantry and one of *jaegers,* was attacked by a squadron of the 18th Light Dragoons, which boldly charged the head of the column when it arrived at Opmeer. This force, led by Lieutenant Colonel Stewart who was wounded in the affair, was too small to be any real threat and was probably only intended to delay the advance of the Batavians. The squadron was soon driven off by volleys from the *jaegers* positioned either side of the road, and galloped back to a village called Aartswoud accompanied by the infantry garrison of Opmeer. Daendels reported that he captured about twenty men and thirteen horses. The Batavians pressed on, clearing the fugitives out of Aartswoud and sending them scurrying for the shelter of the entrenchments behind the dyke.

It was now the turn of the Batavians to complain about the state of the roads. Daendels said their condition prevented him from getting his troops in position to attack the entrenchments at Aartswoud, and a village further to his left called Langereis, until three o'clock in the afternoon. Wishing to force the prince from these positions before nightfall, Daendels persevered with his attack; splitting his column into three, falling on the entrenchments with his right and attempting to storm the bridges at Langereis with his left and centre. Again he was impeded by the terrain. The British had begun to flood the area and had fortified the approaches to Langereis so the attacks in that sector could make no headway and were bloodily repulsed by 35th foot, commanded by Prince William.

The right had been fortified with a position created behind the dyke and artillery emplaced above it. However, with some difficulty, Daendels was able to bring up a howitzer to fire into the entrenchments and attack them with his infantry, who threw bridges over the canal. This, said Daendels, caused the positions to be 'abandoned with the utmost precipitation' but the fall of night and the failure of the attacks on Langereis prevented his pursuit. Prince William, however, seeing his position was now almost surrounded was compelled to retire allowing Daendels to capture Winkel. The abandonment of this post meant that the enemy now occupied the ground overlooking the right of the Anglo-Russian position, necessitating the inundation of the land east of Schagen.[5] There was further desultory skirmishing at outposts such as Haring's-Karspel, which changed hands twice, but the allies now restricted themselves to digging in and strengthening their defences.[6]

Resorting to inundation, the breaking down of dykes to flood the low-lying land, was a sure sign that York had all but given up. The Dutch lived in constant fear of flooding so to deliberately flood the country was an acknowledgement that there was no hope of counter-revolution. Grenville's fifth column had never materialized and the feelings of the local inhabitants were now subordinated to cold military necessity.

The army had returned to their position on the Zype Canal and York held a further conference of his generals to discuss the options that remained open to the expedition. Resuming the offensive looked out of the question so the alternatives were: remaining on the defensive on the Zype, transferring the theatre of operations to another part of the Netherlands or evacuating in the face of the enemy.[7]

The conclusion of the council of war was that there was no sense in continuing. With naval support, the army could have held the Zype position against attack almost indefinitely. However, they would need to be well supplied and they simply weren't. In the course of the government enquiry held after the expedition it emerged that, owing to a miscalculation by the commissary general, a large portion of the supplies allocated to the army had been kept on the ships.[8] This, sensibly, was to cover the possibility of overloaded troop transports being blown off course and having to spend any length of time at sea. Unfortunately these rations had been included in the calculation of the supplies required by the troops on land and so by 14 October the army had only around eleven days worth of rations remaining.[9] The country they were now defending had been exhausted by their previous occupation and this situation would not be improved by the suggested inundation. A huge quantity of flour had been purchased on the Elbe before the expedition sailed but there had been no sign of its appearance, and if the wind was against the convoy there was no telling when it would arrive. This clearly illustrated the difficulties inherent in supplying an army by sea on that coast.[10]

Efforts to fortify Helder town were redoubled, not to withstand an assault but to cover the re-embarkation of the army.[11] The council of war had decided that they must seek the permission of the government to re-embark and return to England, so Colonel Brownrigg was sent to London to present their opinions to the government. The following is taken from York's letter to the ministers:

'From the prisoners taken upon the 6th instant, I learnt the certainty of the enemy having been reinforced since the action of the 2nd by two Demi-Brigades, amounting to about six thousand infantry, and of their having strengthened the position of Beverwyk, and fortified strongly in the rear of it. Points which it would still be necessary to carry before Haerlem could be attacked.

'It ought also be stated, that the enemy had retired a large force upon Purmirind in an almost inaccessible position, covered by an inundated country, and the debouches from which were strongly fortified and in the hands of the enemy; and further, that as our army advanced this corps was placed in our rear.

'But such obstacles would have been overcome, had not the state of the weather, the ruined condition of the roads, and total want of necessary supplies arising from the above causes, presented difficulties which required the most serious consideration.'

The result of York's consideration was that, in consultation with Abercromby 'and the lieutenant-Generals of this army, I could not but consider (and their opinion was unanimous in this) that it would be for the benefit of the general cause to withdraw the troops from their advanced position, in order to await His Majesty's further instructions.'[12]

Abercromby also wrote to Dundas explaining the situation from his perspective:

'I do not imagine you have been for some time very sanguine in your hopes of our succeeding in the conquest of Holland. The grounds on which this great undertaking were founded have failed. We have found no co-operation in the country and the French have found the means of sending a powerful force to maintain their authority on the Batavian Republic.'

The old general highlighted the difficulties that had been experienced with supplying the troops through the Helder and stressed that he did not envisage this situation improving, even if the port of Haarlem were to be taken. He added that although the troops had performed well and 'maintained their national character', he felt that if they were to suffer a serious defeat 'I much doubt if their discipline would have been able to prevent a total dissolution of the army. This is a melancholy fact, and is the natural consequence of young soldiers and inexperienced officers, all powerful when they attack, but without resource if they are beaten.'

He was, he wrote, not alone in these opinions and had expressed them to the Duke of York: 'I scarcely believe there is a difference of opinion amongst us, and all those whose rank entitles them to be consulted are unanimous in approving the measures which have been taken since the affair of the 2nd.'[13]

The allied army in Switzerland had been completely defeated at Zurich on 2 October and just a fortnight later Brune received his first reinforcements from the Army of the Rhine. Not only did that mean the French were now free to turn their attention onto York's army but it also meant that another of the expedition's objectives, that of diverting resources from the southern front, was now also irrelevant. The army's sick and wounded, its women and the Orangist battalion on Texel were sent to England to reduce the number of mouths to feed.[14]

It was the lack of supplies that weighed most heavily upon York's mind though and it was this that made him decide to open negotiations with Brune, rather than await the ministry's decision. Even if leave to re-embark reached the Helder before the food ran out, the operation would be immensely risky. The engineers, Colonel Twiss and the one-legged Major Finlay, had expressed the opinion that the defences at Helder could not be maintained for more than three days in the face of concerted attack, which, if the winds were against them, would not give the fleet enough time to evacuate the army.[15] Lord Chatham, writing to his brother Pitt, estimated that such an evacuation would cost the army their rearguard (around 3,500 men) all their horses and most of their cannon.[16] Under such circumstances a negotiated capitulation seemed the most sensible option.

Major General Knox, who had played little part in the campaign up to this point, was selected to carry out the negotiations and was sent to Brune's headquarters on 15 October. After a few days of intense negotiation a deal was struck, whereby the Anglo-Russian forces would evacuate all Dutch territory by 30 November 'without committing any devastation, by inundations, cutting the dykes, or other ways injuring the sources of navigation.' As noted previously, this was a particular fear of the Dutch and had been raised as a threat during the negotiations. However, it was pretty toothless as the British lacked the will to carry it out and even whilst uttering the threat, York had written that 'the strongest sense of duty could alone induce us to adopt a system repugnant to the sentiments which have ever directed the conduct of the English nation.'[17]

Perhaps sensing York was bluffing, Brune imposed some fairly odious conditions on the British negotiator, which made it feel to many reading of the capitulation in London that this was a surrender rather than an armistice. One of these conditions was the return of 8,000 French and Batavian prisoners, captured during the campaign, from camps in England. Another was the restoration of the Dutch batteries at the Helder.[18] One of the campaign's chroniclers, Colonel Krayenhoff, was actually sent to oversee the handover of stores and magazines at the Helder and almost caused a diplomatic incident by his reaction to the condition in which they had been left.[19]

Despite the distasteful conditions, the armistice was agreed and was felt by most to be the best possible outcome. Lord Chatham wrote to his brother, the prime minister, that:

'I concurred entirely in opinion, with the other General Officers whom H.R.H. consulted, as to the feasibility of adopting this measure, which was become unavoidable, in order to save the army from imminent danger.

'The only thing, as it stands, which is painful, is the being obliged as the price of not being molested, to give up a certain number of French and Dutch prisoners now in England, as it carries with it, something more like a condition imposed. But when it is remembered that though we might threaten, we never could have brought ourselves, under any circumstances almost, to have cut the great dykes and destroyed the whole of North Holland, and that the loss of our rear guard of perhaps three or four thousand men, was inevitable without an agreement, I hope the measure taken however it may be lamented, cannot be disapproved.'[20]

Both sides were able to observe that there were no further defences created and the evacuation was carried out in a largely amicable atmosphere. This was only marred by the resumption of republican control over the towns liberated by Mitchell where, despite his threats of bombardment, members of the provisional regency were imprisoned. With little further incident the fleet finally departed on 20 November and the expedition returned to Britain to face its final battle.

Chapter 17

Opinions and Debate

The withdrawal of the army to their position on the Zype and the ending of the expedition had, as Lord Chatham predicted, caused some dismay and even outrage in England. Many commentators rushed to present their opinions on what had gone wrong or to simply point out the mission's flaws.

From his position on the army's staff, Bunbury reckoned that the Helder could have been held by a small part of the army while the remainder crossed the Zuider Zee and operated along the river Yssel around a town called Zwoll, where they could have threatened Arnhem, Utrecht or Amsterdam from the other side.[1] The naval commander Admiral Mitchell believed that the army had failed as they had shown too little initiative, remained concentrated and been too easily discouraged. He complained that his requests for troops to support his activities on the Zuider Zee were consistently rebuffed and as result he had long had 'doubts of success'. Mitchell thought that the campaign had begun to unravel the moment Abercromby was withdrawn from Hoorn and that he should instead have been reinforced. From this position, he believed that with the support of his squadron, Abercromby could have repelled any attempt to 'disturb' him and been ideally placed to fall on Amsterdam.[2] He was bitterly disappointed by the army's decision to retreat to the Zype and, even as they awaited instructions from London, had urged immediate action to widen the campaign, making a diversion in Friesland using the transports with the shallowest draft. Like Grenville, he thought if this failed, a further attempt should be made in the spring.[3] The historian and military theorist Baron Jomini joined the chorus of criticism; expanding upon Mitchell's view and saying that maritime expeditions would always fail if they acted with too much caution instead of pushing quickly inland before the enemy could organize their defences.[4]

Whilst some parts of the press merely moderated their previously triumphant tone, *The Evening Mail* confessed that it had always felt that the expedition's failure was inevitable. It expressed the conviction that 'the troops should be withdrawn, and the willing slaves of that country be left to their fates ... and the farther fruitless destruction of our brave and gallant countrymen be terminated.'[5] It was a view that held weight in many quarters.

Certainly the failure of the expedition was a gift for the opposition. In a House of Commons debate, MP Richard Sheridan proclaimed that: 'It was a humiliating thing, after such proud expectation, to fail in our design and to fail too amidst such an accumulation of disgrace.'[6] He called for an enquiry, describing the expedition as 'a waste of blood, and expense of treasure' adding that it had squandered one tenth of every man's income.[7]

They weren't even impressed by the capture of the Dutch fleet:

'I cannot conceive, that the corrupt and clandestine surrender of the Dutch fleet will be viewed as the attainment of our wishes. Yet I see, that the Lord Lieutenant tells the Irish Parliament, that the expedition to Holland will prevent the invasion of Ireland. He speaks as if the main object of our policy was not the deliverance of the Dutch from the yoke of France; not the restoration of the house of Orange to their right; not the protection of religion, or the defence of social order; but the capture of a few Dutch ships of war.'

The lack of intelligence was also picked up on pretty quickly:

'Were not all the circumstances which pointed out the certain conclusion, that the expedition could not be successful, known previous to the sailing of the Duke of York? If there was not a secret motive for persevering in the expedition, which no common understanding can suspect, why did not ministers profit by their experience to avoid further disaster? If they did know all the circumstances, they must stand convicted of a negligence no less criminal than the presumption of persisting after so many warnings to desist.'[8]

Certainly, these are charges that can be laid at the door of the political leadership of the expedition. Indeed Thomas Grenville was already plotting further intrigues, regarding the betrayal of the fortress of Delfzijl by its largely German garrison, as he waited at Emden for passage to the Helder on 7 October. This was despite his own admission that there had been no 'great convulsion' in favour of the Prince of Orange and that in fact there had been 'no movement … of any sort'.[9] This too came to nothing and even he came to understand that the Dutch would do nothing unless the British liberated the whole country:

> 'I see that no human means will make them move with any exertion attended with risk to their persons or property … if they would not stir till the whole business was done into their hands, there was no reason why they should stir afterwards. Such a wretched and lamentable want of all zeal and spirit, public or private, I could never have believed if I had not been an unwilling witness to it.'[10]

Despite this, he expressed the opinion (and indeed gave assurances to the Hereditary Prince of Orange) that the 'expedition will be resumed in the spring'![11]

With the many voices raised against the expedition, questions must be asked, such as whether there was ever any chance of success and if so, why did it fail? Certainly, many factors contributed to this costly and embarrassing debacle not least the choice of the Helder itself. This narrow peninsula was particularly detrimental to the successful conduct of military operations by an eighteenth-century army. The roads were terrible and the port was unsuitable for provisioning such a large force. Additionally, the weather was appalling throughout although, as Sheridan pointed out, this shouldn't have been much of a surprise (my own visit to the Helder in August 2015 was plagued by driving rain alternating with a penetrating drizzle).[12] However, it seems that Abercromby chose to land there as a last resort. It had been suggested by Dundas and all the other options seemed unworkable.

Whether a landing in the east of the country would have been any more successful is debatable but once the decision was made to move methodically through the Helder with an inexperienced army and without any significant assistance from the local populace, failure became almost inevitable. The capture of the Dutch fleet was significant and went some way to compensate for the military shortcomings of the expedition but was not ever considered the principal target. The Dutch people's apparent lack of interest in being liberated undermined the whole basis on which the expedition was conceived. Grenville's strategic aim of distracting French reinforcements from the fighting in Switzerland also became irrelevant when the Austro-Russian forces were defeated at Zurich. Although this does not seem to have featured in the decision to withdraw from the Helder, the fact that the expedition was now the sole focus of the French military effort meant that its days were numbered.

Many laid the blame at the door of the Russians. Perhaps the majority view amongst British observers was that 'during the campaign we should have been better without them' but there could have been no expedition in that case, as Britain was in no position to furnish another 17,000 troops from its meagre resources.[13] Certainly, their part in the campaign caused a great deal of controversy and their performance fell well below expectations. Abercromby believed that 'I have been cautious about blaming the Russians. I must however, acknowledge that I have seen nothing to admire.'[14] They were, it seems, a blunt instrument and York was unable to get the best out of them, largely as a result of his inability to interact with them on a diplomatic level, which was in part his fault. Whilst it could be said that the Russians ensured the attack on Bergen was not a success and they precipitated the Battle of Castricum, they cannot be considered a principal cause of the expedition's failure.

The British Army was absolved of all blame by its commanders, the press and parliament (and even Sheridan) but whilst the conjuring of this force into existence was near miraculous its performance also left something to be desired. Those who praised them did so in the knowledge (and with the proviso) that these were raw troops, barely trained and completely inexperienced. Even though the same could be said of much of the opposition, their performance should be seen in this light. It would have been hard to have done anything else with these troops without putting the whole army in danger of disintegration. Unlike the French, whose ability to raise enormous forces on an annual basis enabled them to be a little reckless with their armies, this was the only one that Britain had and, as Chatham pointed out to his brother, it was the duty of its commander to preserve it.[15]

If the army were not to blame, then what of the Royal Navy? The Netherlands has a long coastline and after the surrender of the Dutch fleet the navy had complete superiority on the sea. They had made their presence felt strongly during the landing but after that they co-operated very little with the army. The Dutch engineer Colonel Krayenhoff, who had been in charge of building the defences at Amsterdam, expressed the view in his history of the campaign, that the navy had missed an opportunity in not attacking Amsterdam when it was almost defenceless immediately after the surrender of the fleet.[16] However, once again they cannot really be blamed. The ministry had issued no instructions to help them in supporting the expedition and they were unaware of the vulnerability of Amsterdam from the Zuider Zee. The waters around the coast were shallow so they could not support the army directly once they moved inland beyond the use of shallow draft vessels and gunboats, which were in fact deployed later in the campaign. There were some minor successes scored by the small ships on the Zuider Zee and by Popham's gunboats supporting the army on the canals.[17] However, beyond this there was little that could have been achieved without detaching troops for marine operations, which would have weakened the army and perhaps ensured that no decisive engagement would have been possible on land.[18] So the lack of co-operation in this matter may also be discounted as anything beyond incidental.

Before leaving this discussion, there is one factor that comes up again and again in accounts of the campaign and it is the attitude of the Dutch. Certainly, the expedition was planned badly and in haste, as Grenville sought to co-ordinate Britain's efforts with those of Austria and Russia in order to have a decisive influence upon events. Yet all of his strategies counted on the co-operation of the Dutch. The majority of the intelligence he received in the two years prior to the expedition told him that the Dutch chafed under French yoke and would need restraining once the allied army landed, such would be their enthusiasm to overthrow the Batavian regime. The minister's unshakable belief that the expedition was going to be a walkover was such that they were already making plans for the subsequent deployment of York's army before it had even sailed. This arrogant presumption overshadowed every part of the expedition's conception, overriding all other considerations.[19] The failure of the Dutch to rise had been anticipated by some, certainly as a possibility, before the expedition sailed but no allowance was made for this contingency.[20] A great deal of rhetoric was expended on the justice of the cause and the certainty that the Dutch people supported it, but no one thought to independently verify their opinion. 'What manifestation,' asked Sheridan, 'had been given of the disposition of the people of Holland?'[21] Such reliance was placed upon their support for the House of Orange that the lukewarm reception of their liberators and the robust defence of the Batavian Republic by their army must be considered a significant factor in the failure of the campaign.

In the final analysis it must be said that the lion's share of blame for the expedition's failure lies with the ministry. The conception and planning of the entire operation was entrusted to this small elite, who lacked knowledge of military matters and had learnt little from their experience of planning operations in the previous six years. A spirit of amateurishness and a naively optimistic belief in the operation's chances permeated the whole process. As Sheridan caustically pointed out in parliament: 'In proportion, however as the chief object was wise and good, must be the criminality of those whose misconduct its failure is to be attributed ... gross negligence, their ignorance, and their presumption.'[22]

A Mr Taylor rounded off a House of Commons debate on the campaign by expressing his hope that 'parliament would inquire into the miscarriage of an enterprise upon which so much of the blood and treasure of the nation had been expended to no effect.' But he was to be disappointed.[23] Parliament preferred to let the matter rest and the Dutch people who had failed to stir themselves in favour of the House of Orange would remain under French domination for another 14 years. The Duke of York would never command an army in the field again but his army would go on to become one of the most celebrated and successful forces to ever fight under the British flag.

Notes

Introduction

1. Introduction: S. Schama, *Patriots and Liberators: Revolution in the Netherlands 1780–1813* (London: Harper Perennial, 2005 [1977]), p.46.
2. Schama, *Patriots*, p.64.
3. Schama, *Patriots*, p.46.
4. Schama, Patriots, p.203 and P. Mackesy, *The Strategy of Overthrow 1798–1799* (London: Longman, 1974), p.128.
5. H. Bunbury, *Narratives of Some Passages in the Great War with France, from 1799–1810* (London: Richard Bentley, 1854), p.xxii.

Chapter 1

1. J. Ehrman, *The Younger Pitt, The Consuming Struggle* (London; Constable, 1996), p.3–5; T. Pakenham, *The Year of Liberty, The Great Irish Rebellion of 1798* (London: Weidenfeld & Nicolson 1997 [1969]), p.107 & p.295–97; Mackesy, *Strategy*, p.5; H. Baring, *The Diary of the Right Hon. William Windham 1784–1810* (London: Longmans Green & Co, 1866), p.401; Anon., *British Minor Expeditions 1746 to 1814: Compiled in the Intelligence Branch of the Quartermaster-Generals Department* (London: HMSO, 1884), p.27–31.
2. Mackesy, *Strategy*, p.30.
3. Mackesy, *Strategy*, p.33–4; A. Alison, *History of Europe from the Commencement of the French Revolution in MDCCLXXXIX to the Restoration of the Bourbons in MDCCCXV* (Edinburgh: William Blackwood, 1854), Vol. IV, p.33 & 218.
4. Mackesy, *Strategy*, p.35.
5. Baring, *Diary*, p.401.
6. Alison, *History*, p.219.
7. Mackesy, *Strategy*, p.36.
8. Schama, *Patriots*, p.347–53.
9. Ehrman, *Pitt*, p.157.
10. Mackesy, *Strategy*, p.44 & 47.
11. W. Fitzpatrick, *Report on the Manuscripts of J.B. Fortescue Esq., preserved at Dropmore, Historical Manuscripts Commission, vol. V* (London: HMSO, 1905), *Introduction*, p.v.
12. Mackesy, *Strategy*, p.54; Captain J. Wallis to Vice Admiral Dickson, Newark Island, 18 February 1799, in I. Schomberg, *Naval Chronology: Or An Historical Summary of Naval and Maritime Events, Vol. III* (London: T. Egerton, 18020 p.187); Duke of Portland to Marquess of Buckingham, 21 March 1799, HO 42/46/172, f 357.
13. Anon., *A Collection of State Papers relative to the War against France, VOL. VIII* (London: Debrett, 1800), p.i–iii.
14. Blanning, *The French Revolutionary Wars 1787–1802* (London: Hodder, 1996), p.231.
15. Thomas Grenville to Lord Grenville, 10 April 1799, Fitzpatrick, *Dropmore*, p.7.

16. Alison, *History*, p.218; the programme of restructuring had been entrusted to Archduke Charles, the Emperor's brother, who took a somewhat pessimistic view of his task. He warned the emperor, Francis, that if war broke out before the reforms were complete 'the army will be in disarray and there will be disaster'; G. Rothenberg, Napoleon's Great Adversary, Archduke Charles and the Austrian Army – 1814 (Staplehurst: Spellmount, 1995), p.66.

17. Mackesy, *Strategy*, p.55; Alison, *History*, p.141.

18. Blanning, *Revolutionary Wars*, p.231.

19. Blanning, *Revolutionary Wars*, p.234; Lord Grenville to Thomas Grenville, 12 April 1799, Fitzpatrick, *Dropmore*, p.10.

20. Lord Grenville to Thomas Grenville, 17 May 1799, Fitzpatrick, *Dropmore*, p.55.

21. Alison, *History*, p.221.

22. Anonymous account of the attack by a French survivor, 29 April 1799, Fitzpatrick, *Dropmore*, p.47.

23. Lord Grenville to Thomas Grenville, 18 April 1799, Fitzpatrick, *Dropmore*, p.14.

24. Blanning, *Revolutionary Wars*, p.238–48.

25. *The Convention between his Britannic Majesty and the Emperor of all the Russias, signed at St. Petersburgh 22nd (11th) of June 1799* in; Anon., *A Collection of State Papers relative to the War against France, VOL. VIII* (London: Debrett, 1800), p.x-xii & Schomberg, *Naval Chronology*, p.224; see Appendix 1 for summary of main clauses.

26. H. Weil, *Le Général De Stamford, D'Aprés sa Correspondence Inédite 1793–1806* (Paris: Payot & Co, 1923), p.14–5; Thomas Grenville to Captain Home Popham, 19 May 1799, Fitzpatrick, *Dropmore*, p.58.

Chapter 2

1. Thomas Grenville to Lord Grenville, 10 April 1799, Fitzpatrick, *Dropmore*, p.8.

2. Charles Bentinck to Hammond, 11 December 1798, H. Colenbrander, *Gedenstukken Der Algemeene Geschiedenis VanNederland, Van 1795 Tot 1840* (The Hague: Rijks Geschiedkundige Publicatien, 1905, p.356.

3. Charles Bentinck to Hammond, 12 May 1799, Colenbrander, *Gedenkstukken*, p.364 & 368.

4. Various reports reproduced in Fitzpatrick, *Dropmore*, p.15–16, 36, 51 & 53–4.

5. Thomas Grenville to Lord Grenville, 27 May & 14 June 1799, Fitzpatrick, *Dropmore*, p.67& 92.

6. Thomas Grenville to Lord Grenville, 14 June 1799, Fitzpatrick, *Dropmore*, p.92.

7. Lord Grenville to Dundas, 30 July 1799, Fitzpatrick, *Dropmore*, p.208.

8. Thomas Grenville to Lord Grenville, Fitzpatrick, *Dropmore*, p.93.

9. Intelligence Report, *Dropmore*, p.169; Thomas Grenville to Lord Grenville, 10 April 1799, *Dropmore V*, p.4.

10. Weil, *Le Général De Stamford*, p.14–5; Thomas Grenville to Captain Popham, 19 May 1799, *Dropmore V*, p.58.

11. General De Stamford to Thomas Grenville, 18 June 1799, Fitzpatrick, *Dropmore*, p.96.

12. Thomas Grenville to Lord Grenville, 21 May 1799, Fitzpatrick, *Dropmore*, p.60–1.

13. Thomas Grenville to Lord Grenville, 20 June, 22 July & 6 August 1799, p.100, 174 & 248.

14. Mackesy, *Strategy*, p.93.

15. Anon., '*Recollections of the British Army, in the Early Campaigns of the Revolutionary War*', Journal of the Royal United Services Institute, 1836, Part 1, p.181.

16. Bunbury, *Narratives*, p.xviii-xx; H. Verney, *The Journals and Correspondence of General Sir Harry Calvert* (Hurst & Blackett, 1853), p.67

17. Ehrman, *Pitt*, p.224; A. Subaltern, *The Campaign in Holland 1799: The British-Russian Expedition against the Gallo-Batavian Forces in the Low Counties* (London: W. Mitchell), p.101.
18. The Duke of York took the unusual step of having all the militia recruits on Braham Downs medically examined to determine their fitness to serve; Calvert to Grey, 26 August 1799, *Grey Papers*, GRE/A 1965/1.
19. J. Fortescue, *A History of the British Army: Volume 4* (London: MacMillan, 1906), p.642.
20. Bunbury, *Narratives*, p.39.
21. William Windham to Lord Grenville, 10 August 1799 & Lord Grenville to Thomas Grenville, 3 June 1799, *Dropmore*, p.271& p.79.
22. Lord Grenville to Thomas Grenville, 19 July 1799, Fitzpatrick, *Dropmore*, p.161.
23. Lord Grenville to Thomas Grenville, 26 June 1799, Fitzpatrick, *Dropmore*, p.108; for the difficulties in transporting the expeditions' supplies see; R. Sutcliffe, *British Expeditionary Warfare and the Defeat of Napoleon 1793–1815* (Woodbridge: Boydell Press, 2016), p.65.
24. Captain Popham to Lord Spencer, 20 June 1799, Richmond, H. *Private Papers of George, Second Earl Spencer, First Lord of the Admiralty 1794–1801, Vol. III* (London: Navy Records Society, 1924, p.139.
25. Henry Dundas to King George III, 10 July 1799, A. Aspinall, *The Later Correspondence of George III, Vol. III 1798–1801* (Cambridge: University Press, 1967), p.225.
26. R. Abercromby, *Note on British Expedition to Holland 6 July 1799*, Fitzpatrick, *Dropmore*, p.128–29.
27. Abercromby, *British Expedition, Dropmore V,* p.128–29; Abercromby to Lord Grenville 21 July 1799, *Dropmore V*, p.165.
28. Minutes of a Conversation at Canterbury, 6 August 1799, *Spencer Papers*, p.150–52.
29. Lord Grenville to Thomas Grenville, 1 July 1799, Fitzpatrick, *Dropmore*, p.114.
30. Abercromby to Dundas, 21 June 1799, Richmond, *Spencer Papers*, p.140–41.
31. C. Duffy, *Eagles over the Alps: Suvarov in Italy & Switzerland 1799* (Chicago: Emperors Press, 1999), p.129–30; Mackesy, *Strategy*, p.165–64; Popham to Spencer, 20 June 1799, Richmond, *Spencer Papers*, p.139.
32. Lord Grenville to Thomas Grenville, 6 August 1799, Fitzpatrick, *Dropmore*, p.247.
33. Pitt to Grenville, 2 August 1799 & Lord Grenville to Thomas Grenville, 6 August 1799, Fitzpatrick, *Dropmore*, p.224 & 247.
34. Dundas to Abercromby, 10 August 1799, Fitzpatrick, *Dropmore*, p.275.
35. Alexander Hope to Abercromby, (National Records of Scotland) GD364/1/1092.
36. Thomas Grenville to Lord Grenville, 16 June 1799, Fitzpatrick, *Dropmore*, p.96.
37. *The London Chronicle*, 5 August 1799, p.122; 10 August 1799, p.141; 12 August 1799, p.245; 15 August 1799, p.158.
38. Richard Sheridan MP to the House of Commons, 10 February 1800, W.Cobbett, *The Parliamentary History of England from the Earliest Times to the Year 1803* (London: Hansard, 1819), p.1398.

Chapter 3
1. Alison, *History*, p.235; J. Dunfermline, *Lieutenant-General Sir Ralph Abercromby, K.B., 1793–1801* (Edinburgh: Edmonston & Douglas, 1861), p.18–9.
2. Dunfermline, *Abercromby*, p.55–8 & 94.
3. A. Burne, *The Noble Duke of York* (London: Staples Press, 1949), p.271.
4. Mackesy, *Strategy*, p.137.
5. Bunbury, *Narratives*, p.45.

6. Fortescue, *British Army*, p.665, Rodger, *Second Coalition*, p.178, Mackesy, *Strategy*, p.138.
7. Schama, *Patriots*, p.395.
8. Bunbury, *Narratives*, p.44; Mackesy, *Strategy*, p.244; R. Phipps, *The Armies of the First French Republic and the Rise of the Marshals of Napoleon I: Volume V* (Pickle Partners, 2011[1939]), p.198; A. Rodger, *The War of The Second Coalition 1798–1801, A Strategic Commentary* (Oxford, 1964), p.186; Fortescue, *British Army*, p.665.
9. Burne, *Noble Duke*, p.265.
10. Bunbury, *Narratives*, pp.23, 33.
11. F. York, *Plain Statement of the Conduct of the Ministry and the Opposition towards His Royal Highness The Duke of York* (B. McMillan, 1808), p.11.
12. Mackesy, *Strategy;* p.314, Bunbury, *Narratives*, p.44; Fortescue, *British Army*, p.665; Cobbett, *Parliamentary History*, p.1404
13. Abercromby to Dundas, 28 August 1799, Fitzpatrick, *Dropmore*, p.333.
14. Bunbury, *Narratives*, p.46–7.
15. Bunbury, *Narratives*, p.45.
16. Abercromby to Dundas, 28 August 1799, Fitzpatrick, *Dropmore*, p.333; J. Maurice, *The Diary of Sir John Moore, Volume 1* (London: Edward Arnold, 1904, p.354, 357 & 358.
17. The appointment of lieutenant colonels Sharpe and Baylis to command these formations occasioned a complaint from an officer who thought he was better suited but the army's commanders felt they were the right men for the task; Brownrigg to Grey, 30 August 1799, *Grey Papers*, GRE/A1984/2.
18. Dunfermline, *Abercromby*, p173.
19. W. Surtees, *Twenty-Five Years in the Rifle Brigade* (Greenhill, 1996 [1833]), p.7.
20. Surtees, *Twenty-Five Years* p.21.
21. Abercromby to Dundas, 4 September 1799, Fitzpatrick, *Dropmore*, p.358.
22. Hope to Abercromby, Report 2 September 1799, SNA GD364/1/1092-54.
23. Anon., *Recollections*, p.188.
24. Anon., *Recollections*, p.325.
25. Hope to Commander in Chief, Reports, GD 364/1/1092-107,112,113,129.
26. Abercromby to Dundas, 11 September 1799, in Aspinall, *Correspondence*, p.265.
27. Charles Grey of Norfolk, Howick MSS. In Aspinall, *Correspondence*, p.293.
28. Dispatch from FM HRH Duke of York quoted in: *The Field of Mars; being an alphabetical digestion of the principle Naval and Military engagements in Europe, Asia, Africa, and America from the ninth century to the Peace of 1801* (G&J Robinson, London, 1801), p.682.
29. F. Walsh, *A Narrative of the Expedition to Holland, in the autumn of the year 1799* (Memphis: General Books, 2010 [1800]), p.25; Surtees, *Twenty-Five Years*, p.8–9; Anon., *Recollections*, p.189 – Recalls that the French referred to the Russians as cornichons (gherkins) because of their long green coats.
30. Dunfermline, *Abercromby*, p.204.
31. D. Milyutin, *Istoriia Voini Rossii s Frantsiei v 1799, Tome II* (St Petersburg, 1857), p.379; Anon., *Recollections*, p.189.
32. Major John Finlay to his wife, 22 & 24 September 1799, quoted in A. Wace, (ed.) *A British Officer on Active Service, 1799* (The Annual of the British School at Athens, Vol.23, 1919), p.134; Anon., *Recollections*, p.189.
33. Walsh, *Narrative*, p.25.
34. Alison, *History*, p.288.
35. C. Krayenhoff, *Geschiedkundige Beschouwingvan den Oorlong op het Grondgebied der Bataafsche Republiek in 1799* (Vieweg en Zoon, 1832), p.180.

36. Anon., *Recollections*, p.189.
37. York to Dundas, 20 September 1799, Fitzpatrick, *Dropmore*, p.416.
38. A. Mikaberidze, *The Russian Officer Corps in the Revolutionary and Napoleonic wars, 1792–1815* (New York: Savas Beattie, 2005), p.153.
39. Mackesy, *Strategy*, p.243.
40. Burne, *Noble Duke*, p.266.
41. Milyutin, *Istoriia*, p.392–95; Maurice, *Moore*, p.353.
42. Mikaberidze, *Russian Officer Corps*, p.100.
43. Phipps, *Armies*, p.199.
44. Bunbury, *Narratives*, p.23.
45. Mackesy, *Strategy*, p.280.
46. Maurice, *Moore*, p.353.
47. Milyutin, *Istoriia* p.380, complains that the British did not honour their agreement; Hope to Knox, 25 September 1799, NAS GD364/1/1092/116, discusses allocating horses intended for the Russians to the British artillery.

Chapter 4
1. Thomas Grenville to Lord Grenville, Berlin, June 14 1799 – Fitzpatrick, *Dropmore*, p.92
2. G. Street and K. Van Overmeire, *Dutch Troops of the French Revolutionary & Napoleonic Wars 1793–1810* (Newthorpe: Partisan Press, 2014), p.87; Charles Bentinck to Hammond, 12 May 1799, Colenbrander, *Gedenkstukken*, p.364; Mackesy, *Strategy* p.190.
3. Intelligence Report, July 1799, Fitzpatrick, *Dropmore*, p.170.
4. Street and Overmeire, *Dutch Troops*, p.114; G. Van Uythoven, *Voorwaats, Bataven! De Engels-Russische invasie van 1799* (Zaltbommel: Europese Bibliotheek, 1999), p.168; Dumonceau to Daendels, 26 October 1798, Colenbrander, *Gedenkstukken*, p.480–82.
5. Mackesy, *Strategy*, p.191.
6. Schama, *Patriots*, p.391; Street and Overmeire, *Dutch Troops*, p.13.
7. Abercromby to Dundas, 28 August 1799, Dunfermline, *Abercromby*, p173.
8. See Phipps, *Armies*, p.204, 256, 286 & P. Griffith, *The Art of War of Revolutionary France 1789–1802* (London: Greenhill, 1998), p.183.
9. Abercromby to Dundas, 11 September 1799, Fitzpatrick, *Dropmore*, p.387; Hereditary Prince of Orange to Abercromby, 9 September 1799, Colenbrander, *Gedenstukken*, p.396.
10. Rodger, *Second Coalition*, p.184; Mackesy, *Strategy*, p.191; A. Shepperd, 'The Patagonian'; *Brune*, in D. Chandler (ed.) *Napoleon's Marshals* (Cassell, 2000 [1987]), p.80–5.
11. Intelligence Report, July 1799, Fitzpatrick, *Dropmore*, p.171.
12. Shepperd, *Patagonian*, p.9.
13. Phipps, *Armies*, p.203.
14. Shepperd, *Patagonian*, p.89.
15. Burne, *Noble Duke*, p.277; Maurice, *Moore*, p.358.
16. Phipps, *Armies*, p.208.
17. Secret Report from France, Fitzpatrick, *Dropmore*, p.142–3.
18. Alison, *History*, p.287.
19. Bunbury, *Narratives*, p.27.
20. Anon., *Recollections*, p.187.
21. Intelligence Report, July 1799, Fitzpatrick, *Dropmore*, p.171.
22. Secret Report from France, Fitzpatrick, *Dropmore*, p.142–3.
23. Surtees, *Twenty-Five Years*, p.17.

24. Griffith, *Art of War*, p.207–14; J. Lynne, *The Bayonets of the Republic: Motivation and Tactics in the Army of Revolutionary France1791–1794* (Westview, 1996 [1984]), p.265–77; G. Duhesme, *Essai sur L'Infanterie Légere* (Paris: Michaud, 1814), p.13–14 & 109.

25. Maurice, *Moore*, p.347.

26. Mackesy, *Strategy*, p.290.

27. Anon., *Recollections*, p.187.

28. P.Mackesy, *British Victory in Egypt, The End of Napoleons' Conquest* (London: Tauris Parke 2010 [1995]), p.149.

29. Phipps, *Armies*, p.204.

30. Griffith, *Art of War*, p.81; A. Forrest, *Soldiers of the French Revolution* (Duke, 1990), p.82–83.

Chapter 5

1. Dundas to Abercromby, 10 August 1799, Fitzpatrick, *Dropmore*, p.273–5; Dundas gives Abercromby a whole list of possible targets but concludes that 'I do not wish to exclude the exercise of your own discretion.'

2. Abercromby to Vice Admiral Mitchell, 14 August 1799, *Spencer Papers*, p.163–64.

3. See Edward Walsh's detailed description: Walsh, *Narrative*, p.14–15 & That of what appears to be a veteran of the 1787 Prussian invasion, reproduced in *The London Chronicle*, 17–19 September 1799, p.294.

4. Alison, *History, p.285.*

5. Mackesy, *Strategy*, p.189.

6. Daendels, p.432 & 434.

7. F. Maule, *Memoirs of the Principal Events in the Campaigns of Holland and Egypt* (London: F.C & J Rivington, 1816), p.3.

8. C. Gardyne *The Life of a Regiment; The History of the Gordon Highlanders from its Formation in 1794 to 1816* (The Medici Society, 1929), p.53.

9. Walsh, *Narrative*, p.15, Maule, *Memoirs*, p.3, Admiral Mitchell also spoke of the arrangements in his report to his superior, Admiral Duncan, dated 29 August 1799 reproduced in Robinson, *Field of Mars*, p.677.

10. Walsh, *Narrative*, p.15; Maurice, *Moore*, p.341–342.

11. Mackesy, *Strategy*, p.196; Anon., *The History of the Campaign of 1799 in Holland, Translated from the French, Vol.V* (London: J. Barfield, 1801), p.69,437 &.446; Bunbury, *Narratives*, p.3 &p.55; M. Dumas, *Précis des énévemens Militaires ou Essais Historiques sur les Campagnes 1799 à 1814, Tome Premier* (Paris: Treuttel & Wurtz, 1817), p.367.

12. Maurice, *Moore*, p.341–342.

13. Maule, *Memoirs*, p.3 and Anon., *Narrative of a Private Soldier in His Majesty's 92nd Regiment of Foot* (Uckfield: Naval & Military Press, 1820), p.36.

14. C. Atkinson, 'The Expedition to Holland in 1799, From the Journal of Lord Dalhousie', Journal of the Society for Army Historical Research, 1958, Vol.XXXVI. No 147, p.100.

15. Mackesy, *Strategy*, p.197.

16. Atkinson, *Dalhousie Journal*, p.101, Brune's ADC reports that they ran off in complete disorder but that is contradicted by Dalhousie's account; Anon., *Mémoires Historiques sur la Campagne du* Général Brune en Batavie, Du 5 Fructidor an7, au 9 Frimaire an 8; Rédigés par un Officier se son état-major (Paris: Favre, 1802), p.10.

17. H. Daendels, *Report of the operations of the division of Lieutenant General Daendels from 22nd August to the Capitulation of the English & Russians on the 18th October 1799*, As an appendix of: Anon., *History*, p.441 (sometimes this officer is referred to as Colonel Luckner).

18. Anon., *Mémoires Historiques*, p.7.
19. Daendels, *Report* p.439.
20. Maule, *Memoirs*. p.4.
21. Dalhousie, *Journal*, p.100.
22. Anon., *Mémoires Historiques*, p.7.
23. Daendels, *Report*, p.144.
24. Anon., *Mémoires Historiques*, p.11; Daendels, *Report*, p.442.
25. Mackesy, *Strategy*, p.198; Maurice, *Moore*, p.342.
26. Atkinson, *Dalhousie Journal*, P.101.
27. Maule, *Memoirs*, p.6.
28. Daendels, *Report*, p.444.
29. See footnotes to Daendels, *Report*, p.444..
30. Maule, *Memoirs*, p.7; Anon., *Mémoires Historiques*, p.11, Daendels, *Report*, p.444.
31. Anon., *Mémoires Historiques*, p.12; Daendels, *Report*, p.445.
32. Walsh, *Narrative*, p.16.
33. Daendels, *Report*, p.445; A dispatch from Abercromby, 28 August 1799, reproduced in Robinson, *Field of Mars*, p.675–676; Atkinson, *Dalhousie Journal*, p.101.
34. Daendels, *Report*, p.445.
35. Maule, *Memoirs*, p.6; Daendels, *Report*, p.446.
36. Atkinson, *Dalhousie Journal*, p.101.
37. Walsh, *Narrative*, p.16.
38. Dispatch from Abercromby, 28 August 1799, reproduced in Robinson, *Field of Mars*, p.676.
39. Daendels, *Report*, p.446.
40. Anon., *Private Soldier in the 92nd*, p.36.
41. Maurice, *Moore*, p.342.
42. Anon., *Private Soldier in the 92nd*, p.38.
43. Maurice, *Moore*, p.342; Anon., *Private Soldier in the 92nd*, p.38.
44. Abercromby to Dundas, 28 August 1799, Dunfermline, *Abercromby*, p173.

Chapter 6

1. Chapter 6: Abercromby to Mitchell, 14 August 1799, Richmond, *Spencer Papers*, p.163.
2. T. Roodhuyzen, *In woelig vaarwater: marineofficieren in de jaren 1779–1802* (Amsterdam: Bataafsche Leew, 1998) p.164.
3. Duncan to Spencer, His Britannic Majesty's *Kent*, Texel, 25 July 1799, Richmond, *Spencer Papers*, p.144.
4. Colenbrander, *Gedenkstukken*, p.343.
5. Thomas Grenville to Lord Grenville, Berlin, 14 June 1799, Fitzpatrick, *Dropmore*, p.92.
6. Lord Grenville to the Lords of the Admiralty, Most secret, 25 June 1799, Fitzpatrick, *Dropmore*, p.101–102.
7. Duncan to Storey, the *Kent*, 20 August 1799, reproduced in Schomberg, *Naval Chronology*, p.225.
8. Story to Duncan, 22 August 1799, reproduced in Schomberg, *Naval Chronology*, p229.
9. Extract from the Register of the Deliberations of the Executive Directory of the Batavian Republic 23 August 1799, reproduced in Schomberg, *Naval Chronology*, p230.
10. Maurice, *Moore*, p.343.
11. Bunbury, *Narratives*, p.5.
12. Vice Admiral Mitchell to the Admiralty, 31 August 1799, reproduced in Robinson, *Field of Mars*, p.671.

13. Mitchell to Admiral Story, Isis, *under sail, in line of battle*, 30 August 1799, reproduced in Walsh, *Narrative*, p.53.
14. Rear Admiral Story to the minister of marine of the Batavian Republic, 31 August 1799, Walsh, *Narrative*, p.85.
15. T. Roodhuyzen, *In woelig vaarwater*, p.166; J. De Jonge, *Geschiedenis van het Nederlandsche zeewezeni* (Haarlem: A.C. Kruseman, 1862), p.470, Story to the minister, Walsh, *Narrative*, p.86.
16. De Jonge, *Geschiedenis*, p.474.
17. Story to the minister, Walsh, *Narrative*, p.86; De Jonge, *Geschiedenis*,p.478.
18. Maitland to Dundas, 9 September 1799, Colenbrander, *Gedenstukken*, p.393.
19. Admiral Story to Vice Admiral Mitchell, the *Washington*, anchored under the Vlieter, 30 August 1799, reproduced in Robinson, *Field of Mars*, p.674.
20. Richmond, *Spencer Papers*, p.184.
21. Vice Admiral Mitchell to the Admiralty, 31 August 1799, reproduced in Robinson, *Field of Mars*, p.674.
22. Vice Admiral Mitchell to the Admiralty, 31 August 1799, reproduced in Robinson, *Field of Mars*, p.671.
23. George III to Earl Spencer (First Lord of the Admiralty), 4 September 1799, Richmond, Spencer Papers, p.182.
24. De Jonge, *Geschiedenis*, p.478.
25. Sheridan to the House of Commons, 10 February 1800, in Cobbett, *Parliamentary History*, p.1398; Maurice, *Moore*, p.351; Bunbury, *Narratives*, p.6.

Chapter 7
1. Abercromby to Dundas, 28 August 1799, Fitzpatrick, *Dropmore*, p.33.
2. Walsh, *Narrative*, p.19.
3. A. Jomini, *Histoire Critique et Militaire des Guerres de la Revolution: Campagne de 1799* (Memphis: General Books, 2012 [1820]), p.41.
4. Rodger, *Second Coalition*, p.186 – claims that Abercromby could have been in Amsterdam within 48 hours.
5. Fitzpatrick, *Dropmore*, p.333.
6. Charles Bentinck to Hammond, 12 May 1799, Colenbrander, Gedenkstukken, p.368; General Stamford to Thomas Grenville 26 July 1799, Fitzpatrick, *Dropmore*, p.197.
7. Proclamations of General Abercromby, The Prince of Orange & the Hereditary Prince of Orange, in Walsh, *Narrative*, p.87–90.
8. Walsh, *Narrative*, p.20.
9. Abercromby to Dundas, 28 August 1799, Fitzpatrick, *Dropmore*, p.333; – Abercromby mentions that a number of former Dutch officers are with him and that he is being advised by Baron de Heerdt.
10. Fitzpatrick, *Dropmore*, p.333.
11. Dundas to Pitt, 28 August 1799, Aspinall, *Correspondence*, p.247.
12. Daendels, *Report*, p.455; Don to Huskisson, 4 September 1799, Fitzpatrick, *Dropmore*, p.357.
13. Dumas, *Précis*, p.380; Schama, *Patriots*, p.394.
14. Dumas, *Précis*, p.380–83; Schama, *Patriots*, p.394.
15. Abercromby to Dundas, 11 September 1799, Fitzpatrick, *Dropmore*, p.387.
16. Mackesy, *Strategy*, p.207.
17. G. Van Setten, *Freule Van Dorth*, Digital Vroulexicon van Nederland URL: http//resources. huygens.knaw.nl (consulted 21 November 2016).

18. *The London Chronicle*, 26 September 1799, p.309 (At the second reading a Mr Nicholls even raised objections to the continuation of the war).

19. Walsh, *Narrative*, p.20; Atkinson, *Dalhousie Journal*, p.102.

20. J. Finlay to H. Finlay, 29 August 1799, Wace, *British Officer*, p.131.

21. Abercromby to Dundas, 4 September 1799, Fitzpatrick, *Dropmore*, p.358.

22. J. Fortescue, *A History of the British Army: Volume IV Maps* (Naval & Military Press, 2004 [1906]), #21.

23. Maurice, *Moore*, p.344; Walsh, *Narrative*, p.22.

24. Maurice, *Moore*, p.344.

25. Maurice, *Moore*, p.345.

26. Mackesy, *Strategy*, p.206; He also feared that the weather would prevent the Russians from joining him and that he would have to rely on contingents of militia volunteers from Barham Downs as his sole source of manpower – Abercromby to Dundas, 18 August 1799, Fitzpatrick, *Dropmore*, p.297.

27. Atkinson, *Dalhousie Journal*, p.103; Walsh, *Narrative*, p.22; Abercromby to Dundas, 4 September 1799, p.358

28. Abercromby to Huskisson, 11 September 1799, Fitzpatrick, *Dropmore*, p.388.

29. Daendels, *Report*, p.452.

30. Maurice, *Moore*, p.345.

31. Abercromby to Dundas, 4 September 1799, Fitzpatrick, *Dropmore*, p.357–58.

Chapter 8

1. Fortescue, *British Army*, p.661; Dumas, *Précis*, p.382; Maurice, *Moore*, p.344.

2. Anon., *Mémoires Historiques*, p.16.

3. Daendels, *Report*, p.456.

4. Anon., *Mémoires Historiques*, p.24.

5. Phipps, *Armies*, p.199.

6. Fortescue, *British Army*, p.663; Daendels, *Report*, p.457; Anon., *Mémoires Historiques*, p.20.

7. Gardyne, *Gordon Highlanders*, p.54; Dalhousie likewise reports that his picquet of sixty men, four subalterns and captain 'stood to' daily just before dawn, Atkinson, *Dalhousie Journal*, p.103.

8. Daendels, *Report*, p.457.

9. Maurice, *Moore*, p.347.

10. Mackesy, *Strategy*, p.217.

11. Maurice, *Moore*, p.347.

12. Daendels, *Report*, p.457.

13. Abercromby to Dundas, 11 September 1799, Fitzpatrick, *Dropmore*, p.385; Subaltern, *Campaign in Holland*, p.36; Anon., *Mémoires Historiques*, p.23.

14. Daendels, *Report*, p.458.

15. Anon., *Mémoires Historiques*, p.23; Daendels, *Report*, p.460.

16. Krayenhoff, *Geschiedkundige*, p.118.

17. Anon., *Mémoires Historiques*, p.24.

18. Maurice, *Moore*, p.346.

19. Maurice, *Moore*, p.347.

20. Anon., *Mémoires Historiques*, p.25.

21. Maurice, *Moore*, p.347.

22. Anon., *Private Soldier in the 92nd*, p.41; Maurice, *Moore*, p.347; Anon., *Mémoires*, p.25.

23. Anon., *Private Soldier in the 92nd*, p.41.

24. *Return of Killed, Wounded, and Missing, of the British Army under the command of Lieutenant-General Sir Ralph Abercromby, in the Action of the Zuype, 10th September 1799*, reproduced in: Subaltern, *Campaign in Holland*, p.347.

25. Anon., *Mémoires Historiques*, p.25 & 26; Uythoven, *Voorwaats, Bataven!*, p.86.

26. Anon., *Mémoires Historiques*, p.26, Bunbury, *Narratives*, p.8; Maurice, *Moore*, p.347.

27. Brune to Bernadotte, 10 September 1799 in A. Du Casse *Le General Vandamme et sa Correspondence, Tome Second* (Paris: Didier, 1870), p.12.

28. Anon., *Mémoires Historiques*, p.26.

29. Du Casse, *Vandamme*, p.12.

30. Anon., *Mémoires Historiques*, p.27, (Clement may in fact be the author of this account; he was promoted to General de Brigade by Brune for his role in the battle of Bergen and was killed in a duel with a fellow officer, whilst serving in Spain in 1811).

31. Abercromby to Dundas, 11 September 1799, Fitzpatrick, *Dropmore*, p.386 ; Bunbury, *Narratives*, p.8.

32. Du Casse, *Vandamme*, p.12; Report of Adjutant General D'Ardenne to the Batavian Directory, 11 September 1799 reproduced in *The London Chronicle*, 26–28 September 1799, p.311.

33. Fortescue, *British Army*, p.663.

34. Anon., *Mémoires Historiques*, p.27.

35. Dumas, Précis, p.378–9; Anon., *Mémoires*, p.28.

36. Bunbury, *Narratives*, p.8.

37. Anon., *Mémoires Historiques*, p.29–30; Abercromby to Dundas, 11 September 1799, Fitzpatrick, *Dropmore*, p.386.

38. Anon., *Mémoires Historiques*, p.30.

39. Du Casse *Vandamme*, p.14; Jomini, *Histoire Critique*, p.42; Subaltern, *Campaign in Holland*, p.36.

40. Vice Admiral Mitchell to Evan Nepean, 10 September 1799, Fitzpatrick, *Dropmore*, p.385.

41. Dumas, Précis, p.378–9; Anon., *Mémoires Historiques*, p.30.

42. Abercromby to Dundas, 11 September 1799, Fitzpatrick, *Dropmore*, p.386.

43. Brune to Bernadotte, 10 September 1799 in Du Casse, *Vandamme*, p.12.

44. Du Casse, *Vandamme*, p.14.

45. *The London Chronicle*, 26–28 September 1799, p.311.

46. Du Casse, *Vandamme*, p.14.

47. Daendels, *Report*, p.461.

48. Maurice, *Moore*, p.345.

49. Daendels, *Report*, p.461.

50. Du Casse, *Vandamme*, p.16.

51. Daendels, *Report*, p.461.

52. Phipps, *Armies*, p.200.

53. Du Casse, *Vandamme*, p.16.

54. Daendels, *Report*, p.461.

55. Abercromby to Dundas, 11 September 1799; reported that 300 had deserted in a short time, Fitzpatrick, *Dropmore*, p.387.

Chapter 9

1. Abercromby to Dundas, Schagen, 11 September 1799, Richmond, *Spencer Papers*, p.265.

2. Fortescue, *British Army*, p.668.

3. Abercromby to Dundas, 4 September 1799, Fitzpatrick, *Dropmore*, p.358.

4. Abercromby to Dundas, Schagen, 11 September 1799, Richmond, *Spencer Papers*, p.265.

5. Fitzpatrick, *Dropmore*, p.338.
6. A. Burne, Noble Duke, p.264.
7. Mackesy, *Strategy*, p.243; Schama, *Patriots*, p.395; Fortescue, *British Army*, p.665.
8. Dundas to Pitt, 28 August 1799, Aspinall, *Correspondence*, p.247.
9. Abercromby to Dundas, 16 September 1799, Colenbrander, *Gedenstukken*, p.400; York to King George, Aspinall, *Correspondence*, p.268.
10. Aspinall, *Correspondence*, p.268.
11. Aspinall, *Correspondence*, p.269.
12. Abercromby to Dundas, 16 September 1799, Colenbrander, *Gedenstukken*, p.401.
13. York to Dundas, 18 September 1799, Colenbrander, *Gedenstukken*, p.401.
14. Anon., *Mémoires Historiques*, p.32–3; Dumas, *Précis*, p.383.
15. Daendels, *Report*, p.462; Anon., *Mémoires Historiques*, p.33.
16. Daendels, *Report*, p.462.
17. Anon., *Mémoires Historiques*, p.33; Daendels, *Report*, p.463.
18. Subaltern, *Campaign in Holland*, p.41.
19. Nowadays this area is a coastal park and can be explored via an extensive network of paths and cycleways.
20. Bunbury, *Narratives*, p.12.
21. Anon., *Mémoires Historiques*, p.34–5.
22. Maule, *Memoirs*, p.15.
23. Bunbury, *Narratives*, p.12.
24. J. Grehan & M. Mace, *Despatches from the Front; British Battles of the Napoleonic Wars 1793–1806* (Barnsley: Pen & Sword, 2013), p.134.
25. Alison, *History*, p.287; Jomini, *Histoire Critique*, p.43.
26. H. Belloc, *Six British Battles* (Bristol: Arrowsmith, 1931), p.226.
27. Jomini describes it as striking a decisive blow ('*frapper un coup décisive*') in Jomini, *Histoire Critique*, p.43.
28. York to Dundas, headquarters, Schagen Brug, 20 September 1799, Grehan & Mace, *Despatches*, p.133–4.
29. Grehan & Mace, *Despatches*, p.134.
30. Mackesy, *Strategy*, p.259; see *General dispositions for the attack upon the enemy's position*, WO1/180, p.199.
31. Abercromby to Dundas, 20 September 1799, Fitzpatrick, *Dropmore*, p.426–7.
32. Phipps, *Armies*, p.201, quoted in Burne, *Noble Duke*, p.266.
33. Bunbury, *Narratives*, p.13–14.
34. Maurice, *Moore*, p.350; Secretary at War William Windham later also wrote that the plan was probably flawed and again blamed the council of war, Windham to Lord Grenville, 29 September 1799, Fitzpatrick, *Dropmore*, p.432.

Chapter 10

1. Dutch veteran of the campaign, Krayenhoff wrote 'That the Russian wing was fired by a great passion to compete with the enemy is beyond doubt': Krayenhoff, *Geschiedkundige*, p.163; Mackesy, *Strategy*, p.254.
2. Milyutin, *Istoriia*, p.379.
3. General Ivan Ivanovitch Herman von Ferzen was a distinguished Russian general of Saxon descent. He is referred to in most contemporary sources as Hermann or d'Herman but I have followed Mikaberidze's more recent rendering: Mikaberidze, *Russian Officer Corps*,

p.153; Captain Herbert Taylor to HRH Field Marshal The Duke of York, 20 September 1799, Fitzpatrick, *Dropmore*, p.417.

4. Fitzpatrick, *Dropmore*, p.418.
5. Milyutin, *Istoriia*, p.384–5.
6. Anon., *Mémoires Historiques*, p.37.
7. Milyutin puts this division at three and a half battalions of infantry and one squadron of cavalry (a total of 2,100 men) but he names the commander Sedmoratsky: Milyutin, *Istoriia*, p.378; Fitzpatrick, *Dropmore*, p.418.
8. Fitzpatrick, *Dropmore*, p.418.
9. Fitzpatrick, *Dropmore*, p.418.
10. Anon., *Mémoires Historiques*, p.38.
11. Fitzpatrick, *Dropmore*, p.418, Bergen is described as a considerable village with a chateau, surrounded by deep woods: Dumas, *Précis*, p.386.
12. Fitzpatrick, *Dropmore*, p.418.
13. Fitzpatrick, *Dropmore*, p.420; Milyutin attributes the Russians' ignorance of their isolated position to the darkness and poor visibility caused by the weather: Milyutin, *Istoriia*, p.384–85.
14. Anon., *Mémoires Historiques*, p.39.
15. Fitzpatrick, *Dropmore*, p.420.
16. Fitzpatrick, *Dropmore*, p.421.
17. Brune's Report to the minister of war, reproduced in L. Bourgoine, *Esquisse Historique sur le Marechal Brune, Tome Premier* (Rosseau, Paris, 1840), p.153; Anon., *Mémoires Historiques*, p.45.
18. Anon., *Mémoires Historiques*, p.46.
19. Walsh was the medical officer with 29th Regiment of Foot, who were part of Coote's brigade on the right of the allied line. He was later to serve as a physician with the British Army at Waterloo and was a pioneer in curing battlefield trauma: Anon., *Edward Walsh* http://www.universitystory.gla.ac.uk University of Glasgow Story People, (Accessed:1 September 2015); Walsh, *Narrative*, p.28.
20. Bunbury, *Narratives*, p.15.
21. Anon., *Mémoires Historiques*, p.47–8.
22. Bunbury, *Narratives*, p.15.
23. Anon., *Mémoires Historiques*, p.48.
24. York to Dundas, Fitzpatrick, *Dropmore*, p.416.
25. Anon., *Mémoires Historiques*, p.48.
26. Mackesy, *Strategy*, p.254.
27. *The Times*, 26 September 1799, Chatham to Pitt, Schagen Brug, 29 September 1799 Dacres Adams MSS, British Library, Add MS89036/1/5(65), York to Dundas, Fitzpatrick, *Dropmore*, p.416, all directly blame the Russians.
28. F. Carr-Gomm (ed.), *Letters and Journals of Field-Marshal Sir William Maynard Gomm, From 1799 to Waterloo 1815* (London: John Murray, 1881), p.36.
29. Carr-Gomm, *Letters and Journals*, p.36.
30. Anon., *Mémoires Historiques*, p.48.
31. Walsh, *Narrative*, p.28.
32. Anon., *Mémoires Historiques* p.49.
33. Carr-Gomm, *Letters and Journals*, p.38–9.
34. York to Dundas, Fitzpatrick, *Dropmore*, p.416.
35. Bunbury, *Narratives*, p.23.

36. Mackesy, *Strategy*, p.267.
37. Anon., *Recollections*, p.186.
38. General Brune to the Batavian Directory, 20 September 1799 quoted in L. Bourgoine, *Esquisse Historique*, p. 154.
39. Anon., *Recollections*, p.189.
40. General Essen to Tsar Paul, Cobbett, *Parliamentary History*, p.1408; A.B. Piechowiak, *The Anglo-Russian Expedition to Holland in 1799* (The Slavonic and East European Review, December 1962), p.191.
41. Milyutin, *Istoriia*, p.380.
42. York tried, unsuccessfully, to arrange with Daendels for Russian generals captured at Bergen to be exchanged for French generals imprisoned in England; *The London Chronicle*, 1 October 1799, p.328.

Chapter 11

1. York to Dundas, 20 September 1799, Grehan & Mace, *Despatches*, p.135.
2. Anon., *History*, p.113.
3. Grehan & Mace, *Despatches*, p.135.
4. Anon., *History*, p.114.
5. Milyutin, *Istoriia*, p.384–85 & p.389.
6. Anon., *History*, p.114–15.
7. Grehan & Mace, *Despatches*, p.135.
8. Bunbury, *Narratives*, p.17; Anon., *History*, p.113.
9. Bunbury, *Narratives*, p.17.
10. The column consisted of: 1st Brigade (Major General Eyre Coote) – 2nd, 27th, 29th & 85th regiments of foot. 2nd Brigade (Major General Don) – 1st & 2nd Battalions 17th foot and 1st & 2nd Battalions 40th foot, Uythoven, *Voorwaats, Bataven!*, p.97; Bunbury, *Narratives*, p.17.
11. Daendels, *Report* p.463–4.
12. Lieutenant General Sir James Pulteney's Report 20 September 1799, quoted in E.Webb, *A History of the Services of the 17th(The Leicestershire). Regiment* (London: Vacher & Sons, 1912), p.1067 – this passage would appear to have been written by Don as it refers to Pulteney in the third person whilst giving the account from a personal perspective.
13. Captain O'Donell, 40th Regiment; listed as missing in *Return of Killed, Wounded, and Missing of the British Army under the command of His Royal Highness the Duke of York, in the Action of the 19th September 1799* in Subaltern, *Campaign in Holland*, p.105.
14. Daendels, *Report*, p.465.
15. Atkinson, *Dalhousie Journal*, p.104.
16. Webb, *History*, p.106.
17. Webb, *History*, p.106; Daendels, *Report*, p.465; A total of three 6 pounders and four ammunition wagons are reported 'disabled by the enemy' in Lieutenant Colonel Whitworth R.A. *Return of English Ordnance lost in the action of 19 September 1799*, GD364/1/1095.
18. Webb, *History*, p.107.
19. Daendels, *Report*, p.466; Maule, *Memoirs*, p.23.
20. Daendels, *Report*, p.469; Webb, *History*, p.107.
21. Daendels, *Report*, p.469.
22. Coote's report, Schagen 20 September 1799, quoted in Webb, *History*, p.107; Atkinson *Dalhousie Journal*, p.104.
23. Manuscript of General G.J.W. Beinen. G.S. Archives, The Hague, quoted in Burne, *Noble Duke*, p.267–8.

24. Webb, *History*, p.107.
25. Maule, *Memoirs*, p.25.
26. Maule, *Memoirs*, p.25; Daendels, *Report*, p.471.
27. Bunbury, *Narratives*, p.19.
28. Daendels, *Report*, p.471.
29. Fortescue, *British Army*, p.673.
30. Maurice, *Moore*, p.350; Bunbury, *Narratives*, p.14.
31. Surtees, *Twenty-Five Years*, p.10.
32. This seems incredible but on a recent visit to the area in similar conditions, the present author noted that from the train, roads and ditches were almost indistinguishable, even in daylight.
33. Bunbury, *Narratives*, p.22.
34. Bunbury, *Narratives*, p.21.
35. Mackesy, *Strategy*, p.273
36. *General dispositions for the attack upon the enemy's position*, WO1/180, p.199.
37. Maurice, *Moore*, p.348–49.
38. Jomini, *Histoire Critique*, p.44.
39. Burne, *Noble Duke*, p.269.
40. Bunbury, *Narratives*, p.22.
41. Maurice, *Moore*, p.349.
42. Anon., Recollections, p.185.
43. Maurice, *Moore*, p.349.
44. Anon., Recollections, p.186.
45. Burne, *Noble Duke*, p.270.
46. Chatham to Pitt, Schagen Brug, 29 September 1799, Dacres Adams MSS, British Library, Add MS89036/1/5(65).
47. Maurice, *Moore*, p.350.
48. Windham to Lord Grenville, 29 September 1799, Fitzpatrick, *Dropmore*, p.432.

Chapter 12
1 Alison, *History*, p.288.
2. Daendels, *Report*, p.473.
3. Burne, *Noble Duke*, p.274.
4. Fortescue, *British Army*, p.682.
5. Maurice, *Moore*, p.350–51.
6. Mackesy, *Strategy*, p.280 & 285.
7. Alison, *History*, p.288.
8. Mackesy, *Strategy*, p.285.
9. Daendels, *Report*, p.473.
10. Walsh, *Narrative*, p.31.
11. Duke of York's official dispatch, Alkmaar, 6 October 1799, Grehan & Mace, *Despatches*, p.140.
12. York's dispatch, Grehan & Mace, *Despatches*, p.140.
13. Bunbury, *Narratives*, p.24.
14. Maurice, *Moore*, p.351.
15. Anon., *Private Soldier in the 92nd*, p. 43–4.
16. Maurice, *Moore*, p.352.
17. Gardyne, *Gordon Highlanders*, p.56.
18. Surtees, *Twenty-Five Years*, p.15.

19. Maurice, *Moore*, p.354; Maule, *Memoirs*, p.31.
20. Half distance means the gap between the companies was half what it would normally be; W. Gilham, *Manual of instruction for the Volunteers and Militia of the Confederate States*, (1861), p.197; 'Sir Ralph's column consisted of the 1st brigade of Guards under Major-General D'Oyley; the 5th, Lord Cavens; the 4th Major-General Moore's; and the reserve, Colonel McDonald's; about 1100 Dragoons [7th], Lord Paget; and a troop of Mounted Artillery; to which were added two 6-pounders, making in all ten pieces of ordnance.' Maurice, *Moore*, p.354.
21. Anon., *Private Soldier in the 92nd*, p.43.
22. Walsh, *Narrative*, p.33.
23. Surtees, *Twenty-Five Years*, p.15; it may also be that there was no attempt to fire at the Light Battalion, for it was reported that the French fired a signal gun prior to retiring and perhaps the inexperienced militiamen mistook it for a barrage: an unknown officer of Abercromby's division quoted in Gardyne, *Gordon Highlanders*, p.57.
24. Anon., *Mémoires Historiques*, p.56.
25. Anon., *Mémoires Historiques*, p.56.
26. Maurice, *Moore*, p.354.
27. Anon., *Private Soldier in the 92nd* , p.44.
28. Maurice, *Moore*, p.354.
29. Bunbury, *Narratives*, p.25, refers to MacDonald as Abercromby's protégé.
30. Maurice, *Moore*, p.355.
31. Anon., *Private Soldier in the 92nd*, p.44.
32. Maurice, *Moore*, p.355.
33. Anon., *Private Soldier in the 92nd*, p.45.
34. Maurice, *Moore*, p.355.
35. Anon., *Mémoires Historiques*, p.62.
36. Anon., *Mémoires Historiques*, p.62–3; Gardyne, *Gordon Highlanders*, p.57.
37. Marquis of Anglesey, *One Leg, The Life and Letters of Henry William Paget, The First Marquess of Anglesey, K.G. 1768–1854* (London: Leo Cooper, 1996 [1961]), p.58; Subaltern, *Campaign in Holland*, p.107 – casualty list.
38. Maurice, *Moore*, p.355.
39. Anon., *Mémoires Historiques*, p.63; Maurice, *Moore*, p.355.
40. Walsh, *Narrative*, p.35; Maurice, *Moore*, p.356.
41. Anon., *Private Soldier in the 92nd*, p.46.
42. Anon., *Private Soldier in the 92nd*, p.46–7.
43. Gardyne, *Gordon Highlanders*, p.58; Walsh, *Narrative*, p.35.
44. Anon., *Mémoires Historiques*, p.65.
45. Anglesey, *Paget*, p.58; Maurice, *Moore*, p.356; Bunbury, *Narratives*, p.28 – the group included Paget, Colonel Erskine and Sir Robert Wilson; Anon., *Private Soldier in the 92nd*, p.48.
46. Gardyne, *Gordon Highlanders*, p.58; Walsh, *Narrative*, p.35.
47. Bunbury, *Narratives*, p.28 – Bunbury identifies the attackers as two squadrons of Chasseurs à Cheval but French sources indicate that there was at least one squadron of Hussars and possibly a squadron of Dragoons involved as well; Anon., *Mémoires Historiques*, p.67.
48. Anon., *Private Soldier in the 92nd*, p.48.

Chapter 13

1. Walsh, *Narrative*, p.33.
2. Bunbury, *Narratives*, p.26.

3. Anon., Recollections, p.187.
4. Surtees, *Twenty-Five Years*, p.16.
5. Anon., Recollections, p.187; Surtees, *Twenty-Five Years*, p.16.
6. Anon., Recollections, p.187, a similar observation was made during the Egyptian campaign; Mackesy, *British Victory*, p.149.
7. Surtees, *Twenty-Five Years*, p.17.
8. Anon., *Mémoires Historiques*, p.61.
9. *Return of the Killed, Wounded, and, Missing of the British Army under the command of His Royal Highness the Duke of York … 2nd October 1799* reproduced in Subaltern, *Campaign in Holland 1799*, p.108.
10. Anon., Recollections, p.187.
11. Anon., *Mémoires Historiques*, p.60.
12. Bunbury, *Narratives*, p.29.
13. Walsh, *Narrative*, p.33.
14. Coote to Lieutenant General Sir Charles Grey, 4 October 1799, Fitzpatrick, *Dropmore*, p.450.
15. Walsh, *Narrative*, p.33.
16. Anon., *Mémoires Historiques*, p.56.
17. Walsh, *Narrative*, p.33.
18. York to Dundas, 6 October 1799, Grehan & Mace, *Despatches*, p.141; Anon., *Mémoires Historiques*, p.57.
19. Anon., *Mémoires Historiques*, p.58.
20. Surtees, *Twenty Five Years*, p.18.
21. Anon., *History*, p.158; Atkinson, *Dalhousie Journal*, p.105.
22. York to Dundas, Grehan & Mace, *Despatches*, p.141–42.
23. Walsh, *Narrative*, p.34; Anon., *Mémoires Historiques*, p.64.
24. Surtees, *Twenty-Five Years*, p.17; York to Dundas, Grehan & Mace, *Despatches*, p.142.
25. Walsh, *Narrative*, p.34.
26. Daendels, *Report*, p.473.
27. *Return of Killed, Wounded, and Missing, of the British Army under the command of His Royal Highness the Duke of York, 2nd October, 1799*, reproduced in Subaltern, *Campaign in Holland*, p.107.
28. Anon., *Mémoires Historiques*, p.64.
29. Maurice, *Moore*, p.356.
30. Maurice, *Moore*, p.357.
31. Captured letter from General Boudet to General Vandamme quoted in; Anon., *History*, p.168.
32. Du Casse, *Vandamme*, p.29.
33. Anon., *Private Soldier in the 92nd*, p.49 – The officer may have been Lieutenant Gordon M'Hardy who is reported to have died in the fighting in the sandhills; a Lieutenant Alexander Fraser also died during the battle, Subaltern, *Campaign in Holland*, p.109.
34. Anon., *Recollections*, p.188; see also Surtees, *Twenty-Five Years*, p.20 who adds that biting the ends of nearly 150 cartridges 'had nearly choked me'.
35. Maule, *Memoirs*, p.34.
36. York to Dundas, Grehan & Mace, *Despatches*, p.143–44.
37. Maule, *Memoirs*, p.33–4.
38. Anon., *History*, p.166.
39. Krayenhoff, *Geschiedkundige*, p.180.
40. Coote to Grey, 4 October 1799, Fitzpatrick, *Dropmore*, p.451.

41. Anon., Recollections, p.189.
42. Count W.G. Bentinck-Rhoon to Lord Grenville, 6 October 1799, Helder (translated from French), Fitzpatrick, *Dropmore*, p.454 (Possibly the meat was refused as the Russian soldiers could not stomach it – see Milyutin p.379).

Chapter 14

1. Duncan felt that his flagship, *Kent* and the larger Russian ships drew too much water to be of much use in the shallow depths around Helder and the Zuider Zee, so returned them all to Yarmouth: Duncan to the Admiralty, 1 September 1799, Fitzpatrick, *Dropmore*, p.344.
2. Duncan to the Lords of the Admiralty, Robinson, *Field of Mars*, p.680.
3. Porlock to Mitchell, Robinson, *Field of Mars*, p.681.
4. Porlock to Mitchell, Robinson, *Field of Mars*, p.681, R. Wilkinson-Latham *British Artillery on Land & Sea, 1790–1820* (London: David & Charles, 1973), p.30.
5. Brune to Bernadotte, 10 September 1799 in Du Casse, *Vandamme*, p.15.
6. Abercromby to Dundas, 4 September 1799, Fitzpatrick, *Dropmore*, p.358.
7. Admiral Young to Spencer, 11 September 1799, Richmond, *Spencer Papers*, p.187.
8. Mitchell to Spencer, 16 September 1799, Richmond, *Spencer Papers*, p.190–191.
9. Mitchell to Duncan 14 September 1799 in Robinson, *Field of Mars*, p.682 (the ships were, the *Dart*, four bomb Ketches, the brigs *L'Espeigle* and the *Speedwell*, the lugger *Lady Anne* and an 'armed ship' *Prince William*). It should be noted that the Duke of York had arrived the day before which may have prompted this spurt of activity.
10. Mitchell to Duncan 14 September 1799, Robinson, *Field of Mars*, p.682.
11. Mitchell to Duncan 14 September 1799, Robinson, *Field of Mars*, p.682.
12. Walsh, *Narrative*, p.31.
13. Mitchell to Duncan, 14 September 1799, Robinson, *Field of Mars*, p.682.
14. Home Popham to Spencer, 12 September 1799, Richmond, *Spencer Papers*, p.188–189.
15. York to Dundas, 20 September 1799, in Walsh, *Narrative*, p.60.
16. Mitchell to Duncan, 14 September 1799, Robinson, *Field of Mars*, p.682; the town in question is now called Stavoren.
17. Captain Bolton to Mitchell, 29 September 1799, Walsh, *Narrative*, p.63.
18. Captain Bolton to the commandant of Lemmer, 29 September 1799, *The London Gazette*, 15191 (1021).
19. Captain Bolton to Mitchell, 29 September 1799, Walsh, *Narrative*, p.64.
20. Mitchell to Spencer, 4 October 1799, Richmond, *Spencer Papers*, p.192.
21. Popham to Spencer, 4 October 1799, Richmond, *Spencer Papers*, p.193.
22. York to Dundas, 6 October 1799, Grehan & Mace, *Despatches*, p.141.
23. Daendels, *Report*, p.454; The Pampus was a channel in the Zuider Zee which led to Amsterdam.
24. Schomberg, *Naval Chronology*, p.237; Campbell to Mitchell, 7 October 1799, Walsh, *Narrative*, p.73.
25. Schomberg, *Naval Chronology*, p.238.
26. Mitchell to Spencer, 10 October 1799, Richmond, *Spencer Papers*, p.194.
27. Boorder to Mitchell, 11 October 1799, in Walsh, *Narrative*, p.74.
28. Mitchell to the regency and inhabitants of Enkhuizen, 12 October 1799, Walsh, *Narrative*, p.74.
29. Krayenhoff, *Geschiedkundige*, p.166.

Chapter 15

1. Jomini, *Histoire Critique* p.46.
2. Jomini, Histoire Critique, p.46; Anon., Mémoires Historiques, p.72.
3. Florent Guiot to Rienhard, 18 October 1799, Colenbrander, *Gedenstukken*, p.104.
4. York, Alkmaar, 7 October 1799, Grehan & Mace, *Despatches*, p.146.
5. Lord Chatham to the Dowager Countess of Chatham (his mother), 4 October 1799, from Lord Ashbourne, *Pitt: some chapters of his life and times* (London, 1898), p.168–69.
6. Maurice, *Moore*, p.358.
7. Christopher Hely-Hutchinson to Lord Donoughmore, 7 October 1799, Donoughmore, MSS T3459/D/43/3.
8. Anon., *Private Soldier in the 92nd*, p.51–2.
9. Maule, *Memoirs*, p.37.
10. Anon., Recollections, p.188–89.
11. Surtees, *Twenty-Five Years*, p.23.
12. All parties involved calculated time differently – probably based on the local time in their respective capitals, making it difficult to establish a strict chronology of events.
13. Krayenhoff, *Geschiedkundige*, p.196; York, Alkmaar, 7 October 1799, Grehan & Mace, *Despatches*, p.146.
14. Krayenhoff, *Geschiedkundige*, p.197; Anon., *Mémoires Historiques*, p.74.
15. Anon., *Mémoires Historiques*, p.80–1.
16. Surtees, *Twenty-Five Years*, p.25.
17. Anon., *Recollections*, p.190.
18. Surtees, *Twenty-Five Years*, p.25–6.
19. Anon., *Mémoires Historiques*, p.82.
20. Surtees, *Twenty-Five Years*, p.26; Anon., *Mémoires*, p.83–4.
21. Hely-Hutchinson to Donoughmore, Donoughmore MSS T3459/D/43/3.
22. Krayenhoff, *Geschiedkundige*, p.199; Anon., *Mémoires*, p.75.
23. Krayenhoff, *Geschiedkundige*, p.200; Anon., *Mémoires*, p.76.
24. Hely-Hutchinson to Donoughmore, Donoughmore MSS T3459/D/43/3; Anon., *History*, p.181–82.
25. Anon., Recollections, p.188–89.
26. Walsh, *Narrative*, p.38.
27. Anon., *Mémoires Historiques*, p.77; Colonel MacDonald to Dundas, 7 October 1799: National Archives of Scotland GD 51/1/710; *The Evening Mail*, London, 15 October 1799.
28. Anglesey, *Paget*, p.59; Anon., *Mémoires*, p.77; Krayenhoff, *Geschiedkundige*, p.200 – credits a Colonel Commings with the charge.
29. Anon., *Mémoires Historiques*, p.78; the French account puts the time at five but it may have been earlier.
30. Anon., *Mémoires Historiques*, p.77.
31. Maule, *Memoirs*, p.38–9.
32. Anon., *Mémoires Historiques*, p.79&75.
33. Krayenhoff, *Geschiedkundige*, p.207.
34. Anon., *Mémoires Historiques*, p.84.
35. Anon., History, p.240.
36. Moore, *Diary*, p.358.
37. Dunbar, *Narratives*, p.32.
38. The British losses were, 92 killed, 724 wounded and 609 missing: Subaltern, *Campaign in Holland*, p.113.

Chapter 16

1. *Military Notes on the Dutch Expedition,* WO1/180, 49, p.12.
2. Maule, *Memoirs,* p.41; Walsh, *Narrative,* p.44.
3. Atkinson, *Dalhousie Journal,* p.106.
4. Maule, *Memoirs,* p.41–2.
5. Daendels, *Report,* p.475–7; Walsh, *Narrative,* p.44.
6. Anon., *History,* p.194.
7. Anon., *History,* p.196.
8. Fortescue, *British Army,* p.703.
9. Anon., *History,* p.199.
10. Fortescue, *British Army,* p.704–06.
11. Major John Finlay to his wife, Helder, 20 October 1799, Wace *British Officer,* p.136–37.
12. York , Schagen Brug, 9 October 1799, Grehan & Mace, *Despatches,* p.147–48.
13. Abercromby to Dundas, 8 October 1799, Colenbrander, *Gedenstukken,* p.428–29.
14. Mackesy, *Strategy,* p.307, Anon., *History,* p.195–96.
15. Anon., *History,* p.202.
16. Chatham to Pitt, Schagen Brug, 19 October 1799, *Chatham Papers* 145, p.133–35.
17. York to Brune, 15 October 1799, Walsh, *Narrative,* p.78.
18. Walsh, *Narrative,* p.75.
19. York to Vice Admiral Dickson, 30 October 1799, Staff Papers, GD364/1/1092, 58.
20. Chatham to Pitt, Schagen Brug, 19 October 1799, *Chatham Papers* 145, p.133–35.

Chapter 17

1. Bunbury, *Narratives,* p.49.
2. Mitchell to Spencer, 10 October 1799, Richmond, *Spencer Papers,* p.194–95.
3. Mitchell to Spencer, 12 October 1799, Richmond, *Spencer Papers,* p.198–99.
4. Jomini, *Histoire Critique,* p.48.
5. *The Evening Mail,* London, 15 October 1799.
6. Sheridan to the House of Commons, 10 February 1800, Cobbett, *Parliamentary History,* p.1406.
7. Sheridan to the House of Commons, 10 February 1800, Cobbett, p.1398.
8. Sheridan to the House of Commons, 10 February 1800, Cobbett, *Parliamentary History,* p.1405.
9. Thomas Grenville to Lord Grenville, 7 & 1 October 1799, Fitzpatrick, *Dropmore,* p.457 & p.446.
10. Thomas Grenville to Lord Grenville, 11 October 1799, Fitzpatrick, *Dropmore,* p.469.
11. Thomas Grenville to Lord Grenville, 20 October 1799, Fitzpatrick, *Dropmore,* p.489.
12. Sheridan to the House of Commons, 10 February 1800, Cobbett, *Parliamentary History,* p.1399.
13. Anon., *Recollections,* p.189.
14. Ibid., p.202.
15. Chatham to Pitt, Schagen Brug, 19 October 1799, *Chatham Papers* 145, p.133–35.
16. Krayenhoff, *Geschiedkundige,* p.166.
17. Mitchell to Admiralty, 20 September 1799, Walsh, *Narrative,* p.61; Subaltern, *Campaign in Holland,* p.54–55.
18. Fortescue, *British Army,* p.682.

19. Windham to Grenville, 30 July 1799, W. Windham, *The Windham Papers, the Life &* *Correspondence of the Right Honourable William Windham* (Herbert Jenkins, 1913); Dundas to Grenville 29 July 1799, Fitzpatrick, *Dropmore,* p.207; Mackesy, *Strategy,* p.149.
20. Windham to Grenville, 18 September 1799, Windham, *Windham Papers*; Dundas to Grenville, 29 & 31 July 1799, Fitzpatrick, *Dropmore,* p.206 & p.215.
21. Sheridan to the House of Commons, reported in *The London Chronicle,* 26 September 1799, p.309.
22. Sheridan to the House of Commons, 10 February 1800, Cobbett, *Parliamentary History,* p.1400.
23. Debate in the Commons on the failure of the Dutch Expedition, 10 February 1800, Cobbett, *Parliamentary History,* p.1415.

Bibliography

Manuscripts:
War Office Papers at the National Archives:
  WO 1/180.
  WO 1/181.
  WO 1/182 .
  HO 42/46/172, Duke of Portland to Marquess of Buckingham, 21 March 1799, f 357.
Dacres Adams MSS, British Library:
  MS89036/1/5 (65) Chatham to Pitt, Schagen Brug, 29 September 1799.
  Chatham MSS PRO 30/8/122 f 145, Chatham to Pitt, Schagen Brug, 19 October 1799.
  Donoughmore MSS (PRONI) T3459/D/43/3,C. *Hely-Hutchinson to Lord Donoughmore, 7 October 1799.*
National Archives of Scotland:
  GD364/1/1092 Alexander Hope to Abercromby, 20 August 1799.
  GD364/1/1095 Staff Papers.
  GD364/2/215 Letter Book of Alexander Hope as Deputy Adjutant General, Helder Campaign.
  GD364/2/216 General Orders for the Helder Campaign.
  GD51/1/703/1-13 Correspondence between General Sir Ralph Abercromby, Henry Dundas, Colonel Robert Brownrigg, HRH Duke of York and the king relative to the Helder expedition.
  GD 51/1/710, MacDonald to Dundas, 7 October 1799.
University of Durham:
  The Papers of the 1st Earl Grey, GB-0033-GRE-A1881-A1989.

Primary Printed Sources:
Anglesey, Marquis of, *One Leg, The Life and Letters of Henry William Paget, The First Marquess of Anglesey, K G 1768–1854* (London: Leo Cooper, 1996 [1961]).
Anon. *The Field of Mars; being an alphabetical digestion of the principal Naval and Military engagements in Europe, Asia, Africa, and America from the ninth century to the Peace of 1801* (London: G&J Robinson, 1801).
Anon. *Narrative of a Private Soldier in His Majesty's 92nd Regiment of Foot* (Uckfield: Naval & Military Press, 1820).
Anon. *Mémoires Historiques sur la Campagne du Général Brune en Batavie*, Du 5 Fructidor an7, au 9 Frimaire an 8; Rédigés par un Officier se son état-major (Paris: Favre, 1802).
Anon. 'Recollections of the British Army, in the Early Campaigns of the Revolutionary War', Journal of the Royal United Services Institute, 1836, Part 1.
Anon. *A Collection of State Papers relative to the War against France, VOL. VIII* (London: Debrett, 1800).
Aspinall, A. *The Later Correspondence of George III, Vol. III 1798–1801* (Cambridge: University Press, 1967).

Atkinson, C.T. 'The Expedition to Holland in 1799, From the Journal of Lord Dalhousie', Journal of the Society for Army Historical Research, 1958, Vol.XXXVI. No 147.

Baring, H. *The Diary of the Right Hon. William Windham 1784–1810* (London: Longmans Green & Co, 1866).

Belloc, H. *Six British Battles* (Bristol: Arrowsmith, 1931).

Bourgoine, L. *Esquisse Historique sur le Marechal Brune, Tome Premier* (Paris: Rosseau, 1840).

Bunbury, H.E. *Narratives of Some Passages in the Great War with France, from 1799–1810* (London: Richard Bentley, 1854).

Carr-Gomm, F.C. (ed.). *Letters and Journals of Field-Marshal Sir William Maynard Gomm, From 1799 to Waterloo 1815* (London: John Murray, 1881).

Casse, A. Du *Le General Vandamme et sa Correspondence, Tome Second* (Paris: Didier, 1870).

Cobbett, W. *The Parliamentary History of England from the Earliest Times to the Year 1803* (London: Hansard, 1819).

Colenbrander, H. *Gedenstukken Der Algemeene Geschiedenis VanNederland, Van 1795 Tot 1840* (The Hague: Rijks Geschiedkundige Publicatien, 1905).

Daendels, H.W. *Report of the operations of the division of Lieutenant General Daendels from 22nd August to the Capitulation of the English & Russians on the 18th October1799*, As an appendix of: Anon., *The History of the Campaign of 1799 in Holland, Translated from the French, Vol.V* (London: J. Barfield, 1801).

De Jonge, J. *Geschiedenis van het Nederlandsche zeewezeni* (Haarlem: A.C. Kruseman, 1862).

Fitzpatrick, W. *Report on the Manuscripts of J.B. Fortescue Esq., preserved at Dropmore, Historical Manuscripts Commission, vol. V* (London: HMSO, 1905).

Grehan, J. & Mace, M. *Despatches from the Front; British Battles of the Napoleonic Wars 1793–1806* (Barnsley: Pen & Sword, 2013).

Krayenhoff, C.R.T. *Geschiedkundige Beschouwingvan den Oorlong op het Grondgebied der Bataafsche Republiek in 1799* (Nijmegen: Vieweg en Zoon, 1832).

Maule, F. *Memoirs of the Principal Events in the Campaigns of Holland and Egypt* (London: F.C & J Rivington, 1816).

Maurice, J.F. (ed.). *The Diary of Sir John Moore, Volume 1* (London: Edward Arnold, 1904).

Randolph, H. *Life of General Sir Robert Wilson, Volume1* (London: John Murray, 1862).

Richmond, H.W. *Private Papers of George, Second Earl Spencer, First Lord of the Admiralty 1794–1801, Vol. III* (London: Navy Records Society, 1924).

Schomberg, I. *Naval Chronology: Or An Historical Summary of Naval and Maritime Events, Vol. III* (London: T. Egerton, 1802).

Surtees, W. *Twenty-Five Years in the Rifle Brigade* (London: Greenhill, 1996 [1833]).

Wace, A. (ed.). 'A British Officer on Active Service, 1799': *The Annual of the British School at Athens*, Vol.23, 1919).

Walsh, E. *A Narrative of the Expedition to Holland, in the autumn of the year 1799* (Memphis: General Books, 2010 [1800]).

Windham, W. *The Windham Papers, the Life & Correspondence of the Right Honourable William Windham* (London: Herbert Jenkins, 1913).

Weil, M.-H. *Le Général De Stamford, D'Aprés sa Correspondence Inédite 1793–1806* (Paris: Payot & Co, 1923).

York, H.R.H. Duke of *Plain Statement of the Conduct of the Ministry and the Opposition towards His Royal Highness The Duke of York* (London: B. McMillan, 1808).

Newspapers:
The London Chronicle 1799 (G. Woodfall, 1799).
The Sun, 15 October 1799.
The Evening Mail, 15 October 1799.
The London Gazette, 5–8 October 1799, no. 15191 (1021).
The London Gazette, 19–23 November 1799, no. 15205 (1193).
The London Gazette Extraordinary, 15 October 1799.

Maps:
Fietskaart 12; Noord-Holland noord; Texel (Den Haag: ANWB, 2015).
Fietskaart 13; Noord-Holland zuid; Amstredam & Kennemerland (Den Haag:ANWB, 2015).

Secondary Sources:
Alison, A. *History of Europe from the Commencement of the French Revolution in MDCCLXXXIX to the Restoration of the Bourbons in MDCCCXV* (Edinburgh: William Blackwood, 1854).
Anon. *British Minor Expeditions 1746 to 1814: Compiled in the Intelligence Branch of the Quartermaster-Generals Department* (London: HMSO, 1884).
Anon. *The History of the Campaign of 1799 in Holland, Translated from the French, Vol.V* (London: J. Barfield, 1801).
Bartlett, K.J. *The Development of the British Army during the Wars with France, 1793 -1815* (Durham, 1998).
Black, J. *Britain as a Military Power 1688–1815* (London: UCL Press, 1999).
Black, J. *European Warfare 1660–1815* (London: UCL Press, 1994).
Blanning, T.C.W. *The French Revolutionary Wars 1787–1802* (London: Hodder, 1996).
Burne, A. *The Noble Duke of York* (London: Staples Press, 1949).
Clausewitz, C. *On War,* edited & translated by M.Howard & P. Paret (London: Everyman, 1993 [1976]).
Colley, L. *Britons: Forging the Nation 1707–1837* (London: Pimlico, 1994).
Cust, E. *Annals of the Wars of the Eighteenth Century: Vol.V. 1796–1799* (London: John Murray, 1869).
Duhesme, G. *Essai sur L'Infanterie Légere* (Paris: Michaud, 1814).
Dumas, M. *Précis des énévemens Militaires ou Essais Historiques sur les Campagnes 1799 à 1814, Tome Premier* (Paris: Treuttel & Wurtz, 1817).
Dunfermline, J. *Lieutenant-General Sir Ralph Abercromby, K.B., 1793–1801* (Edinburgh: Edmonston & Douglas, 1861).
Ehrman, J. *The Younger Pitt, The Consuming Struggle* (London; Constable, 1996).
Forrest, A. *Soldiers of the French Revolution* (Durham:Duke, 1990).
Fortescue, J.W. *A History of the British Army: Volume 4* (London: MacMillan, 1906).
Fuller, J.F.C. *The Conduct of War 1789–1961: A Study of the Impact of the French, Industrial, and Russian Revolutions on War and its Conduct* (New York: Da Capo Press, 1992 [1961]).
Gardyne, C. *The Life of a Regiment; The History of the Gordon Highlanders from its Formation in 1794 to 1816* (The Medici Society, 1929).
Glover, R. *Peninsular Preparation: The Reform of the British Army 1795–1809* (Cambridge: Ken Trotman, 1988 [1970]).
Graves, D. *Fix Bayonets, A Royal Welch Fusilier at War, 1796 -1815* (Stroud: Spellmount, 2007).
Griffith, P. *The Art of War of Revolutionary France 1789–1802* (London: Greenhill, 1998).
Hague, W. *William Pitt The Younger* (London: Harper Collins, 2004).
Haswell, J. *The British Army: A Concise History* (London: Thames & Hudson, 1975).

Jomini, A.H. *Histoire Critique et Militaire des Guerres de la Revolution: Campagne de 1799* (Memphis: General Books, 2012 [1820]).

Knight, R. *Britain against Napoleon: The Organisation of Victory 1793–1815* (London: Allen Lane, 2013).

Liddell-Hart, B. 'Economic Pressure or Continental Victories', *Journal of the Royal United Services Institute*, 76:503(1931).

Limm, A. The British Army, 1795 -1815: An Army Transformed?, in M. Locicero, R. Mahoney & S. Mitchell ed., *A Military Transformed? Adaptation and Innovation in the British Military, 1792–1945* (Solihull: Helion, 2014).

Lynne, J.A. *The Bayonets of the Republic: Motivation and Tactics in the Army of Revolutionary France 1791–1794* (Westview, 1996 [1984]).

Mackesy, P. *The Strategy of Overthrow 1798–1799* (London: Longman, 1974).

Mendels, L. *Herman Willem Daendels, Voor Zijne Benoeming Tot Gouverneur-General Van Oost-Indie, 1762–1807* (S-Gravenhage: Martinus Nijhof, 1890).

Mikaberidze, A. *The Russian Officer Corps in the Revolutionary and Napoleonic wars, 1792–1815* (New York: Savas Beattie,2005).

Milyutin, D. *Istoriia Voini Rossii s Frantsiei v 1799, Tome II* (St Petersburg, 1857).

Pakenham, T. *The Year of Liberty, The Great Irish Rebellion of 1798* (London: Weidenfeld & Nicolson 1997 [1969]).

Phipps, R.W. *The Armies of the First French Republic and the Rise of the Marshals of Napoleon I: Volume V – The Armies of the Rhine in Switzerland, Holland, Italy, Egypt, and The Coup D'Etat of Brumaire (1797–1799).* (USA: Pickle Partners, 2011 [1939]).

Piechowiak, A.B. 'The Anglo-Russian Expedition to Holland in 1799' *The Slavonic & East European Review.* Vol.41. No. 96, (1962).

Rodger, A.B. *The War of the Second Coalition 1798 to 1801: A Strategic Commentary* (Oxford: Oxford University Press, 1964).

Rodger, N.A.M. *The Command of the Ocean, A Naval History of Britain, 1649–1815* (London: Allen Lane, 2004).

Roodhuyzen, T. *In woelig vaarwater: marineofficieren in de jaren 1779–1802* (Amsterdam: Bataafsche Leew, 1998).

Rothenberg, G. Napoleon's Great Adversary, Archduke Charles and the Austrian Army 1792–1814 (Staplehurst: Spellmount, 1995 [1982]).

Subaltern, A. *The Campaign in Holland 1799: The British-Russian Expedition against the Gallo-Batavian Forces in the Low Counties* (London: W. Mitchell, 1861).

Schama, S. *Patriots and Liberators: Revolution in the Netherlands 1780–1813* (London: Harper Perennial, 2005 [1977]).

Schneid, F.C. (ed.). *European Armies of the French Revolution 1789–1802* (Norman: University of Oklahoma, 2015).

Shepperd, A. 'The Patagonian', Brune, in D. Chandler, ed., *Napoleon's Marshals* (London: Cassell, 2000 [1987]).

Steppler, G.A. *Britons to Arms: The Story of the British Volunteer Soldier* (Stroud: Sutton Publishing, 1992).

Street, G. *Dutch Troops of the French Revolutionary & Napoleonic Wars 1793–1810* (Newthorpe: Partisan Press, 2014).

Sutcliffe, R. *British Expeditionary Warfare and the Defeat of Napoleon 1793–1815* (Woodbridge: Boydell Press, 2016).

Turton, R. *The History of the North York Militia* (Stockton-On-Tees: Patrick & Shotton, 1973).

Uythoven, G. Van *Voorwaats, Bataven! De Engels-Russische invasie van 1799* (Zaltbommel: Europese Bibliotheek, 1999).

Webb, E.A.H. *A History of the Services of the 17th (The Leicestershire). Regiment* (London: Vacher & Sons, 1912).

Western, J.R. *The English Militia in the Eighteenth Century, The Story of a Political Issue 1660–1802* (London: Routledge & Kegan Paul, 1965).

The War in General:

Best, G. *War and Society in Revolutionary Europe 1770–1870* (Stroud: Sutton, 1998 [1982]).

Bowen, H.V. *War and British Society, 1688–1815* (Cambridge: Cambridge University Press, 1998).

Cust, E. *Annals of the Wars of the Nineteenth Century: Vol II. 1807–1809* (London: John Murray, 1862).

Duffy, C. *Eagles over the Alps: Suvarov in Italy & Switzerland 1799* (Chicago: Emperors Press, 1999).

Glover, M. *Britannia Sickens: Sir Arthur Wellesley and the Convention of Cintra* (London: Leo Cooper, 1970).

Mackesy, P. *British Victory in Egypt; The End of Napoleon's Conquest* (London: Tauris Parke, 2010 [1995]).

Nosworthy, B *Battle Tactics of Napoleon and his Enemies* (London: Constable, 1995).

Phipps, R.W. *The Armies of the First French Republic and the Rise of the Marshals of Napoleon I: Volume I – The Armee Du Nord* (USA: Pickle Partners, 2011 [1939]).

The Convention Between His Britannic Majesty and the Emperor of All the Russias, Signed at St. Petersburgh 22nd (11th) of June 1799

'His Majesty the King of Great Britain and his Majesty the Emperor of all the Russias, in consequence of the friendship and the ties of intimate alliance which exist between them and their common and sincere co-operation in the present war against the French, having constantly in their view to use every means in their power most effectually to distress the enemy, have judged that the expulsion of the French from the Seven United Provinces, and the deliverance of the latter from the yoke under which they have so long groaned, were objects worthy of their particular consideration. ...

[His] Imperial Majesty, notwithstanding the efforts which he has already made, and the difficulties of his employing an additional body of forces to act at a distance from his dominions, has, nevertheless, in consequence of his constant solicitude in favour of the good cause, consented to furnish seventeen battalions of infantry, two companies of artillery, one company of pioneers, and one squadron of hussars, making in all 17,593 men, to be destined for the said expedition to Holland. But as that number of troops, according to the plan proposed by his Britannic Majesty, is not sufficient, and as it has been judged that 30,000 men would be necessary for that purpose, his said Majesty will on his side, furnish 13,000 men of English troops. ...

In order to enable his Majesty the Emperor of all the Russias to afford to the common cause this additional and efficacious succour, his Majesty the King of Great Britain engages to furnish the undermentioned subsidies. ...

[T]o pay the first and most urgent expenses, the sum of £ 88,000
sterling.'

To be followed by a subsidy of £44,000 a month to be paid from the time the
troops were ready to sail until the point at which they returned to Russian
ports.

There was also a specific provision for Britain to supply horses which
became contentious later in the campaign:

'As the transport of the horses necessary for the officers, the artillery and
the baggage, would require a great many vessels, and as that arrangement
would lead to many other inconveniences, and more particularly to that
of a delay … his Britannic Majesty engages to furnish, at his own expense,
the necessary number of horses … and to have them conveyed to the
place where the Russian troops are to act.'

British Order of Battle

		Initial Numbers	Date Arrived
Cavalry	7th Light Dragoons	approx. 500	03/09/99
Paget	11th LD	539	25/09/99
	10th LD	101	15/09/99
	15th LD	193	25/09/99
	18th LD	Unknown	
1st Bde	Guards Grenadiers	922	27/08/99
D'Oyly	3/1st Guards	955	27/08/99
2nd Bde	2nd Guards	927	27/08/99
Burrard	3rd Guards	954	27/08/99
3rd Bde	2nd Foot	582	27/08/99
Coote	27th Foot	867	27/08/99
	29th Foot	595	27/08/99
	69th Foot	593	27/08/99
	85th Foot	559	27/08/99
4th Inf Bde	2/1st Foot (The Royals)	666	27/08/99
Moore	25th Foot	551	27/08/99
	49th Foot	518	27/08/99
	79th Foot	437	27/08/99
	92nd Foot	764	27/08/99
5th Inf Bde	1/17th Foot	636	28/08/99
Don	2/17th Foot	636	28/08/99
	1/40th Foot	639	28/08/99
	2/40th Foot	620	28/08/99

		Initial Numbers	Date Arrived
6th Inf Bde	1/20th Foot	701	29/08/99
Lord Cavan	2/20th Foot	762	29/08/99
	63rd Foot	774	29/08/99
(Reserve Bde)	23rd Foot	868	29/08/99
Macdonald	55th Foot	283	29/08/99
7th Inf Bde	1/4th Foot	594	15/09/99
Chatham	2/4th Foot	541	15/09/99
	3/4th Foot	540	15/09/99
	31st Foot	794	15/09/99
8th Inf Bde	1/5th Foot	386	15/09/99
Prince William	2/5th Foot	466	15/09/99
	1/35th Foot	607	15/09/99
	2/35th Foot	614	15/09/99
9th Inf Bde	1/9th Foot	624	15/09/99
Manners	2/9th Foot	625	15/09/99
	56th Foot	676	15/09/99
Advanced	Combined Grenadiers	627	15/09/99
Guard	Combined Light Infantry	633	15/09/99
Knox	6/60th Rifles	Unknown	

Appendix III

Russian Order of Battle

Division	Brigade	Regiment (Battalions)	Date arrived
1st Jerepsoff	Fersen	Jerepsoff 2	13/09/99
		Fersen 2	13/09/99
	Dubiansky	Grenadiers 3	13/09/99
2nd Essen	Sedmoratsky	Sedmoratsky 2	15/09/99
		Grenadiers 2	15/09/99
	Darbinioff	Darbinioff 2	15/09/99
		Grenadiers 1	15/09/99
3rd Emmé	Capzewitz	Emmé 2	21/09/99
		Grenadiers 2	21/09/99
Advanced Guard	Soudhoff/Suthoff	Jaegers 2	21/09/99
		Grenadiers 1	21/09/99
Artillery	Regiment of Capzewitz		21/09/99
Cavalry	Hussars – 4 squads		21/09/99
	Cossacks – 6 squads		21/09/99

Appendix IV

Franco-Batavian Order of Battle

CinC – Brune				
Division	**Brigade**	**Unit**	**Inital Numbers**	**Date arrived**
1st Batavian Division				
Daendels	1st Bde – Van Guericke			
		2nd Jaegers – Chassé	674	27–Aug
		5th Halve Bde – Crass		27–Aug
		1st Bn– Nijholt	618	27–Aug
		2nd Bn – Herbig	600	27–Aug
		3rd Bn– Van Sandwick	583	27–Aug
		7th HB – Gilquin		27–Aug
		1st Bn– Verhorst	617	27–Aug
		2nd Bn– Lambrechts	534	27–Aug
		3rd Bn– Zeebis	664 (300 detached)	27–Aug
	Cavalry	1st Regt 'Zware' Cavalrie, 4 sqns – Du Rij	411	27–Aug
	Artillery	4x6pdr, 2x24pdr Howitzers.		27–Aug
	2nd Brigade – Van Zuylen Van Nijvelt			27–Aug
		1st Jaegers – Luck	741	27–Aug
		1st HB – Rietvelt		27 Aug
		1st Bn – Nicolson	579	27–Aug
		2nd Bn – Step	590	27–Aug

Division	Brigade	Unit	Inital Numbers	Date arrived
		3rd Bn– Van Till	865	27–Aug
		1/3rd HB– Abbema	604	27–Aug
		1/4th HB– Pitcairn	740	27–Aug
		3/6th HB– Carteret	686	27–Aug
	Cavalry	2nd Regt 'Zware' Cavalrie, 4 sqns – Broux	488	
	Artillery	24x6pdr		
2nd Batavian Division				
Dumonceau				
	Advanced Guard– Gilquin			
		4th Jaegers	511	
		Grenadiers	489	
		Hussar Sqn	114	
		Artillery	2 guns	
	1st Brigade– Bonhomme			
		1/6 Halve Brigade	509	
		3/6 HB	550	
		1/7 HB	502	
		2/7 HB	375	
		Hussar Sqn x3	372	
		Artillery	2 guns	
	2nd Brigade – Bruce			10–Sep
		3rd Jaegers	298	10–Sep
		Grenadiers	208	10–Sep

Division	Brigade	Unit	Inital Numbers	Date arrived
		1/2 HB	474	10-Sep
		2/2 HB	421	10-Sep
		3/2 HB	449	10-Sep
		2/6 HB	582	10-Sep
		Art	2 guns	10-Sep
		1st Zware Cav x 4 Sqn	434	10-Sep
1st French Division – Vandamme				
	Aubrée	42e Demi-Brigade (3)	1835	10-Sep
		3/48e DB	740	10-Sep
	Michel	49e DB (3)	2130	10-Sep
		54e DB (3)	2306	10-Sep
		3/60e DB	587	10-Sep
		72e (grenadiers)	37	10-Sep
	Capt. Neller	90e (2)	1370	19-Sep
Cavalry				
	Godard	10e Dragoons (4)	487	19-Sep
		5e Chasseurs a Cheval	87	10-Sep
		16e Chasseurs a Cheval	175	19-Sep
Artillery		2 companies foot		
		2 companies horse/light		
Gen de Brigade Gouvion (promoted GdD after Bergen)				

Division	Brigade	Unit	Inital Numbers	Date arrived
Gen de Brigade Barbou (promoted 14 Vendemiaire				
Gen de Division Boudet (arrived later)				
Gen Mortot				
		22e DB (1)		02-Oct
		51e DB (1)		02-Oct
		72e DB (2)		02-Oct
		90e (1)		02-Oct
		4e Chasseurs a Cheval (4)		02-Oct
		16e Chasseurs a Cheval (1/2)	3509	02-Oct
		98e DB (2)		06-Oct
		60e DB (2)		06-Oct
		4e (3)		06-Oct
		66e DB (3)	8756	22-Oct

Appendix V

British Losses

Numbers represent those killed/wounded/missing

Unit	Callantsoog	Krabbendam	Bergen	Egmond	Castricum
11th LD		0/0/0	0/1/0	one/four	8/18/7
10th LD				0/0/0	0/0/0
7th LD			0/0/0	2/11/1(horse)	2/7/2
15th LD			0/0/0	2/10/2(horses)	2/0/0
Guards Grenadiers	3/51/1	6/15/0	13/48/27	1/19/0	1/18/0
3/1st Guards	0/14/0	0/5/0	2/49/43	6/55/8	3/28/22
2nd Guards	0/7/1	1/8/0	10/23/14	0/0/0	1/13/3
3rd Guards	0/0/0	2/4/0	2/19/0	0/0/0	5/20/0
2nd Foot	2/24/0	0/0/0	0/0/0	2/16/2	0/1/8
27th Foot	8/45/7	0/0/0	0/1/0	4/45/1	0/0/17
29th Foot	3/36/0	0/0/0	0/0/0	8/35/11	0/0/0
69th Foot	0/14/0	0/0/0	0/0/0	0/0/0	0/0/0
85th Foot	8/33/16	1/3/0	0/0/0	7/71/9	0/0/25
2/1st Foot (The Royals)	0/0/0	0/4/0	0/0/0	7/72/10	
25th Foot	0/0/0	0/0/0	0/0/0	36/67/13	
49th Foot	0/0/0	0/0/0	0/0/0	33/58/21	
79th Foot	0/0/0	0/0/0	0/0/0	14/53/2	
92nd Foot	0/0/0	1/4/0	0/0/0	60/193/39	
1/17th Foot		2/0/0	6/42/3	0/0/0	0/0/0
2/17th Foot		2/18/0	10/25/0	2/7/0	0/0/0
1/40th Foot		1/10/0	17/55/13	0/3/0	0/0/30
2/40th Foot		0/0/0	10/47/11	0/1/0	0/0/0

Unit	Callantsoog	Krabbendam	Bergen	Egmond	Castricum
1/20th Foot		14/31/14	0/0/0	0/11/1	9/54/9
2/20th Foot		4/36/5	0/0/0	5/30/3	7/71/32
63rd Foot		0/0/0	0/0/0	1/39/2	10/149/45
23rd Foot	18/77/0	0/0/0	0/0/0	7/55/7	6/36/0
55th Foot	13/69/0	0/0/0	0/0/0	3/19/0	0/12/0
1/4th Foot			0/0/0	1/4/1	15/45/19
2/4th Foot			0/0/0	1/5/2	3/42/184
3/4th Foot			0/0/0	1/1/4	2/37/148
31st Foot			0/0/0	2/7/5	11/89/33
5th Foot			4/5/6	0/0/0	
35th Foot			0/8/3	0/0/0	
1/9th Foot			2/3/214		
2/9th Foot			18/52/98		
56th Foot			30/36/57		
Combined Grenadiers			0/0/0	13/64/37	4/52/10
Combined Light Infantry			0/0/0	4/61/5	5/40/9
6/60th Rifles				6/7/4	0/0/0

Index